MODERN SCHOOL ORGANISATION

MODERN SCHOOL ORGANISATION

[For B.Ed. Course]

By

UDAI VEER

ANMOL PUBLICATIONS PVT. LTD.

NEW DELHI - 110 002 (INDIA)

ANMOL PUBLICATIONS PVT. LTD.
4374/4B, Ansari Road, Daryaganj
New Delhi - 110 002
Ph.: 23261597, 23278000
Visit us at: www.anmolpublications.com

Modern School Organisation

First Published, 2004

ISBN 81-261-1948-9

PRINTED IN INDIA

Published by J.L. Kumar for Anmol Publications Pvt. Ltd., New Delhi - 110 002 and Printed at Mehra Offset Press, Delhi.

Contents

Preface

Education is a vast discipline and Teachers' Training is a vital part of it. The responsibilities of the educationists and educators are focused on the task of providing better training to the future teachers for their better learning and proper development. Needless to say that this responsibility can only be exercised, if the trainers are equipped with the required knowledge of the subject concerned. That's why it becomes essential for making adequate provisions for each course to the student-teachers or teacher trainees. The present series is designed for providing a solid workable base for all course-papers. It has been prepared strictly according to the syllabus of the B.Ed class, prescribed by the UGC for different universities.

No doubt, there are so many other books on the subject, available in the market, written by worthy authors. However, every writer has his or her own style and way of presentation. The present work also has its own features and characteristics.

In preparation of this series of texts, the editor had to refer to the works of other authors and information sources. The editor feels a deep sense of gratitude for incorporating their ideas in the text. Hopefully, this series would serve as a 'ready to refer' tool for all teachers, teacher-students and others.

– Editor

1

Introduction

The present age is the age of rapid changes—cultural, political, scientific, social and technological. Dynamism is the main characteristic of the changed situation. It is, therefore, very essential that school management must conform to the changing times and the head of the school must be very dynamic.

School management is the embodiment of an ideal and of a spirit. It must enable different limbs of the school organism to function harmoniously in happy coordination blending themselves into a composite personality like the different rivulets which join together.

School management implies the practical measures which the school takes to ensure that the system of work which it uses will be of the greatest possible assistance in fulfilling its objectives and of the greatest possible value to the students.

Management means an organised body or system or structure or arrangement or framework which is used for ensuring unity of effort, efficiency, goodwill and proper use of resources.

Management may primarily be composed of men, materials, ideas, concepts, forms, rules, principles or more often of a combination of these.

Management of a school has five aspects, i.e. management of 5 M's. These are as under:

Management of Men. This includes school staff, students and their parents, members of the community, members of the governing body and departmental officials.

Management of Money. This is concerned with school finances.

Management of Machines. The present day schools are expected to possess different kinds of machinery for carrying out programmes related to work experience and socially useful productive work.

Management of Material. A variety of material in the form of furniture and stationery etc. exists in the school. School plant also comes under this category.

Management of Methods. This means organisation of ideas and principles into school system-curriculum, methods of teaching etc.

Fundamentally the purpose of school management is to enable the right pupils to receive the right education in the right way at the right time from the right teachers by bringing them together at a cost within the means of the state at a place specifically designed for the purpose of education. This objective can be achieved only when four categories of relationships within the school community, i.e. relations between organisers, and teachers, relations between teachers and teachers, relations between pupils and pupils and relations between pupils and teachers are pleasant and constructive based on mutual goodwill and cooperation.

The objectives of school management may be seen from the point of view of the society, the students and their parents.

Broadly speaking the objectives of school management from the point of view of society are :

1. Consolidating the spiritual strength of the society.
2. Maintaining the historic continuity of the society.
3. Securing the past achievements of the society.

4. Ensuring modernisation of the society.

5. Guaranteeing bright future of the society.

Objectives of the school management from the point of view of the students and their parents are :

1. To develop aesthetic sense.

2. To refine cultural values.

3. To cultivate appropriate ethical values.

4. To sharpen intellect by training various faculties.

5. To build strong physical strength.

6. To train in spiritual values.

7. To form suitable habits.

8. To strengthen vocational efficiency.

9. To develop values of democracy, socialism and secularism.

School administration lays more emphasis on the rigidity of rules and regulations. Management stresses human relations and organisation highlights coordination. It must, however, be noted that all these elements are present in varying degrees in all these concepts.

Educational administration or school administration lays down the aims, policies and guidelines of educational institutions. School management is concerned with the achievement or realisation of these.

Educational administration is more concerned with rules and regulations while school management is concerned with the realisation of objectives.

School administration, because of its emphasis on rules is generally rigid and traditional. In school management innovative ideas are appreciated.

In school administration, results are not easily measurable. In school management results are easily measurable. Bureaucratic has six characteristics :

(a) There is the rigidity of official behaviour.

(b) There is resistance to the adoption of innovations and change.

(c) There is a rigidity of rules and regulations.

(d) The decision is taken by a hierarchy of officers and officials.

(e) There is the levelling of talent. This system tends to reduce the performance of bright workers to the level of mediocrity.

(f) The consequence is the 'red tape' which is never in the straight line. All feel entrapped and helpless.

2

The Fundamentals

"School administration which does not facilitate education is a parasite and a debauchery of public funds. School administration, therefore, exists only for the pupil and its efficiency must be measured by the extent to which it contributes to teaching and learning."

- P. C. Wren

Basic Issues

Every institution has certain aims and ideals before it and for the speedy and successful achievement of these ideals, some sort of administration is essential. The school is one of the important social institutions and as such it must have a well organised administrative machinery. Without an efficient administrative machinery there is bound to be chaos and confusion in the school life. An efficient administrative machinery brings systematic work in the school. It places right persons at their right places at right time and in the right manner.

Aims and Objectives

The one and the sole objective of school administration is to realize faithfully the goals which are laid down in the country.

Education in a democracy has to fulfil the democratic ideal. Educational administration must be referred to as social statesmanship. Educational administrator must not be thought of in operational terms. The management of educational institution is only a part, although an important part of educational administration. Educational administrators must have a broad social perspective before them. They should bear in mind the following objectives :

1. To organise the school life in such a way as to provide social life to the students so that they may be prepared in the 'Art of Living Together'. The school has its own community life which can be used as an excellent training ground for citizenship.
2. To make the school a place of Community Centre.
3. To provide initiative and freedom to the students and the teachers.
4. To organise co-curricular activities.
5. To help each pupil in the unfolding and blossoming of his personality.
6. To prepare the students for vocation in line with their abilities and aptitudes.
7. To develop ethical judgement and aesthetic appreciation based on a correct philosophy of life.
8. To train students in scientific attitude towards life and its problems.

The objectives of the school administration may be summed up in the words of P.C. Wren as "organise the school to benefit the scholar, to train his faculties, to widen his outlook, to cultivate his mind, to form and strengthen his character, to develop and cultivate his aesthetic faculty, to build up his body, and give him health and strength to teach his duty to himself, the community and the State. Organise the school for this and not to prepare him for the Matriculation Examination."

Significant Factors

(a) Principles of democratic administration. (b) Scientific collection of the data. (c) Efficient use of the school machinery. (d) Judicious use of money. (e) Target fixing. (f) Periodic checking or evaluation. (g) Flexibility.

Important Principles

An efficient administration must be based on the following principles of democratic administration :

(i) Principle of sharing responsibility.

(ii) Principle of equality.

(iii) Principle of freedom.

(iv) Principle of cooperation.

(v) Principle of justice.

(vi) Principle of recognizing the individual worth.

(vii) Principle of leadership.

Scientific Collection of the Data. This implies that the school records must be maintained in a proper manner. They must be up-to-date, complete in all respects and quite accurate. Any lapse in this direction is likely to upset the whole planning of organisation. The administrator, that is, the head of the school must devote adequate attention to this aspect of school administration.

Efficient Use of the School Machinery. What is school machinery ?

By school machinery we mean the building, the teachers and the students. The work of the school should be distributed among the members of the staff in such a way that the right teacher teaches the right class. This implies that work should be distributed among the members of the staff according to their qualifications and experience. A good time-table will enable the head to make the best use of the school building.

Attempt should be made to associate the students with the organisation of different school activities. A limited form of self-government is very helpful in enlisting their cooperation.

Judicious Use of Money. The school money is a trust in the hands of the school authorities. Most of the troubles in schools may be attributed to the wrong use of the funds, especially the Boys' Fund which gives a handle to the students to create mischief and cause indiscipline. It is, therefore, very necessary that the Boys' Fund must be spent for the welfare of the students.

Target Fixing. Term-wise programme should be chalked out. The entire syllabus to be covered during the academic year should be divided into four terms.

Periodic Checking. Terminal and monthly tests should be conducted to judge the progress of the students as well as teachers.

Flexibility. It must be stressed that administration is a means and not an end. It must not dominate the end. The end is the many-sided development of the personality of the child. The curriculum, the methods of teaching, the examinations, the time-table and in fact every aspect of school administration is devoted to this end. Therefore, it is but proper that the administration should be kept flexible. H.G. Stead has rightly stated that administration should be fluid. Freedom should be given to the teachers to use their own methods of teaching. Similarly, students should not be forced to obey a multiplicity of rules and regulations. At some other place it has been discussed that self-discipline cannot be achieved through rod and punishment. It can only be realised through love and sympathy.

Similarly, monthly tests should not be treated all in all. They are a means to the end as enumerated above. All the aspects of school administration and the administration itself is the servant of the students, the teachers and the Head and as such it must not be given the place of a master. It should be dynamic and static and should change according to the circumstances.

In the end we may emphasise that there must be a right cooperative spirit behind the school administration. All the organisational agencies must work in team-spirit. Then and only then the functions of the school will be really achieved.

The Difficulties

In the past the life of the community was very simple and the school administration was also a simple affair. At present, the modern life has become very complex and the school system has also become very complicated. Democracy and science have given birth to new outlook and broader visions. In education, a host of theories regarding child development, methods of teaching, curriculum construction, etc., have brought new educational awareness. The following factors have greatly influenced the problems of school administration :

(i) Increase in the school going population. People are becoming increasingly education conscious. Today we find a large number of students attending the school. They differ in tastes, needs, aptitudes and in various other ways. Family and social backgrounds of the students also vary. This has made the problem of educational administration very complex.

(ii) The school of today is not only concerned with the intellectual development of the child but is to train him in the 'art of living together' which in itself is a complicated affair.

(iii) Growing recognition of new demands upon administration and the necessity of an imaginative response in transforming the job of the head of an institution.

(iv) Schools are expected to help in achieving goals of secularism and national unity and as such the importance of its impact on educational administration can hardly be ignored.

(v) The school is devoted to and engaged in the service of the basic democratic principles and goals, recognising, at the same time, its service to the individual and to the progressive improvement of society. Looking at the functions of school from this angle we find that they present many administrative problems.

It is quite evident from the above that new situations demand new techniques and are a challenge to the old, rigid and dogmatic practices which we have followed so far.

Changed Conception

Change is the order of the day. Our conception and procedures of school administration must be in accordance with our particular culture and traditions. Neither a system of education nor its administration should be imported. To be authentic and effective they must be indigenous. Revolutionary changes have taken place in our country and accordingly our objectives and procedures of school administration must undergo a radical change to be in conformity with the changing needs of the times.

The Vigilance

P.W.L. Cox and R.E. Langfitt write, "Administration executes, directs, supervision advises with, stimulates, explains, leads, guides and assists. Both plan, both diagnose, both inspect, but administration decides and orders execution, while supervision helps to decide and assist in improving institution."

Administration represents the whole enterprise of school management and the supervision represents a portion of it that is delegated to others by the administrators. Supervision represents a practical part of the over-all direction of the school enterprise.

Different Types

External administration implies control from above governmental control through the Department of Education. The issues like framing of rules and regulations, enforcement of compulsory education, prescription of textbooks, framing of courses of studies, fixation of salaries and service conditions of teachers, fixation of school working days etc., are decided and controlled by the Department of Education and the educational institutions are required to conform to the departmental rules and regulations.

Internal control implies the management of the day-to-day school programme and activities through the head and his assistants.

Democratic Administration and Monarchical Administration. Prof. Humayun Kabir writes, "If our democratic way of life is to survive and prove effective it is essential that our children grow up using and understanding its techniques. If our children are, during their school lives, in the position of subjects to an autocratic rule, no matter how benevolent, they are not learning to fill their place adequately in a democracy." According to principal R.R. Kumria, the democratic administration differs from monarchical administration in four respects. The first is that in a monarchical administration, the will of one man reigns supreme while in a democratic administration, the will of the group counts. Secondly, in a monarchical administration, there are social grades of high and low and in a democratic administration, all members are equal and there are no such social grades. Thirdly, in a monarchical administration emphasis is on personalities, while in a democratic administration, rules and codes govern and not the whims of personalities. And fourthly, there are special privileges for the administrators in a monarchical administration whereas there are no special privileges for anybody in democratic administration.

Why Democratic Educational Administration? In a democracy all institutions, social, economic, political, educational, and others should be organised from the democratic standpoint. The school is no longer regarded a place where students receive formal instruction but it is regarded to be "devoted to and engaged in the service of the basic democratic principles, and goals, recognising at the same time its service to the individual and to the progressive improvement of society."

This implies that the administration of a school should be done in such a way as it helps in the realization of the aims for which the school exists. In a society where the dominant ideals are democratic, the administration of education will be essentially democratic whereas in a society favouring the autocratic pattern of living and thinking, the administrative organisation for education is necessarily autocratic. Since independence we have evolved a new pattern of social and political ideals and the philosophical foundations of our educational administration which must be modified accordingly. In the words of Chitra Naik, an educational administrator "is more than an official, punctilious about administrative routine, he is a leader, guiding and directing a sacred undertaking. The official apparatus that is at his disposal, the education department that is under his control, is more than a bureaucratic machine. It is an instrument of social service."

There is a close relationship between school administration and objectives of education in a community, and between social and political objectives of a community and its educational objectives. The objectives of the educational system of our country have been beautifully described by the Secondary Education Commission. These objectives are based on the fact that India had decided to transform herself into a secular democratic republic according to the constitution. This means that the educational system makes its contribution to the development of habits, attitudes and qualities of character which will enable its citizens to bear worthily the responsibilities of democratic citizenship and to counteract all those fissiparous tendencies which hinder the emergence of a broad, national and secular outlook. The educational administrators must understand the implications of these objectives and discard their traditional attitude and approach and should reorganise their entire administrative machinery in such a way as these objectives are realised.

3

Administrative Setup

Report of Commission

Ramamurthi Report 1990 has laid great stress on the decentralisation of administration and management of education in view of the "sheer size and diversity of the country". It has observed, "In the sphere of education, the size and diversity of the country get reflected in the magnitude of the population to be provided education, number of the educational institutions to be established from the primary to the university level, the number of languages in which delivery services have to be organised, the cultural and regional diversities which have to be linked to the content and process of education etc. Decentralisation is the only solution to these problems. There is need for decentralisation of educational planning and management all the way down at all levels, from the centre to the states, from the states to the districts, from the districts to the blocks, from the blocks to the panchayats/villages and habitations.

Decentralisation in the university system would mean autonomy for the universities and colleges as well as for the respective facilities and individual teachers. Examination reforms including establishment of continuous, comprehensive internal evaluation cannot come about unless delegation of authority and decentralisation of functions becomes real down to the level of teachers. Educational complexes recommended by the Committee are construed as an instrument of bringing about decentralisation.

Services taken Together

Side by side with emphasising decentralisation as the cornerstone of planning and implementation of educational programmes, the Committee has laid much stress on convergence of services already available through the parallel infrastructure created in several departments vitally connected with education. This would call for institutionalised coordination mechanisms to be evolved and to be set into operation as a rule of practice.

Management in Cooperation

The Committee has envisaged the concept of participative educational order as being relevant to every stage of education as only involvement through participation can bring about the environment for genuine reform. Important modalities contemplated in this regard are involvement of the colleges and universities in issues of regional development and improvement of school education; creation of school complexes, bringing about mutual coordination between primary schools, middle schools, high schools, colleges and universities (the universities affiliating themselves, as it were, with these complexes so that management of education becomes a job of the professional); forging education-industry interactions for the purpose of bringing about cost effective and practice-oriented vocationalisation of school education, involvement of the village communities in working for the goal of universal elementary education; non-formalising the formal school system so that the system itself reaches out to the door-steps of those who are out of school, apart from being attractive to, and also be capable of retaining them; assignment of meaningful role to genuine voluntary agencies engaged in educational development programmes; and, of course, the teacher being placed at centre-stage in educational reform at all levels with careful attention devoted to their status, recruitment modalities, service conditions and training.

The Coordination

The Ministry of Human Resource Development should undertake a serious review of the situation regarding inter-departmental coordination to bring about convergence of services coming within the purview of the individual departments under the Ministry. The Ministry should also lay down specific modalities of bringing about this coordination and convergence of services. An appropriate institutionalised mechanism should be created for the purpose by the Ministry. Interdepartmental coordination should percolate down to the grass root levels for the purpose of bringing about convergence of services, particularly, for facilitating girls' universalisation of elementary education through support services such as provision of access for them to water, fodder and fuel.

Central Institutes

Institutions like the NCERT and UGC should bring about a sea change in their style of functioning, confining themselves to the role of coordination and providing resource support. They should allow institutions in the State and sub-State levels areas of their competence in a way relevant to the local circumstances.

Educational Counselling

Instead of creating the Indian Education Service, Cadres of Educational Advisory Service should be created in the States on the model of the Government of India. (In the Government of India, larger number of posts should be operated, under the Advisory Service.)

Role of Voluntary Organisations

While liberal flow of funds for securing people's participation through voluntary agencies is unobjectionable, care should be taken to see that the same does not dilute the voluntary spirit of these institutions or distract them from their originally chartered course of action.

In the matter of securing participation of voluntary agencies, the preferred path should be for the Government to respond to the initiatives of voluntary organisations with reference to their own programmes.

Various Complexes

The Committee has recommended educational complexes in place of school complexes as envisaged by the Education Commission 1964-66.

School System for All

The Review Committee has recommended the common school system on account of the following benefits :

1. It is open to all children irrespective of economic, social and other differences.
2. Access to education depends on merit.
3. It is possible to maintain standards.
4. No tuition fee is charged.
5. The ordinary parent would not ordinarily feel the need of sending his children to expensive schools outside this system.
6. This system has been prevalent in the U.S.A., U.S.S.R. and some European countries in some form or the other.

Reasons why the Common School System has not gained ground so far, are the following:

Economic and social disparities; the well-to-do communities send their children to schools with better infrastructure, teachers and teaching standards; ordinary schools are not sought after; and in turn, results in low investments in them.

The constitutional protection given to the minorities to establish and administer their own educational institutions etc. does not go with the concept of the Common School System.

In Government schools, the quality of education has remained poor.

Lack of political will.

Public schools, privately managed English medium schools, schools charging capitation fees and those having expensive coaching classes have proliferated.

Growth of institutions in the Government sector like the Sainik Schools and Kendriya Vidyalayas meant for separate categories of students.

Recommendations for Popularising Common School System

Provision of significantly increased outlay for elementary (particularly primary) education. This would help in the building up of the required levels of infrastructure and quality of education, thereby transforming Government, local-body and aided schools into genuine Neighbourhood Schools.

Provision of special allocations for improvement of school system in backward areas, urban slums, tribal areas, hilly tracts, desert and marshy areas, drought and flood-prone zones, coastal belts and islands.

Ensuring instruction for all in the medium of mother tongue at the primary level, particularly for linguistic minorities; active encouragement of teaching in the regional languages at the secondary levels; and discontinuance of State aid to the schools imparting education otherwise than in the medium of mother tongue/ regional language.

Phased implementation of the common school system within a ten year time frame.

Exploring ways of including the expensive private schools into the common school system through a combination of incentives, disincentives and legislation.

On a pilot basis, at least one Educational Complex may be established in every district during the Eighth Five Year Plan so as to develop a functional model. At the pilot stage full administrative and financial support should be given to these Complexes. The features of these Complexes are described below:

1. The Management model may be that of a local college, a high school or group of high schools and the associated middle and primary schools coming together in a cluster. The Complex may work in coordination with Panchayati Raj institutions as well as local development and social welfare agencies, voluntary or Government. The university serving the region may affiliate itself with this Complex. The university may help in the development of the Complex through its faculty, students and technical resources. There could be a memorandum of understanding between the Complex and the university on the one hand, and the Complex and the local body, on the other. The Complex will follow its own self-monitoring system. Parallel systems of monitoring through the university, District Board of Education, local body, resource agencies (SCERT SIE/ DIET) etc., could coexist. The Complex should be provided with adequate intellectual resources as well.
2. In the long term, these Educational Complexes may come under the umbrella of Panchayati Raj institutions/ local bodies. The details of devolution of responsibilities at different tiers of education will no doubt depend upon the legal framework that may be designed by the State for the purpose.
3. The management of education in the Complexes should be the job of professionals, i.e. the teaching community. Various aspects like curriculum; syllabi, content and process, evaluation, monitoring, teacher training and modes of delivery of education to different segments of the society will be the responsibility of the teaching community itself.

4. In discharging this responsibility, teachers will closely interact with the community they are serving. In this arrangement, the quality of education will not be determined by a body of inspectors or functionaries external to the education system. Consequently, education being directly in the hands of those for whom it is a matter of day-to-day concern, its quality should significantly improve.
5. While the running of the Educational Complexes will be the joint concern of the community and the teachers who are internal to the system, their funding will necessarily come from the State Governments and other local bodies that may have jurisdiction. For the purpose of ensuring that the financial resources deployed by them really result in efficient delivery of education, the State Governments and the local bodies may interact with the Educational Complexes through District Boards of Education and Block-level and Village-level Education Committees. These bodies will consist of educationists, teachers, social workers, representatives of voluntary organisations, trade unions and official development sections such as Scheduled Castes and Tribes, Other Backward Classes, women etc.
6. The Head of the educational institution, the Headmaster/ Headmistress/Principal shall have meaningfully delegated authority with the teachers being centre-stage.
7. The community also will need to be made aware of simple parameters with reference to which they can make their own assessment of the learning outcome from the schools, in both the cognitive and the affective domains.

The Educational Complexes should be autonomous registered societies in structures and they should be vested with the following powers :

(i) To take decisions, in Council, on all matters on which powers have been delegated which should include powers for recruitment of teaching and non-teaching staff, their transfers within a well defined transfer policy, discipline, control, finance etc.

(ii) To organise professional orientation and updating of all the teachers and administrators, so as to make them perform better on the job and to increase their sense of professionalism.

(iii) To develop suitable support materials and teaching aids.

(iv) To engage in mutual and on-going administrative and academic supervision of schools, through a systematic and agreed programme of action, using the resources of DIETs and SCERTs, where available.

(v) To mobilise resources from within the community, to supplement and complement the Government grants.

(vi) To prepare and implement the action plans for universalisation of education, for those who come within the area of the Complex.

(vii) To plan action programmes for adult and continuing education, aiming at functional education for all and where possible also literacy; and accordingly, to organise programmes of skill, aptitude and knowledge education for the various sections in the area of the Complex.

4

The Management

School administration lays more emphasis on the rigidity of rules and regulations. Management stresses human relations and organisation highlights coordination. It must, however, be noted that all these elements are present in varying degrees in all these concepts.

Some writers mention the following differences :

Educational administration or school administration lays down the aims, policies and guidelines of educational institutions. School management is concerned with the achievement or realisation of these.

Educational administration is more concerned with rules and regulations while school management is concerned with the realisation of objectives.

School administration, because of its emphasis on rules is generally rigid and traditional. In school management innovative ideas are appreciated.

In school administration, results are not easily measurable. In school management results are easily measurable.

Administrative Trends

Authoritarianism. In this type of management, the subordinates usually use terms like 'Malik', 'Huzoor', 'Annadata', 'Sarkar' etc. The behaviour of the administrators and the managers is autocratic and hurts the dignity and self-respect of the workers. The administrators and the managers thrive by creating terror in the minds of the workers.

Bureaucratic. It has six characteristics :

(a) There is the rigidity of official behaviour.

(b) There is resistance to the adoption of innovations and change.

(c) There is a rigidity of rules and regulations.

(d) The decision is taken by a hierarchy of officers and officials.

(e) There is the levelling of talent. This system tends to reduce the performance of bright workers to the level of mediocrity.

(f) The consequence is the 'red tape' which is never in the straight line. All feel entrapped and helpless.

Cultural Ethos. Management is also influenced by the cultural ethos of a country. Traditionally, it is not considered fair in India to terminate the services of an employee whereas 'hirings' and 'firings' are very common in the U.S.A.

Scientific. Two mechanical Engineers, Henry R. Towne and Frederick W. Taylor are the pioneers of the scientific management. Scientific management involves criticism, modification or revision of existing or new methods of doing jobs and of the flow of inputs in relation to men, machines and processes. This approach treats man as a machine.

Bagley used the term scientific management in educational management in his book, Classroom Management which was released in 1907. The book became so popular that it underwent 30 reprints in a short period. Such terms as 'raw material' and 'financial products' came to be used for pupils and 'supervisor' for principal.

Motivational. As a result of Haorne studies emphasis began to be laid on motivation as an important factor in exhorting workers by treating them as human beings. These studies were conducted by George Elton Mayo and F.J. Roethlisberger, Professors of industrial research at Harvard Graduate School of Business Administration. Effects of important factors like physical environment, proportion of work and fatigue, wage incentives etc. on the productivity of workers were found out.

Following are the three modern theories of management:

Theory of Management by McGregor. Its basic assumptions are given below:

(i) The average human being has an inherent dislike of work.

(ii) The average human being avoids work if he can.

(iii) Because of the human characteristics of dislike of work, there arises the need for coercion, control and direction of individuals. The individuals are threatened with punishment to get them to put forth adequate effort for the achievement of objectives of an organisation.

(iv) The average human being wants security.

'Y' Theory of Management by Douglas. Following are its

(i) The average human being does not inherently dislike work.

(ii) Self-control and self-direction are perhaps more powerful means than external control and the threat of punishment for bringing about better results.

(iii) Self-actualization is the highest level need of the worker.

(iv) The average human being works under proper conditions not only to accept but also to seek responsibility.

(v) The capacity to exercise a relatively high degree of imagination, ingenuity and creativity in the solution of organisational problems is wisely distributed in the management personnel.

(vi) Under the modern industrial life, the intellectual potentialities of the average human being are only partially utilised.

'Z' Theory of Management. This theory has been evolved by William G. Ouchi, Professor at the University of California, Los Angeles. Its salient features are given below:

(i) Employment is life-time.

(ii) There is slow promotion.

(iii) There is no evaluation for the first ten years of service.

(iv) An individual has adequate opportunities in the organisation to move from one speciality to another.

(v) There is participative decision-making.

(vi) All significant achievements are outcomes of team work and group effort.

(vii) There is holistic concern for the employee which means that the employer not only provides work to the employee but also accepts the obligation of looking after his physical, intellectual and moral development. A public announcement to this effect is made at the time of the induction of the employee.

Principle of Sharing Responsibility. A democratic administrator acts upon the principle of sharing responsibility. He does not himself usurp all powers but shares control and responsibility not only with his colleagues but also with the students. He does not make the mistake of thinking that he is born to rule. He delegates some of his powers to his colleagues. He avoids to be on the top of everything in the school. He introduces student government in the school under the guidance of expert teachers.

Principle of Equality. R.R. Kumria writes, "A democratic administrator should look upon the personnel as socially equal to himself, he should not take decisions by himself, but with his colleagues; he should make them feel responsible and share in administration; he should have a code of set rules of administration which he and his colleagues should follow rigidly, making no discrimination in their application, and lastly, he should want no special privilege." He should avoid all 'bossing tendencies'. He should treat all those who work under him as his 'co-workers' as in democracy there are no subordinates.

Principle of Freedom. People are at their best when they have freedom to exercise their powers and talents. Unnecessary restraints imposed by the administrators curb all initiative and enthusiasm of their subordinates. The power of critical thinking to arrive at the proper decisions which is an important feature of democratic education can only be cultivated by individuals in an atmosphere of freedom.

The Principal will not command or force or impose his will upon the students and the teachers. The Principal should give freedom to the teachers to ask questions, to criticise, to reason and to differ in viewpoints with him. According to Ryburn, both headmasters and inspectors should give due recognition to any signs of display of initiative on the part of a teacher. The teachers should be given sufficient amount of freedom in classroom procedures. They should be encouraged to try all the modern methods of instruction.

A democratic administrator will also give a fair amount of freedom to the students to exercise their powers.

Principle of Cooperation. A democratic head will stress the importance of working together in a spirit of mutual help and cooperation. The school is said to be cooperative society in which every member must work for all and all for each. A cooperative spirit must be reflected in every activity of the school - cooperation between the head and the staff, head and the students, head and the parents, head and the managing committee, head and the inspector, etc. All engaged in the field of education have the same interests and purposes and there is no reason why there should not be cooperation at all levels of educational administration.

Ryburn writes, "The pupils of the school, if they are to develop the characteristics of cooperativeness must live when in school in a society which in a practical way provides a living example of cooperation." Dewey tells us, "A society which makes provision for participation in the good of all its members on equal terms and which secures flexible readjustment of its institutions through interaction of the different forms of associated life is in so far democratic. Such a society must have a type of education which gives individuals a personal interest in social relationships and control, and habits of mind which secure social changes without introducing disorder."

Principle of Justice. A democratic administrator will not show undue favours to some. All will be treated on the same footing. All points of disputes should be promptly and judiciously settled. Lack of justice breeds disgust and frustration among the service personnel. Individual worth and not birth should be given due importance. No person should be above rules and regulations. All matters should be investigated thoroughly before decisions are given.

The teachers and the students should feel that the head is an embodiment of fair play and justice. Most of our troubles in our educational institutions will vanish if once we recognise the importance of fair play and justice.

Principle of Recognition of the Individual Worth. The democratic administrator will respect the individuality of his co-workers. He will not injure their self-respect. He will realise the necessity of studying his co-workers individually. Knowledge of home conditions, cultural and social background, psychological traits and temperamental characteristics of the teachers and the students aids in his task considerably.

The merit of the individual should be given its due recognition. Ryburn writes, "Nothing will more encourage a man or a woman, a boy or a girl, to great effort, than an encouraging recognition of good work done, of sincere effort made, of good qualities shown. If those in charge of institutions, and those carrying on the administrative work of department wish to enable those working with them to do their best, they should always realize the value of ungrudging recognition of all that merits such recognition."

The Principle of Leadership. An educational administrator is a leader of various groups and he must possess qualities of leadership so that others may also follow him. In every sphere of human activity, leadership is beset with difficulties. The adminis-trator must have a grasp of group and individual psychology, if he is to be successful.

Chitra Naik enumerates in detail the qualities needed in a person who hopes to exercise effective administrative leadership as "Desire to serve the people, identification with their problems, ability to think more and more creatively than others, courage of convictions, courage to shoulder responsibility, tenacity of purpose, high intelligence, personal dignity and charm, maturity in social behaviour, emotional stability, faith in cooperative action, faith in the dependability of people, willingness to delegate responsibility as well as authority, ability to supply new ideas and ability to supply solutions to problems as they arise, acquired qualities needed for leadership, thorough knowledge of field work, clear vision of goals, competence in planning, good grasp of methods to be used in organising planned work, ability to see and relate goals to existing situations, sound knowledge of the individual and the groups involved in the work of reaching the goals, knowledge of methods for guiding cooperative action, competence in using all the media for inter-personal communication such as speech-making, writing, organisation of social functions, conferences, etc., ability to choose and train workers, ability to do maximum work possible within the framework of rules and regulations and knowledge of how to keep on adding to one's own knowledge as a specialist."

The democratic administration develops friendly relationships among all the members working in every enterprise, educational or otherwise. In a school, if the Principal follows the democratic principles, he is sure to be successful in harnessing the talents and powers of the students and the teachers both to the maximum extent. In a democratic atmosphere everybody works in a spirit of joy and makes a distinct contribution to the progress of the school. The moral enthusiasm of the teachers and the students is raised.

The teachers become professionally mature when they share the planning of the school. The public in general also takes a keen interest in the school, if the head seeks its cooperation.

In the autocratic administration, the personality of the teacher is violated and he occupies a subordinate position. The personality of the child is also violated. The autocratic administration breeds the cult of blind obedience. Books which encourage freedom of thought are condemned. The school becomes merely an arm of the central ministry of propaganda.

> "The boss drives his men, the leader coaches them.
>
> The boss depends on authority, the leader on goodwill.
>
> The boss inspires fear; the leader inspires enthusiasm.
>
> The boss assigns the task; the leader sets the pace.
>
> The boss says, 'Get here on time; the leader gets there ahead of time.
>
> The boss fixes the blame for the breakdown; the leader fixes the breakdown.
>
> The boss makes work a drudgery; the leader makes it a game."

The scope of school administration is sufficiently wide and it includes the administering of a total programme of education fulfilling the needs of democracy. School administration concerns all relationships in school system, i.e. relationship between the Head and the students, between the staff and the students, between the school and the community, between the menial staff and the teaching staff, between the Head and the staff, between the school and the State or the university and so on. It involves the following functions :

1. Formulation of the purposes of the school administration.
2. Coordination of work among teaching personnel.
3. Classification and grouping of pupils.
4. Organisation of a systematic co-curricular programme.

5. Planning the curricula and distribution of work.
6. Providing various services, i.e. responsibilities with regard to building and equipment, laboratories, library sanitation, ventilation, etc.
7. Maintaining discipline at school.
8. Organising the programme for health and health education.
9. Maintenance of school office.
10. School building.
11. Coordinating the work of home, school and community.
12. Initiating students into social service programmes.
13. Providing opportunities to the students to get training in the 'art of living together'.
14. Evaluating pupil achievement.
15. Assigning teacher's work in a way so that each can achieve maximum efficiency.
16. Formulating school policies democratically.
17. Encouraging teachers to exercise freedom in the performance of their duties within the limits of school policy.
18. Making education a cooperative enterprise involving both faculty and students.
19. Making school policies consistent with present day educational philosophy.
20. Supervising teachers in classroom and conferences.
21. Cooperating with departmental authorities.

Picture of a Well Managed School as Visualised by the Secondary Education Commission 1952-53 and the Role of the Educational Administrator

The following points taken from the Report of the Secondary Education Commission fully illustrate the picture of a secondary school as visualised by the Commission and the role of the educational administrator to do this end.

Provision of a Stimulating Environment. The first concern of the school should be to provide for its pupils a rich, pleasant and stimulating environment which will evoke their manifold interests and make life a matter of joyful experience.

Development of Child's Entire Personality. We would like the school to see if it can provide a richly varied pattern of activities to cater to the development of its children's entire personality. It has to formulate a scheme of hobbies, occupations and projects that will appeal to draw out the powers of children of varying temperaments and aptitudes.

Training in the Art of Living Together. We do not visualize this school as merely a place of formal learning, whose main concern is to communicate a certain prescribed quantum of knowledge but rather as a living and organic community which is primarily interested in training its pupils in what we have called the gracious "art of living."

Activity School. The secondary school of the future must be transformed into an "activity school" because activity has an irresistible appeal for every normal child and is his natural path to the goal of knowledge and culture.

Intrinsic Relationship

We do not visualize that these schools will have dull, routine-ridden formal lessons in the class plus a number of independent unrelated extra-curricular activities which have no intrinsic relationship with them either in contents or methods. The entire programme of the school will be visualised as a unity and inspired by a psychologically congenial and stimulating approach, the so-called 'work' being characterised by the feeling of joy and self-expression usually associated with play and hobbies, and these later having something of the meaningful and purpose which are normally considered a special feature of academic work. Thus by planning a coherent programme of these different activities, rich in stimuli, the school will not be fritting away either the time or the energy of the pupils but will be heightening their intellectual powers also side by side while training them in other fine qualities.

The School Laboratory. The school laboratory will not be a toy-affair, where a few simple and carefully planned experiments are performed under vigilant eye of the teacher who sees that the prescribed routine is followed. It will endeavour to give them something of the thrill and joy of discovery and the educative experience of learning through trial and error.

Self-discipline. Discipline in the school will not be a matter of arbitrary rules and regulations enforced through the authority of the teachers helped by the lure of rewards or the fear of punishment. The students will be given full freedom to organise functions, to conduct many of the school activities through their own committees and even to deal with certain types of disciplinary cases. In this way, discipline will be maintained through the influence of the social group and it will gradually lead to the development of self-discipline.

No school can develop into an educative community, capable of releasing the students' creative capacities, if the teachers maintain a stiff, forbidding attitude towards their pupils and try to maintain their authority through various kinds of punishments whilst the pupils on their part, stand in awe of them and are not prepared to share their problems and difficulties with them.

The Teacher. The good teacher, in our reorganised school, will endeavour to win the love and confidence of his children and establish his prestige on sincerity, integrity, hard work and a sympathetic handling of their problems.

Assessment of the Day-to-Day Work. In this school the emphasis will shift from examination to education, teachers and children will concentrate on the real purpose of the school and will take examination in their stride. Much greater credit can be given to the actual work done by the students from day-to-day, of which careful and complete records should be maintained. Moreover, in assessing his progress and his position, factors other than academic achievement should be given due weight, his social sense, initiative, discipline, cooperation, leadership, etc.

Library as the Hub of School Activities. The library will be the hub and the centre of the intellectual and literary life of the reorganised school and play the same role vis-a-vis all other subjects as the laboratory plays for science subjects or the workshop for technical subjects. In fact, even in the case of scientific and technical subjects it will have a very important role.

Provision of Craft and Productive Work. We expect this school to devote special attention to craft and productive work and thus redress the balance between theoretical and practical studies which have been upset for many years.

Every well-established and reasonably well-financed school will have workshops and craft-rooms where students will learn to handle tools and to fashion different kinds of material into form.

The School as a Centre of Community Service. Another thing which will distinguish this school from most of the existing schools is that it will be organised as a community.

Manual Labour. We have no doubt that under proper encouragement students all over India can, if necessary, carry out minor repairs, whitewash school rooms, keep the school garden and compound in good shape, paint and polish the furniture, decorate the bare walls of their rooms with charts, picture and illustrations and enliven them with flowers wherever this loveliest of Nature's gifts is available.

The Commission concluded by stating, "This is the picture of the reorganised secondary school as we visualise it. We realise that all schools may not be able to work up to it immediately. But it is not an impossible or unduly idealized picture and it does point the correct direction of advance. If the educational authorities and the teachers accept this conception of the school, we are of the opinion that, in spite of the many difficulties and handicaps that exist, it will be possible to bring about many welcome improvements in our schools."

5

Institutional Leadership

"By virtue of his office, he has to be a nexus between the government and the school authorities, the management and the staff, the masters and pupils, and the parents and teachers character rather than capacity, tact rather than authority, sympathy rather than severity are his forte."

-S. Balakrishna Joshi

Significance of the Post

"The Headmaster or the Principal of a school is the hub of the education process."

-Jaswant Singh

"Just as every group needs a leader, so also a school must have a leader who would stimulate and direct its work."

-Mohi-ud-din

"Schools are good or bad, in a healthy or unhealthy mental, moral and physical condition, flourishing or perishing as the headmaster is capable, energetic and of high ideals or the reverse."

-P.C. Wren

"Schools rise to fame or sink to obscurity as greater or lesser headmasters have charge of them."

-P.C. Wren

"The character of the school reflects and proclaims the character of the headmaster."

-P.C. Wren

"He is the seal and school is the wax."

-P.C. Wren

"What the main spring is to the watch, the flywheel to the machine or the engine to the steamship, the headmaster is to the school."

-P.C. Wren

"On him the proper working of the school ultimately depends."

-Secondary Education Commission 1952-53

"The reputation of the school and the position that it holds in the society depends in a large measure on the influence that he exercises over his colleagues, his pupils and the general public."

-Secondary Education Commission

"He acts as a liaison between it (the school) and the department and the general local community."

-Secondary Education Commission

"He holds an important place in the life of the community, where he can exercise a very healthy influence."

-Secondary Education Commission

"By his contact with the parents and the general public he can help to forge that link between the school and the larger community which we have repeatedly stressed."

-Secondary Education Commission

"The Headmaster is a link between internal and external administration of the school."

-S.N. Mukherjee

"The Headmaster is a keystone of the arch of school administration."

-S.N. Mukherjee

The Headmaster is in the strategic centre of a web of instructional inter-relationships - teacher-pupil, teacher-teacher, teacher-supervisor, teacher-parent and teacher-superintendent.

The school may be called the lengthened shadow of the Headmaster.

The Headmaster is the solar orb round whom all the planets (teachers) revolve.

An Ideal Head

1. The Head is the hub of the education process.
2. The Head is the leader of the school.
3. The Head is the seal and the school the wax.
4. The Head is like the main spring of the watch.
5. The Head is like flywheel to the machine.
6. The Head is like the engine to the steamship.
7. The Head is a liaison.
8. The Head is the strategic centre.
9. The Head is the solar orb.
10. The Head is a link.
11. The Head is a key-stone.

Common Responsibilities

According to the Punjab Education Code, it is the duty of the Headmaster to exercise general control of the school and boarding house in his charge; to maintain discipline among the staff and pupils; to organise and supervise the instruction; to prescribe the textbooks; to take a regular part in the teaching work especially in classes and subjects in which his personal guidance is desirable; to arrange for the games and other extra-mural activities of the pupils; to see that all registers are regularly and accurately maintained; to keep strict accounts of all moneys entrusted to him, and to see that they are properly disposed of in accordance with the rules laid down in that regard; and generally to promote the physical, intellectual and moral welfare of the people under his charge.

Organizational Administration

School Office. 1. The Principal should see that a spacious, airy and well-furnished room has been provided for the school office.

2. He should see that records are properly maintained and kept up-to-date.
3. He should be prompt in official correspondence.
4. He should not, as far as possible, entrust office work such as collection of fees, maintenance of fee registers, keeping supplies and stores, to his teachers.
5. He should give every facility to teachers to use school office as service agency.

Time Table. 1. He should see that school time-table is kept and bell rings at the appointed time.

2. He should take care to see that the school time-table is operative on the very opening day of the school.
3. He should equalize working load of teachers as far as possible.
4. He should make routine administrative assignment fairly to all teachers.
5. He should arrange his time and work in office in such a way that teachers may see him conveniently as often as necessary.
6. He should prepare the school time-table in consultation with teachers.
7. He should make school time-table suitable to local conditions.

School-Budget. 1. He should have the school budget for the whole school-year carefully prepared well in advance.

2. The pupils as well as teachers should be allowed to participate in the preparation of the parts of the school budget which concern co-curricular activities.
3. He should see that provision is made in the school budget for all regular and anticipated needs so that the necessity

of reallocations and reappropriations may be minimised during the school year.

School Supplies. 1. He should purchase educational supplies, viz., paper, pencils, pens, ink, chalk, dusters, black-board paint and laboratory chemicals, etc., only from reliable firms offering lowest quotations.

2. He should invariably ask the firms to submit specimens of the commodities to be purchased.
3. He should always insist on good quality of the materials to be purchased for use in the school.

School-Plant. 1. Head should make arrangements for checking the cleanliness of classrooms, laboratory and playground regularly.

2. He should see that pupils' desks and seats and other articles of furniture in the school are kept in proper repair.
3. He should see that toilet and lavatory arrangements are suitable and adequate to the needs of the school.
4. He should see that the supply of drinking water is adequate for students and staff and it is maintained in proper sanitary condition.
5. He should see that school building is kept in good condition.

6. He should see that the school campus is beautiful and attractive with shady trees, ornamental bushes, hedges and ornamental flowering plants.

School Library. 1. The Principal should see that the school library is made a functional part of the school.

2. He should see that the person in charge of the library is well-acquainted with the classroom programmes.
3. He should see that adequate instructions are made available to the pupils on the use of the library.

Teaching and Learning

Classroom Visits. 1. The Principal should regularly pay supervision visits to the classrooms to acquaint himself with the learning situations provided to pupils.

2. He should stay in the classroom long enough to get an adequate picture of the teaching- learning situations of the class.
3. He should not interfere with the regular class work during his supervision visits.
4. He should inspire confidence and friendliness in the teacher by his attitude during the class visits.
5. His class visits should result in practical assistance to teachers.

Demonstration Lessons. He should regularly arrange for demonstration lessons for the benefit of the teachers.

In-service Education. 1. He should recommend suitable instructional materials and professional books for the use of the teachers and should see that those are provided in time.

2. He should hold teachers' meeting to inspire and stimulate them in their educational thinking.
3. He should use democratic ways of discussion in these meetings.
4. He should see that findings of research studies on "instruction and learning" are made available to teachers.
5. Classroom supervision should lead to research on problems existing in the school.

Human Relations

1. The Principal should be ever ready to consider new ideas on education from others and should be willing to try out those which seem to be usefui.
2. He should consistently hold a "progressive" view in educational matters.
3. He should try to apply such new methods as are suitable to Indian conditions.
4. He should encourage teachers to experiment with new procedures and techniques of education.

5. He should keep in touch with the latest developments in the field of education.
6. He should be democratic in his relations with teachers.
7. He should prove by his actions that he always means what he.
8. He should not favour any of the teachers unduly.
9. He should show by his actions that he has confidence in his teachers.
10. He should give proper recognition to the good work done by the teachers.
11. He should not keep himself aloof from the other members of the staff.
12. The principal should show in his dealings a real respect for the opinion of others.
13. He should not attempt to dominate his teachers by the force of his position.
14. He should have a due regard for the feelings of others.
15. He should never play one teacher against another in order to maintain his official superiority.
16. He should try to mutually reconcile differences, if they arise among teachers, between teachers and parents, and between teachers and the employer.
17. He should be ready to share with his co-workers the responsibility for any deficiency or weakness in the school programme.
18. He should share his work with and delegate responsibilities to suitable staff members and committees.
19. He should provide all possible assistance to new teachers.
20. He should encourage and provide opportunities for in-service education of teachers.

Relationship with Pupils

Health Service and Physical Education. 1. The principal should see that provision for regular and thorough medical check-up of the pupils is made.

2. He should plan for a follow-up programme of medical check-up.
3. He should see that equal opportunities are provided to all pupils under physical education programme.
4. He should see that the energies of the teacher in charge of games, sports and physical education are directed towards the physical development of all pupils and not to the production of winning teams or individuals.

Curriculum. 1. The principal should develop a curriculum which provides experiences to meet the mental as well as physical development of the pupils.

2. He should see that curriculum provides experiences which inculcate healthy moral and ethical standards.
3. He should see that curriculum provides ample opportunity for creative activities of the pupils.
4. He should as far as conditions allow develop a curriculum suited to the needs of pupils of ranging academic ability.
5. He should see that vocational subjects, appropriate to the community, are included in the curriculum.

Co-curricular Activities. 1. He should provide for a varied programme of co-curricular activities in the school to develop the different talents of all pupils.

2. He should get the entire programme of co-curricular activities prepared cooperatively by teachers and pupils.
3. He should not use the co-curricular activities primarily to publicize the school or glorify his position.
4. He should see that all pupils are encouraged to participate in co-curricular activities.

Evaluation and Guidance. 1. The principal should see that the evaluation programme of pupils is a continuous activity.

2. He should see that results of evaluation lead to a guidance programme.
3. He should encourage teachers to construct their evaluation instruments.
4. He should see that pupils are assessed and guided before they choose different subjects for study.
5. He should see that school-leavers get guidance on vocational choices.
6. He should see that school provides for individual and personal guidance to the pupils.

Discipline. 1. The principal should encourage constructive solutions for solving disciplinary problems of pupils met by the teachers.

2. He should allow teachers to deal with the disciplinary cases of pupils and should deal himself only with cases of serious nature.
3. He should develop such traditions in the school as will socially shape conduct of the pupils.

Relations with Community

1. The principal should encourage the parents of the pupils to visit the school frequently.
2. He should see that parents are cordially received when they visit the school.
3. He should regularly inform the parents of the progress of their wards.
4. He should encourage the parents to consult the teachers on special problems of their wards.
5. He should visit the homes of the pupils and should suggest to the teachers also to do the same.
6. He should organize parent-study-groups from time to time.
7. He should provide adequate facilities for the organization and proper functioning of the Parent-Teacher Association in the school.

8. The principal should plan school programme with reference to the needs of the community.
9. He should encourage the use of community resources for vitalizing classroom instruction through excursions, field trips, study of local history, etc.
10. He should encourage and organize social service programmes to render public services.
11. He should allow the community to use school facilities and services like school-building, library, and dispensary seeing at the same time that the work of the school does not suffer.
12. He should organize social and cultural activities in the school to interpret the school programme to the community.
13. He should actively participate in the social and cultural functions of the community.
14. He should be above politics and religion in organizing school programmes.
15. He should not allow the school to become a tool in the hands of any pressure group.
16. He should not allow his political beliefs to influence his administration of school.

Responsibilities towards Managing Body

1. The principal should raise funds and secure donations on behalf and with the consent of the managing body to finance the school programme.
2. He should present the case of the school fully to the Department of Education for getting timely grant-in-aid, recognition for teaching new subjects and opening new sections when needed.
3. He should acquaint the managing body with the school programmes.

4. He should give proper advice to the managing body in the selection and appointment of teachers.
5. He should inform the managing body about the work and conduct of the teachers.
6. He should regularly present to the managing body the various financial accounts of the school.
7. The principal should carry out the orders of the Department of Education in time.
8. He should know the school-law well and should keep the school in tune with it.
9. He should act as campaign manager of various drives initiated by the Department such as 'small saving', 'shramdan' and literacy.
10. He should adhere to the Departmental rules.
11. He should submit such information about the school and its programme in time as required by the Department.
12. He should keep the Department well-informed with the school programme and its working.

Five-fold Division of Problems

I. Problems relating to administrative and financial aspects.
II. Problems relating to teachers.
III. Problems relating to students.
IV. Others.
V. Problems relating to double shift schools.

Various Problems

Problem No. 1 : The Principal has to spend too much time on clerical work.

Suggested Solutions. (a) School clerks should be better trained for the special work required in a school. All clerks should know how to type. Senior clerks should pass efficiency tests in typing and in keeping accounts of finances and school supplies.

(b) The number of clerks allotted to a school should depend on the enrolment and nature of school programmes. Up to 500 students, one clerk; 500 to 1,000 two clerks; and 1,000 and over three clerks.

(c) The post of Vice-principal should be created in schools with more than 750 students.

(d) Part-time bursars should be provided in large schools as soon as possible.

(e) The principal should divide his work into different categories. Certain jobs not involving policy making may be distributed among senior teachers.

Problem No. 2 : Paucity of funds for additional projects.

Suggested Solutions. (a) There should be one consolidated fund and the principal should be free to make expenditure on specified and also on special items according to the dictates of need.

(b) Where government aid is necessary, planning should be done early and requests be sent well in advance of the time they will be needed.

Problem No. 3 : Shortage of time for linking the school with the public and parents.

This is more a problem of available facilities than of lack of time. The second Saturday of each month can conveniently be utilized for this purpose provided proper accommodation, seating arrangements and certain funds are made available.

Problem No. 4 : Apathy of parents towards the school.

This apathy may be due to lack of initiative on the part of the school in making parents interested in education. In some instances it is due to their children's lack of interest.

In other cases, the school is unable to satisfy the parents' expectations. In most cases they don't know the teachers or what goes on in the school.

Suggested ways of improving these conditions. (a) Invite parents to the school. Make them feel that they are welcome and interest them in what the school is doing for their own children.

(b) Arrange informal talks and discussions on problems of special interest to parents.

(c) Request parents to join their children in the school's celebration of community festivals.

(d) Open the school library for the use of parents as well as students.

(e) If there is a school magazine, give parents the opportunity to write articles for it.

Problem No. 5 : Lassitude on the part of class IV servants to work efficiently in schools.

Suggested Solutions. (a) Class IV staff should be categorised into two distinct categories - vocational and non-vocational. The principal should be free to allocate duties of such workers as waterman, farash and peon to anyone in class IV. The mali and sweeper should be treated separately.

(b) Hours of duty should be fixed by the principal.

(c) The minimum of class IV workers in a school of 750 pupils should be a total of five including peon, farash, chowkidar, waterman, etc., one or two sweepers depending upon the spaciousness of the school premises and a whole or part-time mali.

(d) Every attempt should be made to build up morale and pride in work class IV workers.

Problem No. 6 : Pressure put by higher authorities or by Management for admission or promotion of students on the Principal.

The headmaster should not submit to pressure by higher authorities regarding admission and promotion of particular students, and that he should be assured of adequate protection if occasion arises.

Problems for Teachers

Problem No. 1 : Lack of interest among teachers in doing their work honestly and sincerely.

This problem is due to the wider opportunities for teachers outside the school. Too often they regard teaching as the secondary job, the primary one being private coaching or other engagements.

Suggested Solutions. (a) Special recognition may be given to teachers who discharge their obligations honestly and sincerely.

(b) Arouse greater interest in the work of the school by decentralising it and entrusting teachers with more responsibilities.

Problem No. 2 : Unsuitable and unqualified teachers.

Unsuitable teachers include those -

(a) Who have not had proper training, i.e. those who pass examination privately without attending formal lectures and classes in organized institutions.

(b) Those who do not possess the aptitude, cultural background and character traits required of a good teacher.

(c) Unqualified teachers are those who have no teaching degree or diploma or who do not possess the requisite qualifications.

Suggestions for improving the situation. (a) Study leaves on full salary with increments may be sanctioned for one or two years, thus permitting unqualified teachers to prepare for examination.

(b) Permission to take M.A., M.Sc. or M.Com. examination may be granted if the teacher had that particular subject at the graduate level.

(c) A selection grade for teachers may be set up so that they do not feel frustrated on reaching the maximum of their grade, in case they are not promoted to a senior grade.

(d) Refresher courses of about three months' duration in some training college may be arranged for those who put in five years of service.

(e) Provision may be made for the more careful selection and recruitment of teachers.

Problem No. 3 : Shortage of science teachers.

Suggestions offered for meeting this situation. (a) A pool of science teachers of a locality may be formed.

(b) B.Sc. teachers may be permitted to continue taking XI class until there is sufficient number of M.Sc. teachers.

(c) Increased increments to science teachers may be offered as a means of attracting and holding them.

(d) Science teachers may be allowed to continue to teach up to age of 65.

(e) Science graduates may be allowed to attend summer training school for two years and some allowance provided for those who attend.

Problem No. 4 : Resentment shown by teachers for extra work and longer working hours.

Practical suggestions which make it easier for teachers to work extra hours. (a) Place teachers in schools which are within a radius of five miles of their homes.

(b) As far as possible, place teachers in schools which are on a connecting bus route with their homes.

Problem No. 5 : Indiscipline among teachers who are more rights minded than duty-minded.

Such cases arise often when the heads of institutions show lack of leadership and do not attend to their duties punctually and regularly.

The heads should set an example for their teachers. They should take teachers into their confidence and explain what is expected of them. Teachers need friendly guidance as well as do students from a head whom they admire and trust and whose character is above reproach.

Problems for Students

Problem No. 1 : Homework and its loadage.

Following are the suggestions on the amount and type of homework to be assigned : (a) No homework should be given on any topic that has not been taught.

(b) Homework can be oral as well as written.

(c) Written homework should not exceed the following limits two hours work for higher secondary classes; one and a half hours for middle classes; and one hour work for primary classes.

(d) Homework should be properly planned and coordinated between subject teachers. A homework time table prepared by them helps to solve the problem.

Problem No. 2 : Absence of proper and correct study habits.

Some time should be spent in teaching children how to study.

Problem No. 3 : Indiscipline, bad manners and lack of courtesy in students.

Good manners and courtesy should be taught by both example and precept. Since 'character is caught rather than taught,' teaching by example is the more effective method. Principals should seek to correct bad manners and lack of courtesy among their teachers and students. Frequently, the whole tone of the school should be improved. This needs cooperation, time and patience.

Other Difficulties

Problem No. 1 : Shortage of time to organise various co-curricular activities in double-shift schools.

Two or three periods a week should be devoted to co-curricular activities. These should be counted as part of the teaching load of the teachers involved.

Problem No. 2 : Inadequate libraries because the authorities do not give freedom to make a good selection of books.

The principal should be authorised to select and buy books in consultation with his teachers. Sanction should be given earlier in the year to give enough time for selection.

With the opening of a new secondary school, an allotment for at least Rs. 9,000 should be made for the purchase of books, and during the first few years, an allotment up to Rs. 5,000.

Problem No. 3 : Frequent transfer of teachers.

Transfer should not be made in the middle of the year and as far as possible none within three years.

Two Shift System

The system was first adopted in Delhi because it appeared to provide a ready solution to a big problem – the problem of providing immediate schooling facilities to tens of thousands of displaced students from West Pakistan. It was, then, perhaps the only solution of the problem in 1948. But its continued adoption to meet the problem of expansion of educational facilities is not justifiable from the point of view of the realization of the aims and objectives of education. The plea of economy of expenditure is not a good enough plea if the normal standards of education are thereby affected. This double shift system is gradually coming up in all the big towns.

The following are some of the defects of the system which inevitably lead to a lowering of standards. They apply to both types of double shift schools -those with a single administration and those with a double administration. They may be classified under two heads (i) educational and psychological defects; and (ii) administrative and other general drawbacks.

The Shortcomings

(i) The school hours under this system are unnatural and are not conducive to effective learning. Both the students and the teachers of the second shift are tired when they come to school at about mid-day, especially in summer. The first shift people find themselves greatly handicapped in winter when they have to come to school by half past seven in the morning.

(ii) The hours of work are shorter in double shift schools than in single shift schools, whereas the curriculum and the syllabi to be covered are the same for both. This has an adverse effect on the achievements of the students which do not compare well with that of students in single shift schools.

(iii) By making the children work under abnormal and difficult conditions we are helping the formation of poor habits of study and wrong attitudes towards work both among students and teachers. It tends to develop an indifferent attitude to, if not a positive hatred of, school work.

(iv) The teachers have either the morning or the afternoon entirely free. This provides a temptation for them to undertake outside work, so that those who have to work in the second shift are too tired to work zealously. Besides, they come to regard school work as secondary and this attitude affects the quality of their effort and output.

(v) Co-curricular activities which should find an important place in the school programme are, to all intents and purposes, stifled for lack of time.

(vi) The ill-effects of the system are accentuated in the case of those schools which are housed in tents.

(vii) There is generally very little time - at the most half an hour between the two shifts. This makes it very difficult to have the school cleaned before the second shift commences. The cleaning and sweeping work often goes on while the school is working. Thus the school does not get properly started.

(viii) The upkeep and repair of the school furniture and other property constitute a disturbing problem. Generally, it is the responsibility of one of the two shifts; but while the wear and tear is double, the contingency provision is the same as for a single shift school, as only the school owning the property can legitimately incur any expenditure under this head. The same is the case with the charges for water and electricity which have to be borne entirely by one of the two shifts.

(ix) The number of children in the various classes in two schools is often different with the result that the seating arrangements require adjustment everyday before each shift begins. This often takes away some time from the already too short hours of work besides creating a great deal of noise and doing damage to the furniture.

(x) There is also a difficulty with regard to the class IV servants. More often than not they do not cooperate and throw the blame on one-another for not doing things like sweeping the floor or cleaning the window panes. Sometimes their quarrels lead to misunderstandings between the heads which result in unfortunate consequences.

(xi) The setting apart of special rooms for subjects like science, domestic science and drawing, and of offices for heads of schools and staff rooms for teachers poses quite a big problem in school buildings which have not been specially constructed with two shifts in view.

(xii) It is extremely difficult, if not impossible, to organise cultural or educational programmes after school hours so that school life remains poor in these respects. This is specially so where one of the shifts is for girls and the other for boys.

Conscious as we are of the fact that it will not be possible to discard the system overnight, we have formulated some suggestions which might be conveniently adopted to minimize or to overcome some of the difficulties listed above. But in no way do they constitute a permanent solution which consists only in the discontinuation of the system.

(i) Though the hours of work may remain more or less as they are, it should be possible for the teachers of the second shift to come about an hour before the school begins and utilize the time in correction of assignments, etc., for which there is hardly any time during the actual school hours. Similarly, the teachers of the first shift may stay back for the purpose. But this cannot be done unless there is a clear departmental regulation fixing the hours of work.

(ii) Both the teachers and the students of the second shift should be asked to plan their work in their free hours in such a way that they have a long period of rest before they come to school. Of course, there can be no binding force to get them to do this; it must be impressed upon them that they need to come to school physically and mentally fresh.

Similarly, first shift students and teachers may be well-advised to have an adequate period of rest before they take up their out-of-school assignments.

(iii) To meet the difficulties of double shift schools of having to cover the syllabus in a shorter period than in single shift schools, it would be advisable:

(a) To plan the syllabus very carefully and thoughtfully avoiding overlapping and repetition.

(b) To plan home assignments very carefully to make up the deficiencies in the work in school.

(c) To adopt a double period time-table, wherever possible. At least those subjects which are allotted more than one period daily should be given consecutive periods.

(d) To make proper lighting arrangements in double shift schools to enable the school hours to be stretched to the utmost extent possible and desirable under the circumstances.

(iv) Teachers should be required to prepare detailed lesson plans to economise on the time available. These should be regularly checked by the head.

(v) The co-curricular programme should be planned co-operatively by the two heads. The activities should be so interwoven into the curricular programme that they do not really need time outside of the school hours. Where a school has playgrounds nearby, the second shift children should be allowed to utilise them when the first shift is on, and vice versa. Of course, the games programme will have to be planned cooperatively by the two heads. In the case of those schools which have no playgrounds of their own, an effort should be made to take the children to nearby public park and give them as much time as possible per week for games and physical education. With thoughtful planning, it should be possible to make some provision in this respect which is better than none.

(vi) If the school is housed in tents, quick growing trees and bushes should be planned to provide protection against the sun and dust-storms.

(vii) There should be close cooperation and communication of ideas not only between the heads of the two shifts but also among the staff of the two shifts. The aim should be to bring about a feeling of oneness and unity among the heads, teachers and students of both shifts. To ensure cooperation between the two heads it is advisable that they meet daily. It should be so arranged that either the second shift head comes an hour earlier or the first shift head stays on for some more time. But to get the best results from this arrangement, it would be necessary to keep records of such meetings and of the decisions taken therein for future reference. These should be open to inspection by the departmental authorities.

(viii) The heads should, in turn, be held individually responsible, though by mutual arrangement, for the cleanliness of the school building for a period varying from one week to a fortnight. The sweepers of both the shifts should work together for a fixed period before each shift and should be held jointly responsible for the proper cleanliness of the school. It would be better if both the sweepers and chowkidars are provided residential accommodation in the premises of the school. The students should be made responsible for picking up pieces of paper, etc. in and around their own classrooms. They should be trained not to throw scraps of paper in the rooms, but to use the dustbins supplied for the purpose. The expenditure on the maintenance of buildings should be divided and a case made out for additional allotment under this head. If the heads cooperate there should be no difficulty in this regard.

(ix) The number of students in the classes in the two shifts occupying a particular room should, as far as possible, be equalized. The numbers in the classes in the two shifts should be an important factor in deciding the allotment of rooms; or the items of furniture supplied to a particular room should be based on the number in the larger section occupying that room. To avoid damage to furniture and to ensure its better care as also to fix the responsibility for breakage, a diary system should be evolved. Each head should make a note of the breakage taking place in his or her shift and pass it on to the other through the chowkidar of the latter.

6

Educational Administration

The head should follow the principles of democratic administration. There is a marked difference between democratic administration and monarchical administration. In a democratic administration the will of the group counts whereas in a monarchical administration the will of one man rules supreme. A democratic Head will not treat the teachers, clerks and peons as his subordinates but will think them to be his co-workers. The work of a democratic administration has been summed up by R.R. Kumria as, "democratic administrator should look upon the personnel as socially equal to himself, he should not take decisions by himself but with his colleagues; he should make them feel responsible and share in administration; he should have a code of set rules of administration which he and his colleagues should follow rigidly, making no discrimination in their application; and lastly he should want no special privilege."

Dr. E.A. Pires calls that system of educational administration good in which there are evidences of democratic leadership in the implementation of educational policies democratically determined. Educational administration at any level should be a cooperative and democratic process. A good administrator would do well if he uses 'we' and not 'I' in emphasising the achievements of the department or of institution. This gives a sense of pride to his colleagues and they think that due regard is given to their merits.

Significant Features

Bossing suggests six characteristics of the leadership needed in the high school principalship :

Ability to Inspire. The principal must be a leader and not an automation or a despot. One crucial test of the principal's competency must be his ability to inspire and lead teachers, not drive them.

Imagination. Imagination must be a second requisite of the leader of the secondary school.

Adventurous Spirit. All this requires a leader for the secondary school who possesses an unflagging adventurous spirit and an experimental attitude toward his problems.

Educational Expert. Contrary to the emphasis of the past the leader of our democracy's school must be first and foremost an educational expert and secondarily a master of administrative technique the principal is above all else an educational leader who must understand the nature of education and the educational process and give leadership to the educational problems of the school and the community.

Man of Contact. To render effective leadership in school and community the principal must be much more than a pusher of buttons. The principal should be a man of wealth of contacts, direct and vicarious.

Social and Educational Philosophy. Finally but not least in importance, the leadership for the secondary school of today must possess a well defined social and educational philosophy. He must have a clear understanding of the basic philosophies of life and values upon which different contemporary societies are based. He should understand the basic difference between the philosophy of fascism and that of democracy. The place and importance of the school in our democratic society and the relationship of such of its parts in the creation of intelligent democratic citizens he must fully appreciate.

Head and Subordinates

Delicate and Critical Role of the Principal. The principal has to play a very delicate and critical role as he has to strike a balance in the practical field among fighting and quarrelling students, grudging and grumbling teachers and complaining parents. The members of the teaching staff have their different whims : some sensitive, some emotional, some enthusiastic, some old, some young, some trained and other untrained and some marking time. The principal has to make the best use of them and seek their whole-hearted co-operation in all the activities of the school : academic, co-curricular and administrative.

"Encouragement in one case, assistance in overcoming difficulties in another, suggestions here, definite orders there, all are necessary," writes H.G. Stead. The principal has to weld the members of the staff into a real team.

The Principal is expected at various times and by various interests to play many roles. He must by nature of his position be

(a) A Teacher of teachers.

(b) A Supervisor not only of teachers but of service personnel.

(c) A Disciplinarian just but effective.

(d) A Psychologist at least to the extent of discovering maladjustments, especially of teachers which hinder progress.

(e) A Financier in organising the school budget.

(f) A Sociologist to the extent of understanding the relationships of the school with social forces.

(g) A Lawyer to the extent of being able to know his own obligations, rights, legal abilities as well as of those of all school personnel.

(h) A Technical Expert in educational measurement and evaluation.

(i) An Expert in Group Dynamics to the extent of working effectively with staff, pupils, public and the authorities.

Relation of the Principal with his Colleagues. Milo Stuart states, "The relation of the principal to his teachers should be the most intimate of any. If a teacher fails, the principal fails; if the teacher succeeds, the Principal succeeds. To sum up what the Principal's job is, I shall call him a referee - the captain of the ship - the boss of the firm - a juvenile judge before whose tribunal come out not only the culprits but the adults who frequently contribute to the pupil's shortcomings. He is a promoter who must project the future of his institution and convert the public to his plan. He is a social physician to every parent who has a wayward son who needs attention. He is a friend in need to pupils and to all the homes in which misfortune comes. His power, his activities, even the good he does, can not be measured by a material yardstick."

Basic Principles

Principle of Democratic Administration. We have already discussed that a Head should follow the principles of democratic administration. According to K.G. Saiyidain, "To my mind a good Headmaster is one who can inspire and enthuse his colleagues without dominating over them like a hard task master."

Principle of Sharing Responsibility. He should be prepared to share the control and authority with his colleagues. He should not think that he is born to rule and should not desire to be on the top of everything in the school, i.e. the president of games, the chairman of literary societies and the patron of social service and health unions, etc. The different departments should be placed under the charge of the senior members of the staff. Principle of 'Sharing Responsibility' should be the keynote of his policy. Supervision of the examinations, school cleanliness, morning assembly, funds, hostel, scouting, literary and social activities are some of the chief duties which would be delegated by the Headmaster to the other members of the staff. This will develop in them a sense of responsibility for the school.

Principle of Mutual Consultation. The Headmaster should frequently consult his colleagues regarding improvement in school discipline and instruction. Such consultations instil in them the spirit that they belong to the school and are as responsible to it as the Headmaster is. Staff meetings should be called from time to time. The teachers should be given full freedom to put forth their problems in these meetings. Briggs found that the teachers expected in a staff meeting (i) help on their problems, (ii) the wider outlook in education, (iii) meeting to be happy and wholesome, (iv) meeting based on appreciation of effort and accomplishment rather than shortcomings and faults. The head of the institution should take note of the teachers' problems and accordingly give his suggestions for the solution of the problems concerned.

Principle of Human Relationships. A good Headmaster keeps in view the humane factor while dealing with the members of the staff. He treats them just like friends and does not say anything to them in the presence of the students and their parents which may lower their prestige. He does not give them suggestions regarding methods of teaching when they are taking their classes but gives the same by calling them in his office and tries to avoid all 'bossing tendencies'. The teacher should come out of the Headmaster's office a better person, wiser and in a more pleasant mood than he was when he went in his office. Autocratic heads are always ready to snub any pupil or teacher who puts questions to them and are easily annoyed when their colleagues differ from them.

Principle of Constructive Criticism. The criticism offered by the Headmaster should be judicious, fair and constructive rather than destructive. Supervision should be a matter of inspiration to teachers. It should be moderate. Excessive supervision kills all the initiative and drive of teachers. The role of a policeman or a military officer does more harm than good.

Principle of Cooperation. On the close cooperation of the Headmaster and the staff depends on the efficiency of the school and the head of the institution is to a great extent responsible for securing cooperation of teachers. According to Reavis, "No matter what his personal characteristics are, he will not be successful unless he is able to inspire his associates and collaborators with the desire to work cooperatively for the goals for which the school stands. He will be judged by his ability to enlist and to utilise their ability in participating in the solution of school problems and in formulating educational policies that have the common objective of advancing the welfare of the children enrolled in the school. He does not attempt to conceal that he is their leader, but he does not on the other hand remind them what he is."

Principle of Friendly Supervision. Speaking about administrators of tomorrow D.I. Lal observes, "He gives up the time-old tradition of checking his teachers, frightening his teachers, weakening his teachers and examining them, but manipulates things so as to train his teachers, inspire his teachers and trust them. In this way he will not only create an excellent professional moral among the teaching staff but will also cultivate a vital interest in them for educational philosophy, so that they can continually test and re-test their plans and purposes, ideas, ideals, methods and procedures, systems and organisations."

Jacobson observes, "The Principal should not interrupt classes, create disturbances on entering and leaving, or to take the class away from the teacher, unless invited to do so. If the Principal stays to the end of the class period he should observe good manners by expressing in a sentence or two his pleasure in visiting the class but refrain from making condemnatory statements until there is sufficient time to discuss them at length, if indeed he indulges in them at all."

1. Take the first step in being friendly.
2. Be cheerful.
3. Remember and use names.
4. Take interest in the out of school activities of the members of the staff.
5. Be easily accessible to the staff.
6. Avoid taking special privileges.
7. Be polite and courteous.
8. Avoid keeping people waiting.
9. Ask persons if they are willing to assume responsibility.
10. Take prompt action on requests.
11. Keep a record of promises and live up to them.

12. Attempt to see actions and decisions from the other persons point of view.
13. Give credit to the persons responsible when the school receives praise.
14. Let people know when their work is good.
15. Be concerned about the way a teacher feels about his job and his out of school life.
16. Be willing to listen.
17. Avoid any evidence of authority.
18. Ask questions that relieve anxiety about discussing a problem.
19. Give praise for reporting facts accurately.
20. Avoid giving advice.
21. Become fully informed about the social structure of the staff.
22. Refuse to accept the assumption that conflicting groups in staff are unavoidable.
23. Offer services to assist in seeking agreement when disagreements arise in the group.
24. Do not show any undue favour to any member of the staff.
25. Inform new teachers on matters of school regulation.
26. Visit teachers who are ill.
27. Keep in mind while preparing your schedule that other teachers are not put to inconvenience.
28. Show consideration for bashful teachers.
29. Give teachers a chance to tell their side of the story.
30. Do not make personal remarks to shame them.
31. Show consideration for the feeling of other teachers.
32. Do not embarrass a teacher of inferior ability or one who has physical defects.

33. Do not laugh at the actions which seem funny to you.
34. Learn to work, to play, to live successfully with your associates.
35. Learn to like people.
36. Find out how different teachers wished to be treated and treat them accoıdingly.
37. Be willing to help teachers secure better positions.
38. Make changes slowly, preferably at teachers' suggestions.
39. Seek the help of teachers as co-workers and special advisers.
40. Be sincerely interested in teachers, like them as persons. Lincoln said, "If you wish to win a man to your cause, first convince him that you are his sincere friend."
41. Give teachers your undivided attention both when listening and when talking to them.
42. Criticise only in private.
43. Smile! As they say in the Navy, "a happy ship is a good ship" so, too, a happy school is a good school.
44. Always ask a teacher's permission to break into a classroom activity.
45. Help teachers in difficulty with pupils, parents or other teachers.
46. Meet staff in informal situations.
47. Use the word 'co-workers' in place of 'subordinates' and treat them as such.
48. Motivate desirable action through commendation.
49. Share knowledge of coming events with colleagues.
50. Give reasons for instructions and orders.
51. Earn respect of colleagues by character and behaviour rather than gain respect through 'position'.

52. Regard yourself as a member of the group rather than command respect through 'position'.
53. Encourage suggestions, evaluate them carefully, and accept them on merit.
54. Deal appropriately with outside criticism of staff members or the organisation.

Gathering of the Staff

Efficient running of the school demands that members of the staff should occasionally meet for sharing responsibilities as well as experiences. These meetings should be presided over by the Principal. These may be convened from time to time.

Briggs found that teachers expected the following things in a staff

(i) Help in their problems.

(ii) A wider outlook on education.

(iii) Meeting to be happy and wholesome.

(iv) Meeting based on appreciation of effort and accomplishment rather than shortcomings and faults.

Planning of Staff Meetings. The teachers should be informed in advance of the problems to be discussed in the meetings. It is very important for the head to listen to every teacher with attention and care. Minutes of staff meetings should be kept if possible.

A limit must be put to staff meetings and the best appears to be once a month. Of course, there need not be any rigidity in observing this principle. Occasional meetings for some particular purposes may have to be called. Sometimes it may become necessary for the head to convey staff meeting to clarify certain points of written order issued by him. An atmosphere of cheerfulness should prevail in all such meetings.

The head of the institution should take note of the teachers' problems and accordingly give his suggestions for the solution of the problems concerned. His attempt should be to help the teachers as much as possible.

Time of meeting should be such as most of the members of the staff find it convenient to attend.

Staff meetings should not be too long. Usually not more than one and a half hours be spent upon these.

Characteristics of Staff Meetings. 1. All discussions should be above the personal level.

2. They should be economical in time.
3. Discussion should not go off the track.
4. They should start in time.
5. They should result in concrete suggestions.

The formation of Staff Club will facilitate intimate contacts between the head and the members of the staff and also among the members of the staff themselves. One member of the staff should serve as a secretary who should be elected every year so that most of the members get a chance of leading others.

The functions of the club would be recreational-cum-educational. It may arrange tea during recess for the staff members. Its another function would be to arrange welcome and farewell parties. Its third function will be to arrange excursions and picnics on holidays. Its fourth function will be to arrange discussions on important school problems.

The Head should not look upon this club with suspicion. He should occasionally attend meetings of the club. Through such informal meetings, he will learn more about the members of the staff and this will also help in cementing the bonds of friendship, goodwill and mutual understanding.

Principal and the Beginning Teacher. 1. Plan a conference with the teacher.

2. Establish friendly relations with him.
3. Discuss the system's educational philosophy and practices with him.
4. Visit the class and hold short conferences after the observation.

5. Arrange for the beginner's observation of successful, and experienced teachers.
6. Help him in making lesson plans.
7. Give a good deal of assistance during the first term.
8. Suggest pertinent educational literature.
9. Give encouragement and appreciation to him.
10. Make him feel that he is capable of becoming a successful.
11. Show patience with his progress.

Relationship with Students

Often it is seen that the Headmaster makes the error of not coming into direct contact with the pupils. He should not forget that he can directly influence them to a considerable extent and as such he must avail himself of every opportunity of addressing them and attending various functions organised in the school. Regarding his work and relations with the students, we may quote Dr. V.S. Jha : "A good Headmaster or Principal is not merely a scholar, he is a man of sound character, deep sympathy and understanding and considerable tact and experience dealing with pupils. He should be profoundly sensitive to the physical, mental, moral and spiritual needs of the pupils and should know how to minister them."

The Headmaster must view the educational programme as a whole and assist students directly in having a balanced experience in terms of individual needs. To accomplish this he should :

– Show by action and in discussion that he places values in educational objectives over and beyond academic achievement : positive attitudes, citizenship skills, aesthetic appreciation, individual initiative, cooperative tendencies, etc.
– Give leadership to planning student activities, clubs and projects which will supplement and complement the academic class work.

— Approach individual student's problems from a guidance point of view, and help teachers to recognize individual differences in teaching and in dealing with students' problems.

— Make it a practice to get to know students personally, showing friendship to them and expressing interest in what they are doing.

— Involve students in real responsibility for the operation of significant aspects of the school, through student government, the house system and other techniques.

Relationship with Parents

Educators and administrators are now fast realising that effective and intimate relations with parents are very necessary for the efficient organisation of school work and activities. The head of an institution must find out ways and means for establishing happy contacts with student's parents and guardians.

His treatment with the parents should be very courteous. As Ryburn puts it, "He should always treat parents with scrupulous courtesy when they come to the school."

Schools serving the public in a democracy should be responsive to the wishes of parents regarding the school programme. Also, the school programme should be related to the community. Towards these ends the headmaster should :

— Arrange a variety of means for keeping the public informed about the school programme; new projects, progress in achieving objectives, and problems should be reported regularly.

— Encourage parents to make constructive suggestions on ways of improving the school, providing avenues through which parents' ideas are reported and discussed.

— Assist the school staff in knowing the community and in teaching students ways in which they can contribute to community development.

— Make the school facilities available for use by appropriate community groups for meetings, recreation and adult education.

– Organize ways in which parents and community groups can help the school, through fund raising for specific activities, making community educational resources more readily available to the school, and assisting teachers and students in studying the community.

Principal's Merits

Hundreds and thousands of eyes watch him, judge him, measure him and are eager to follow his noble example.

He has to be sweet and soft as well as stiff and stem.

Unless he has a seeing eye, an understanding heart and an all adjusting mental poise, he is bound to falter and tumble.

He should be firm in his dealings, resolute in his conviction and decisions, relentless in their execution.

"Oil, vinegar, sugar and saltness in him do agree."

- Goldsmith

Academically and Professionally Well-equipped. He must familiarise himself with the methods of teaching different subjects. Through the study of educational journals and periodicals and latest literature, he should keep himself well-posted regarding the latest developments in the field of education. He reads a lot and travels a lot.

(i) Possesses extensive knowledge in the field of education.

(ii) Possesses extensive knowledge of a school subject of his choice.

(iii) Possesses extensive knowledge in broad areas of fields and experiences other than education.

(iv) Applies scientific methods in dealing with problems.

(v) Respects men of scholarship.

(vi) Encourages through scholarship rather than superficiality.

Administrator's Vision. "No scheme of educational reconstruction will produce the desired results unless it is administered with vision and efficiency."

- Central Advisory Board of Education (Report) 1944

(i) Attends to matters in order of importance.

(ii) Clearly defines the duties of his co-workers and prevents overlapping.

(iii) Delegates responsibility with the necessary authority for effective action.

(iv) Distributes work in a way that every member of the staff makes use of his talents.

(v) Maintains an organisation according to current needs.

Aware of What a Good Organisation is. To quote J.B. Sears, an ideal head recognises that, "a good organisation is an arrangement of persons wherein its members may work effectively, economically and harmoniously together to achieve a common purpose, an arrangement of persons, which, as far as possible, may guard effectively against interference with its purposes and processes, an arrangement of persons which relies as much upon the common will, the initiative and the understanding of its members as it does upon authority, to energize or guide it and that applies to the concepts, also in its relations with those whom it serves."

Capacity to Make Favourable Impression Upon Others. An ideal Headmaster is able to make favourable impression upon all those who come in contact with him. His words, manners and behaviour win confidence of others. His talk is cultured, behaviour dignified, manners affable, conversation engaging, disposition amiable, imagination enlightened and attitude flexible.

Sultan Mohi-ud-din states, "Dignity does not consist in aloofness and in maintaining air of superiority; it rather consists in being helpful and doing the right thing. Great Headmasters have always been great friends of their pupils."

Communication of Ideas and Attitudes. (i) Has a pleasing and clear voice.

(ii) Speaks directly and concisely.

(iii) Uses vivid and suitable vocabulary.

(iv) Writes without ambiguity.

(v) Uses refined language.

(vi) Writes correct and free of grammatical mistakes.

(vii) Organise his thoughts properly before speaking.

(viii) Listens patiently.

(ix) Talks when must.

(x) Respects the point of view of others.

(xi) Keeps the trend of discussion on the track and not off the point.

(xii) Harmonises opposite and conflicting points of view.

(xiii) Does not allow passions to run high level of discussion.

Considers no Aspect of his Work as Trivial. The same writer further writes, "Since he ceaselessly strives to be a model to others, he regards no aspect of his work as trivial or insignificant which can conveniently be passed on to others to be done well or ill." He is too well aware of the truth of that wise statement, "Trifles make perfection and perfection is no trifle." Hence every item be it the folding of a sheet or the writing of a circular - is done with meticulous care as if it were a religious act.

Considers the Administrative Machinery as an Instrument of Social Service. "An educational administrator is more than an official punctilious about administrative routine, he is a leader guiding and directing a sacred undertaking. The official apparatus that is at his disposal, the education department that is under his control, is more than a bureaucratic machine. It is an instrument of social service."

- Chitra Naik

Cooperative Attitude. "The leader of the school can be successful only when he secures willing cooperation from his co-workers; when he makes those co-workers feel that the problems of the school are theirs and not his own."

- Mohi-ud-din

"Dignity does not consist in aloofness and in maintaining an air of superiority; It rather consists in being helpful and doing the right thing."

- Mohi-ud-din

Courteous Treatment with Parents. "He should always treat parents with scrupulous courtesy."

- Will Ryburn

Democratic Attitude. "A democratic administrator should look upon the personnel as socially equal to himself, he should not take decisions by himself, but with his colleagues, he should make them feel responsible and share in administration, he should have a code of set rules of administration which he and his colleagues should follow rigidly, making no discrimination in their application, and lastly, he should have no special privilege."

- R. R. Kumria

Educational Statesman. In the words of E.P. Cubberly, "He must learn to lead by reason, by his larger knowledge and courageous enthusiasm rather than to drive reason of his superior power.... He must reach up out of the routine of school supervision and execute duties into the higher level of educational statesmanship."

Expert in Human Relations. An ideal head always remembers that all people cannot be equally intelligent and hard working. A trouble shooter needs to be handled firmly in the very beginning. Praise and appreciation sometimes help even if a person does not deserve it. Sometimes sympathetic hearing is all that is needed to blow off the steam of emotions. Sometimes valuable suggestions help in easing the tension.

Faith in Human Nature. "It is essential, therefore, that he be a man of faith, faith in his vocation, faith in his pupils, faith in human nature and faith in himself"

"He must have unlimited faith in himself and his creator."

- Jaswant Singh

Firm Attitude. He should be firm in his dealings, resolute in his conviction and decisions, relentless in their execution.

Friend of the Students. The great Headmasters have always been great friends of their pupils. The Headmaster should possess the following skills:

1. Loves them intensely.

2. Shows interest in student activities.
3. Shows due regard to their personality.
4. Shows friendliness towards individual students.
5. Shows a spirit of 'oneness' and 'belongingness' with them.
6. Gives due regard to student opinion.
7. Takes a keen interest in the welfare of the students.
8. Spares time for conferences.
9. Shows a keen interest in solving their problems.

Gives Recognition to Good work Done. Ryburn writes, "Nothing will more encourage a man or woman, a boy or a girl, to greater effort than an encouraging recognition of good work done, of sincere effort made, or good qualities shown. If those in charge of institutions and those carrying on the administrative work of departments wish to enable those working with them to do their best, they should always realize the value of ungrudging recognition of all that merits recognition."

Good at Office Correspondence. Office work is becoming a very taxing job day by day for the headmaster. Filing work should be maintained systematically and scientifically so that promptness is achieved in correspondence.

1. Decides cases promptly.
2. Gives judgment only after weighing and considering relevant evidence.
3. Perceives true qualities of people.
4. Decides cases on the basis of principles rather than expediency.
5. Makes decisions without bias and prejudice.

Headmaster not by Appointment but by Superior Ability. "It must not be known by his staff and scholars that he is their headmaster by appointment but felt that he is their master by superior ability, energy and character."

- P.C. Wren

"He is the organiser, leader, governor, business director, coordinator, superintendent teacher, guide, philosopher and friend."

- P.C. Wren

Health. "A person with indifferent health and poor stamina will not be able to discharge his own or discharge the multifarious and heavy responsibilities of his office."

- Jaswant Singh

His Life is One of Immolation. In the words of S. Balakrishna Joshi, "The progress of the school community is his thought by day and dream by night, and his aching passion is to wear himself out in the service of the shrine in which he feels spiritually wedded. It is his conviction that while the life of a teacher is one of consecration that of the Headmaster should be one of immolation."

Humorous Nature. "It will enable him to get over an impasse with the help of a smile, a light hearted chuckle, or a jocular remark that will ease the tense atmosphere."

- Jaswant Singh

Leader by Courage and Reason and not by Power. "He must learn to lead by reason, by his larger knowledge and courageous enthusiasm rather than to drive by reason of his superior power. He must reach up out of the routine of school supervision and execute duties into the higher level of educational statesman."

- E P. Cubberly

"The successful administrator gets people to work with him, not primarily because he has power over them and can order them about, because he is the kind of leader for whom they want to do their best."

- Pagors and Myers

Man of Integrity. He fights all temptations to pad his purse with money to which he is not entitled. To quote S. Balakrishna Joshi, "He does not try to exploit school influence for private gains because he realizes that if he does it, he signs his moral death-warrant. The result is that no amount of pressure can wean him from the path of duty and justice. Authority cannot coerce him, nor can temptation reduce him into any course of conduct, nor conducive to the highest interests of the school."

Optimistic Outlook. He has unlimited faith in himself. He does not accept defeat. He always thinks of success all the time. Ryburn stresses, "It is essential, therefore, that he be not only a man of high character but also that he be a man of faith; faith in his vocation, faith in his pupils, faith in human nature, and faith in his staff."

Patience. "Patience is a virtue that will pay very generous dividends to assist, not to control the educative process."

- Reaves

"Go slow the first day, the first week, the first month, and even the first year, make changes slowly and always with the cooperation of the faculty."

- William T. Melchor

Philosophy of Education. "A good Headmaster needs to have a sound philosophy of education."

-Jaswant Singh

Planning Capacity. "If a Principal is not careful, he will find himself spending much of the time in answering telephone, running errands for teachers, signing excuses, making repairs to the buildings, handling money, raising campaigns, and performing other minor duties and then budget his time accordingly."

- Margaret Grag

Professional Devotion. "He should drive the same satisfaction from working for institution as the artist or the sculptor derives when working late hours over his handiwork, fully attentive to the smallest detail, never tiring."

-Jaswant Singh

Progressive Outlook. "It is reasonable to expect that a Head master should be progressive in his outlook."

-Mohi-ud-din

Recognition for Good Work Done. "Nothing will more encourage a man or woman, a boy or a girl, to greater effort, than an encouraging recognition of good work done, of sincere effort made, or good qualities shown. If those in charge of institutions and those carrying on the administrative work of departments wish to enable those working with them to do their best, they should always realize the value of ungrudging recognition of all that merits such recognition."

-*Ryburn*

Rises Equal to Any Occasion. "He rises equal to any occasion, and by his resourcefulness and readiness to render service, solves knotty problems. To him it is not beneath his dignity to strike the gong in time if the peon is engaged otherwise, or to lead a band of devoted volunteers to flush the latrines if scavenger is absent. Again he is prepared to 'referee' a match if the umpire has not turned up or step into a class and teach any subject if a teacher is called suddenly. Thus his willingness and ability to do any piece of work pertaining to the school, wrest for him the confidence and regard of all concerned."

Scientific Attitude. An ideal head is particularly careful in making judgement about persons for whom he cherishes a positive like or dislike. He observes correctly without letting personal feelings, prejudices, and wishes to influence him, draws valid conclusions from given facts and makes sound generalizations as the facts warrant. He does not see things through coloured spectacles. He is able to detach his personal likes and dislikes from the performance of others. He is conscious of the fact that monopoly of truth is not held by anyone.

Sense of Humour. Dr. Jaswant Singh writes about this quality, "It will enable him to get over an impasse with the help of a smile, a light hearted chuckle, or a jocular remark which will ease the tense atmosphere. The sense of humour will help break resistance, overcome opposition by injecting a spirit of camaraderie into the situation. Many a difficult situation can be resolved by a witty remark."

Sensitive to the Needs of the Community. "In whatever community the Principal finds himself, he should study the characteristic social conditions and needs of his pupils and endeavour in appropriate ways to secure increased cooperation between the school and the community in meeting these needs."

-*W. Johnson Frank*

Sensitive to the Needs of the Students. "A good Headmaster should be profoundly sensitive to the physical, mental, moral, intellectual and spiritual needs of his pupils and should know how to minister to them."

- V. S. Jha

Sensitive to the Needs of Teachers. "The Principal should not interrupt classes, unless invited to do so."

- Jacobson and Others

"If the Principal stays to the end of the class period he should observe good manners by expressing in a sentence or two his pleasure on visiting the class."

-Jacobson and Others

Sensitive to the Many Sided Development of the Child. According to Dr. V S. Jha, "He should be profoundly sensitive to the physical, mental, moral, intellectual and spiritual needs of the pupils and should know how to minister to them."

Source or Inspiration. The members of staff should look to him for guidance, help and inspiration. "Under any authoritarian regime, where basis of relationship is fear of one sort or another, it is often possible to get certain routine done efficiently. But under such conditions it is impossible to bring into rapport the best elements in the personality of the teacher, thus education loses its formative influence."

"He gives up the time-old tradition of checking his teachers, frightening his teachers, weakening his teachers and examining them; but manipulates things so as to train his teachers, inspire his teachers, encourage his teachers and trust them."

- D.I. Lall

Thinking Capacity. "Experience is an indispensable qualification for a headmaster. This is certainly true. But experience alone without the capacity to think out and plan out new progressive programmes is inadequate."

-Mohi-ud-din

Vision and Imagination. 1. Makes decisions which later events show to be sound and reliable.

2. Searches new practices and techniques.

3. Seizes opportunities to develop new patterns of action.

Qualities of the Headmaster

To justify his place as the inspiring leader and guide, the Head master must have a strong personality. R.A. Lamb remarks. "To make the perfect head of the school, there is needed in addition to all these, a quality which is undefinable - and which resides in the personality of the individuality. It is not possible to analyse this quality any more than it is possible by dissecting a man's brain to find wherein resides the soul or the spirit of life. But that it exists is beyond question."

Not an awful man. "In a school worth its name the Head will neither sit in his room like a large spider waiting for a chance to pounce on his prey nor he like an awe inspiring god on the Olympian Heights who visits the earth once in a way to thunder disapproval or to subjugate the people by his presence."

-A.M.D. Razario

Significance of the each letter of the word "Headmaster".

H stands for

(i) Hard work (ii) Helpfulness iii) Honesty (iv) Humility (v) Humorous nature

E stands for

(i) Enthusiasm (ii) Ethics of the teaching profession (iii) Experimental attitude

A stands for

(i) Accuracy (ii) Adaptability (iii) Alertness (iv) Amicability (v) Attentiveness (vi) Attractive manner

D stands for

(i) Definiteness of aim (ii) Dependability (iii) Desire for self-improvement (iv) Devotion to the democratic ideal (v) Devotion to the profession

M stands for

(i) Mastery of the subject matter (ii) Mental development

S stands for

(i) Self-discipline (ii) Self-reliance (iii) Sincerity (iv) Sociability

T stands for

(i) Tact (ii) Truthfulness (iii) Teaching skill (iv) Training

R stands for

(i) Reasoning (ii) Resourcefulness (iii) Relationships

Need for Raising the Status of Headmasters. The Education Commission felt, "It is also essential to give wider powers to Headmasters and greater freedom to schools. At present, the Headmasters as a class have been neglected. It will be seen that in our proposals, better scales of pay have been recommended... The general principle should be ... to vest them with necessary authority. They might commit mistakes - as all human beings do. But unless the freedom to commit mistakes is given, no headmaster will be able to take deep interest in the school and in its improvement."

Principal's Ideal Character

The progress of the school community is his thought by day and dream by night, and his aching passion is to wear himself out in the service of the shrine to which he feels spiritually wedded. It is his conviction, that, while the life of a teacher is one of consecration, that of the Headmaster should be one of immolation. Responsibilities and not rights, duties and not privileges ever loom large in his mind because he regards himself as the humblest servant of the school. Aware that he has to deal with several agencies like the department, the pubnic and the parents, he strains every nerve of his to guard the reputation of the institution and to maintain the prestige of the profession to which he is privileged to belong. He does not stop to exploit school influence for private gains because he realises that, if he does it, he signs his moral death-warrant. The result is that no amount of pressure can wean him from the path of duty and justice. Authority cannot coerce him, nor can temptation seduce him into any course of conduct, not conducive to the highest interests of the school.

He is dignified in his dealings, and maintains a poise of reserve in his manner without being distant or cold. While willing to be friendly with all he is not familiar with anyone because he knows that indiscriminate fraternisation will land him in embarrassing situations which in turn will adversely affect his work.

He rises equal to any occasion, and by his resourcefulness and readiness to render service, solves knotty problems. To him it is not beneath his dignity to strike the gong in time if the peon is engaged otherwise, or to lead a band of devoted volunteers to flush the latrines if the scavenger is absent. Again, he is prepared to 'referee' a match if the umpire has not turned up or step into a class and teach any subject if a teacher is called suddenly. Thus his willingness and ability to do any piece of work pertaining to the school, wrest for him the confidence and regard of all concerned. Since he ceaselessly strives to be a model to others, he regards no aspect of work as trivial or insignificant which can conveniently be showed on to others to be done well or ill. He is too well aware of the turth of that wise statement, "Trifles make perfection and perfection is no trifle." Hence every item, be it the folding of a sheet or the writing of a circular, is done with meticulous care as if it were a religious act.

7

Teacher's Role

The National Commission on School Teachers 1983-85 has described the role of the teacher in the context of the present needs of India as :

> "For the proper fulfilment of the national goals mentioned above (A United Secular India, A Modern Nation, A Productive People, and A Humane and Caring Society) and for their proper fulfilment of which education must mediate, the teacher's role assumes great significance. Today the average teacher's perception of his role and responsibility is far too limited and is concerned with his own immediate tasks, namely the teaching of the 3 R's and later, covering the subject matter prescribed for the examinations. The teacher must actively and feelingly associate himself, as an essential and responsible partner, in the great tasks which face the nation. If the four national goals were to become the actual motive force and the ideals that every man, woman and child in our land would live by, the teacher must intervene in a big way. The formation of character, a character evolved in response to the national goals, would constitute his primary task. He will indeed prepare students for

examinations, and open to them the world of knowledge. But these will count for little unless he has helped them become persons of character. There is the personal aspect of character-building to develop qualities like honesty and integrity and there is the social aspect which defines national character. Such a character identification must not be based on cultural and religious traditions of any one group but must find acceptance by all sections of the people."

The National Commission on Teachers for Higher Education (1983-1985) listed the following roles of teachers in national development:

1. Teacher as an agent of change.
2. Teacher in the context of explosion of knowledge—to remain up-to-date.
3. Teacher to adopt new methodology to utilize interactive methods of instruction.
4. Teacher to use his creative ability.
5. Teacher as a procurer of knowledge to enlarge the sphere of his knowledge.
6. Teacher as an agent of cooperation with community.
7. Teacher to undertake problem-solving research.
8. Teacher to initiate management change.
9. Teacher to discharge his responsibility with an urgent sense of social purpose.

Different Roles

Parent Surrogate (Parent substitute). A teacher is expected to act as a parent of the students and treat them with affection and care.

Ego-supporter. He is expected to build up and maintain a healthy and strong 'ego' and 'self-concept' among children.

Helper. The teacher is expected to be a helper to students by way of providing them academic and personal guidance.

Resource Person. He is expected to play the role of a resource person who possesses knowledge of the subject-matter and skills better than the pupils.

Detective. He acts as a detective in detecting offences and rule breakers.

Facilitator of Learning. He is expected to promote significant learning among his students.

Limiter or Reducer of Anxiety. He is expected to assist students to control their impulses and reduce anxiety about conduct and performance in different problematic situations.

Referee. He is expected to settle disputes among students in an objective and fair manner.

Group Leader. He is expected to act as a leader in developing suitable climate and cohesion in the class as a social group.

Inspirer and Exemplar. He is expected to behave in a manner whereby the traits exemplified by him may be emulated by the students.

Judge. He is expected to evaluate the academic and other performance of the students in an impartial manner.

Confidant. He is expected to win and share the confidence of the students.

Friend and Philosopher. He is expected to play the role of a friend, philosopher and guide to the students.

Upholder of the Norms and Values. He is expected to uphold the norms and values of the society.

Moral Educator. He is expected to inculcate the attitudes and moral values cherished by the society among the students.

Democrat. He is expected to play the role of a democrat.

Rationalist. He is expected to play the role of a rationalist by basing his actions on reason.

Secularist. He is expected to play the role of a secularist by having an open mind on the beliefs of all religions.

Initiator. He is expected to play the role of an initiator by exploiting the new technology to the best advantage of the students and the purposes of education. He should play the roles of a planned organizer of curricular innovator of educational ideas, practices and systems, writer of Radio and T.V. lessons and programmes, user of video-tapes and computers etc.

Reformer. In a country like India, where conservatism and superstitions prevail, a teacher is expected to play the role of a social reformer.

Equalizer. He should act as equalizer by working for minimising inequalities in the educative process and by building up an egalitarian, secular and socialist society.

Various Responsibilities

I. Character and personality of the students.

II. Classroom management.

III. Professional growth and ethics.

IV. Community relationship.

V. Total school effectiveness.

Development of Character and Personality of the Students

1. To create an environment of purposeful order, to enlist pupil's assistance in orderly, friendly, courteous and cooperative interpersonal relations.
2. To develop a respect for the rights, privileges, opinions, property and individualities of others.
3. To create group situations which will develop desirable leadership and followership qualities in the pupils.
4. To set a standard of classroom and school environment behaviour which conforms to socially acceptable behaviour.
5. To direct discussion and develop understanding on moral and other ethical issues in order to develop understanding of the reasons for ethical standard.

6. To encourage individuality in each pupil's thinking and action.

The Teacher and Classroom Management. This implies the creation of an environment in the class as it allows for the best display of the students' abilities in the teaching- learning process. There is the maximum involvement of the students in the classroom activities. The teacher and the students are full of enthusiasm. The classroom environment is based on mutual goodwill and faith. The teacher gives due regard to the individuality of the students and the students in turn show spontaneous respect for their teacher. The teacher in the true sense is the friend, philosopher and guide of the students.

Management of the Class

These roles may be listed as under:

- Communicator of attitude, knowledge, skills and values
- Coordinator
- Curriculum planner and implementer
- Democrat
- Disciplinarian
- Evaluator of attitudes, knowledge and skills
- Facilitator
- Guide
- Helper
- Improviser
- Innovator
- Integrater of knowledge
- Leader
- Motivator
- Observer
- Programmer
- Researcher
- Scientist

Broadly speaking an effective classroom management include:

1. Curriculum Development and Implementation.
2. Adjustment to Individual Differences and Development.
3. Dynamic Techniques of Instruction.
4. Use of Technology of Teaching.
5. Evaluating and Discussing Pupils' Performance.
6. Maintaining Class Discipline.

Curriculum Development and Implementation. This implies:

1. Participation in grade level or subject matter study of existing curricula and in the development of improved expanded curricula.
2. Determining the object, scope and methods of the grade and subjects to be taught.
3. Devising assignments, when necessary, in order to enrich the teaching programme for the pupils.
4. Correlating his subject matter curriculum with the curriculum of other subjects.

Adjusting to Individual Differences and Development Levels. This calls for :

1. Drawing upon and applying basic knowledge of the psychology of the child in order to establish readiness for learning.
2. Making an effort to know as much as possible about the background and out-of-school environment of each child, in order to improve the teaching learning process.
3. Developing in each pupil a sense of personal growth and value.
4. Maintaining discipline by being consistently friendly, fair.
5. Handling behaviour problems in a controlled manner.

Dynamic Techniques of Teaching (Effective teaching learning) This includes :

1. Selecting materials, teaching aids and methods which will facilitate the learning process and stimulate the desire for further learning.
2. Meeting the needs, backgrounds and capacities of the children , being taught.
3. Teaching by use of a suitable variety of lectures, discussions, demonstrations, visual and oral presentations, recitation, directed group effort, experimentation, special projects and field trips.
4. Analysing and evaluating the effectiveness of various teaching techniques in order to improve the learning process.
5. Endeavouring to obtain and maintain pupil interest and attention so that teaching is done in a receptive atmosphere.
6. Endeavouring to assure that material taught is applied in such a manner as to develop a pattern of understanding for future use in other areas.
7. Encouraging and guiding critical thinking by pupils.
8. Developing desirable work and study skills and habits.
9. Enlisting pupil participation in the lesson planning process.
10. Developing broad outlines and objectives to be attained within prescribed limits, for a subject or skill area based upon the needs and interests of a specific group of pupils.
11. Making suitable lesson plans.

Use of Techniques of Teaching. This relates to

1. Use of blackboard.
2. Use of charts, models, graphs etc.
3. Use of new technology, i.e. computer, radio and T.V.

Evaluating and Discussing Pupils Performance. This comprises:

1. Devising and administering appropriate tests to measure the level and quality of pupil's learning.
2. Interpreting test results and related findings to pupil progress in order to improve the teaching learning process.
3. Reporting pupil's achievement and progress to parents by means of progress reports.
4. Discussing pupil's achievement with the parents individually, in groups and conferences.
5. Cooperating and enlisting the cooperation of school specialist in the process of evaluation.

Maintaining Discipline. This implies:

1. Basing discipline on 'do's' rather than 'don'ts'.
2. Showing due regard to the personality of each student.
3. Insisting on good conduct and manners.
4. Displaying sympathetic but firm attitude.
5. Maintaining a certain reserve but friendly environment.
6. Becoming fair and just.
7. Using polished and sweet language.
8. Showing humour.
9. Keeping the class busy.
10. Avoiding threats.
11. Avoiding discussing family problems.
12. Avoiding discussing colleagues.
13. Avoiding sarcastic remarks.

Community Relations. 1. To participate in parent-teacher and similar activities.

2. To participate in community affairs.
3. To make himself available to parents at scheduled times to discuss pupil progress and behaviour.

4. To evince a sympathetic, helpful and understanding attitude towards parents and their children schooling problems.
5. To establish and maintain a good relationship with parents and conducting reporting of pupil progress, problems and needs.
6. To assure through personal behaviour in the community that the public school staff-image in the community is favourable.

Professional Growth and Ethics. 1. To keep abreast of the developments in the teaching profession.

2. To maintain membership in key professional organizations relevant to his subject or area of speciality.
3. To manifest ethical behaviour in his relations with fellow teachers and educational associates.
4. To exercise professional discretion in his relations with parents and town's people.
5. To keep abreast of subject matter by study of books, periodicals, newspapers and other sources concerning development in his field.
6. To utilise films, filmstrips, TN. and radio as a means of keeping abreast of new and advanced knowledge in his field.
7. To attend conferences, workshops, seminars and meetings; to take field trips which tend to broaden his knowledge.

Total School Effectiveness. (1) To accept responsibility for pupil discipline throughout the school and in the interest of the school as a whole.

(2) To cooperate with all co-workers and to exchange ideas in order to improve and provide variety of approach on the teaching situation.

(3) To execute all required school regulations and assignments on time.

(4) To accept his full share of pupil's activity participation, such as attending athletic contests, etc.

(5) To contribute constructively to committees, faculty meetings and other school system groups.

(6) To take the positive steps in developing and maintaining faculty and student morale.

(7) To provide his fair share of dependable and effective participation in activities involving the general welfare of the school.

Teacher in Older Days

Modern educators emphasize participative methods. Following are the chief points of difference between a traditional teacher and a participative teacher :

Traditional Teacher	*Participative Teacher*
1. Works on the formulated objectives.	Formulates clearly defined objectives based on the needs of students.
2. Focuses on the presentation of content, facts and information.	Focuses on the process of learning - learning how to learn.
3. Assumes the responsibility	Involves the student's actively in assuming the responsibility of their own learning.
4. Decides what the students need and provides it through lectures etc.	Assists the students to learn to be active information seekers and makes use of all available resources.
5. Stresses memorisation as a method of learning.	Motivates the students to learn by discovery and exploration, asks questions, formulates problems.
6. Emphasises group performance.	Emphasises individual achievement in relation to the student's own needs and objectives.
7. Promotes competition with peers for achievement, recognition, grades and other rewards.	Promotes group work on problem-solving activities and learning effectively.

Teacher's Merits

To play their part fully and effectively, the teachers are expected to possess these qualities.

Character and Personality. Character and personality of the pupils cannot be developed if the teacher who is the model to be followed lacks character and personality. 'Example is better than precept' is an old saying and is absolutely true in the teaching profession. No amount of sermons from the teacher can make much headway. A teacher teaches not only by 'what he says and does' but very largely by 'what he is'. Children are imitative and suggestive by nature. They imitate the dress, voice, habits and manners of their teachers. The likes and dislikes of the teachers become their likes and dislikes. Children who are in the plastic period of their life are easily influenced by their teachers. The teachers should teach what they practise. Gandhiji strongly denounces those teachers who teach one thing with lips and carry another in their heart. Man know thyself is the advice given by Socrates in Greece and Yajnavalkya in India. The teachers must undergo an inner training. They should try to find out their own shortcomings and try to remove them. Ryburn puts it, 'Self-analysis on the part of a teacher is a necessary equipment'. Montessori stresses that every teacher worth his salt must destroy these sins: pride, anger, sloth, sensuality, gluttony and envy. The teacher should be partly a scientist, partly a doctor and completely religious. He must acquire a moral alertness; mingling of patience, love and humility. He should always be frank, sincere and honest. Prof. Raymount urges that the teacher must avoid everything that is petty and mean.

Gandhiji observes, "Woe to the teacher who teaches one thing with the lips and carries another in the heart."

Arthur B. Moehlmann states, "The teacher and the principal are always on exhibition, observed by hundreds of eyes. The position involves the strain of producing effect upon others not only through the use of specific methodologies, but also through the extension of teacher personality."

In the words of Dr. Rajendra Prasad, "Their (teacher's) own character should be such that there is no difference between what they say and do. When we act upon this ideal then alone we can be sure of a bright future for our own country."

The Secondary Education Commission observes, "The teacher has always to realise that all his actions are being watched by his pupils."

Love for the Profession. The teacher should feel the importance of his profession. He must give his exclusive attention to the growth and development of the personalities of the children under his charge. He would be showing a dishonesty of purpose if once having entered it, he is engaged in other pursuits. Without an exclusive attention to his job he would fail in bringing forth a fine harvest of young men and women who are able to contribute their best for the welfare of mankind. If a teacher takes to his work just to make his living because nothing else is available, he will lack the essential zeal required by the teaching profession. He must be a teacher first and the teacher last. A person who wants to join this profession must feel the call for it. "If a teacher has not an ideal aim, he had better to take to shopkeeping at once, he will there doubtless find an ideal within his capacity," says Laurie.

In the words of the Secondary Education Commission, "They will not look upon their work as an unpalatable means of earning a scanty living but as an avenue through which they are rendering significant social service as well as finding some measure of self-fulfilment and self-expression."

Love for Children. It has been said that if a teacher does not actually like boys and girls, he should give up teaching. He must enjoy their company in groups. A good teacher feels that some sort of energy is constantly supplied by the young. "Love the child and the child will love you; hate the child and the child will hate you," is a famous maxim. One who does not like children should not stay in teaching.

The Secondary Education Commission remarked, "The good teacher in our reorganised school will endeavour to win the love and confidence of his children and establish his prestige on sincerity, integrity, hard work and a sympathetic handling of their problems."

Respect for the Individuality of the Child. A child should not be treated just like dumb driven cattle. His soul which is pure and very sensitive requires our most delicate care. He has his own individuality. His sense of respect should not be injured. Emerson states, "the secret of education lies in respecting the pupils." A child wants to be heard and his opinion should not be brushed aside merely because he is a child.

K.G. Saiyidain writes, "Under any authoritarian regime, when basis of relationship is fear of one sort or the other, it is often possible to get certain routine done efficiently. But under such conditions it is often impossible to bring into rapport the best elements in the personality of the teacher."

Knowledge of Psychology. Knowledge of psychology goes a long way in providing that basic orientation towards problems of education and child development without which there would be a considerably waste of time, energy and human resources. With a knowledge of child psychology, a teacher will be in a better position to understand and appreciate the individual differences of children, their nature, temperaments, habits and manners.

Intimate Knowledge of the Child. Children are now miniature adults. Their peculiar patterns of thoughts and emotions must be studied. Their names must be learnt and faces recognised. They must not be made to feel that the teacher is indifferent to them. Every source should be tapped to know about them to the fullest possible extent.

Fully Conscious or the Rights of the Child. A teacher must accept his duty to meet his obligations to the child in the following respects as proclaimed by the International Union of Child Welfare which a federation of national and international organisations to promote the physical, moral and spiritual welfare of the child : (i) The child must be protected beyond and above all considerations of race, nationality or creed. (ii) The child must be given the means requisite for its normal development— materially, morally and spiritually. (iii) The child that is hungry must be fed; the child that is sick must be nursed; the child that is physically handicapped must be helped; the maladjusted child must be educated; the orphan and the waif must be sheltered and succoured. (iv) The child must be the first to receive relief in time of distress. (v) The child must enjoy the full benefits provided by social welfare and social security schemes, the child must receive a training which will enable it, at the right time to earn a livelihood and must be protected against every exploitation. (vi) The child must be brought up in the consciousness that its talents must be devoted to the service of fellowmen.

Emotional Stability of the Teacher. It is said in The Education and Training of Teacher published by UNESCO, "Various researches show clearly that the emotional stability of teachers affects that of pupils. Unhappy, frustrated, dissatisfied teachers cannot help their pupils to become happy, well-adjusted young people." The teachers should try to find out their own shortcomings and try to remove them so that the students may be saved from the adverse influence of their unbalanced personality.

K.G. Saiyidain has observed, "You cannot pour out of a vessel except that you have put into it and, if a teacher is poor and shallow from within, if there is no sparkling wire in him, he cannot quicken the mind or humanize the emotions of his children—if he is not a lighted candle himself, he will never be able to light up the flame in others."

Grasp Over the Method. The Secondary Education Commission states, "Any method good or bad links up the teachers and his pupils into an organic relationship with constant mutual interaction, it reacts not only on the minds of the students but on their entire personality, their standard of work and judgement, their intellectual and emotional equipment, their attitudes and values. Good methods which are psychologically and socially sound may raise the whole quality, bad methods may debase it."

The creative teacher always keeps himself in touch with the latest methods of teaching and uses them in his class. Good methods, which are psychologically sound, facilitate learning and inculcate 'love of work". Two farmers may possess an equal amount of land, an equally great desire for rich harvest but the one who uses the best method of farming will, other things being equal, get better results. Similarly, a teacher who adopts proper methods of teaching will show better results and make his teaching more interesting and effective. A teacher should not be wedded to any particular method and must not have a conservative outlook but use every developed and progressive method in his class as required by the intellectual attainment of the particular students in the particular environment. He ought to devote some of his time in exploring new methods which may be of more help to him.

Mastery of the Subject-matter. A teacher must be a master of his subject. Any weakness on his part will lower his prestige in the eyes of his students. Besides, he must love his subject. A teacher who does not love his subject fails to inspire his students and runs the risk of becoming a hypocrite.

According to the University Education Commission, "No teacher who is not a master of the field, who is not in touch with the latest development in his subject and who does not bring to bear upon his duties a free and untrammeled mind will never succeed in inspiring youth with the love of truth which is the principal object of all higher education."

Daily Preparation. Perhaps there is no type of work where the results of poor planning are so devastating as in teaching. Careful and systematic arrangement of the subject-matter and the classroom activities is conducive to creative discipline. A well-prepared lesson helps to overcome the feeling of nervousness and insecurity especially so common in the first attempt at teaching. Bagley emphasises the importance of daily preparation in these words, "However able and experienced the teacher, he could do never without his preliminary preparation."

Democratic Attitude. A teacher cannot afford to be an autocrat. Present day education lays much stress on the inculcation of democratic ideals in the students. A teacher who is to show the way of democracy to the students must develop in himself a democratic attitude. His role is of a friend, philosopher and guide and not of a policeman.

Skill in Questioning. The success of a class teacher in the class also depends on the art of questioning. One who questions faultlessly, teaches effectively. With the help of right type of questions a wise teacher can lead the students from dark and unknown regions to known and bright ones.

Use of Material Aids. Various teaching aids bring clarity and vividness. It is a great asset to the teacher to narrate stories and anecdotes which appeal to children at different ages and attainment levels. Abstract words and phrases can be made clear by illustrations.

Good Vitality. In the opinion of Arthur B. Moehlman, "Good vitality is essential to successful teaching, not only in its reflex influence upon the children but also in making possible continuity of work with the fewest possible interruptions from illness because of general fatigue."

Good Memory. A teacher with a poor memory is ridiculous. It becomes easier for a teacher having good memory to correlate many things. A good creative memory is one of the qualities that differentiates the good teacher from the mediocre.

Good Voice. The voice of a teacher should be clear, moderately pitched and well-modulated. A thin low voice develops dullness and monotony in the class. A very high pitched voice or shrill one must be avoided. It distracts the minds of the students and does not appeal to their aesthetic sense. Plenty of variety must be introduced in voice. A teacher must be slow and emphatic when he is making statements he thinks worth copying. No effort should be spared to cultivate a pleasant musical tone. Anything which adds pleasure is an additional attraction for the attention and especially with children.

In the words of Mohi-ud-din, "The best voice for the classroom is one which is clear, pleasantly toned, fairly even in its general pitch and yet capable of modulation in order to express different shades of meaning and emphasis. A monotonous voice tires the pupils very soon and is not impressive."

The intelligent teacher should know the value of pause. He should know when to raise his voice and when to drop it a little or when to drop it altogether. He should adjust his voice according to the size of the room. Often a good speech fails because it cannot be easily heard especially by those who sit at the back. But it does not mean that a teacher should always be shouting. There are three ways of changing the voice—in pitch, in loudness and in speed.

Optimistic Outlook. Dr. E.A. Pires thinks that the teacher who can infuse happiness into the work of his pupils because he himself enjoys his work is sure to be a successful and popular teacher.

According to S. Balakrishna Joshi, "A teacher whose soul is wrinkled and whose heart is atrophied, who is devoid of energy and enthusiasm, capacity and character and who simply marks time, his eyes fixed on the calendar, is a disgrace to the profession and a curse on society." "The great teacher lives and breathes the spirit of creativity and adventure," writes Dr. E.A. Pires.

Laughter. A tactful teacher never hesitates to laugh, when there is an occasion for it. Laughter done in an unhealthy spirit defeats its own purpose. A teacher should never make the mistake of laughing at the pupils. He should laugh with them and should also see that they laugh with him and not at him.

R.R. Kumaria thinks laughter to be embellishment that lends charm to the teaching profession.

Humour keeps the pupils attentive. A very wise teacher once remarked, "I consider a day's teaching is wasted if we do not at all have a hearty laugh." Sarcasm is to be avoided.

Thirst for Knowledge. A teacher must refresh himself by constant reading not only about his subjects but books which touch life at every point. It would be very helpful if he would get opportunities of attending educational seminars, refresher courses and the like which enable him to get a good grip of his own thoughts and to see his own working in relation to others in the same sphere.

"A teacher can never truly teach unless he is still learning himself" remarks Rabindra Nath Tagore. A teacher should not feel shy to learn from others. There is no end to knowledge and his attitude should be like that of Newton: "I am only a child, playing in the sand by the sea-shore, picking up a pebble here and there with a vast ocean of truth lying undiscovered before me."

Books, Magazines and Newspapers. Although he should read books, magazines and newspapers for his own enjoyment and profit, he must keep in mind his responsibilities as a teacher. His reading must be wide enough so that he can guide his students' reading tastes.

Travel. The summer vacation usually is regarded rightly by most teachers as a period of deserved and needed rest and relaxation. However, an interested and efficient teacher is primarily a teacher for twelve months of the year. Even during his period of relaxation he makes it a point to combine pleasure with education. During summer, winter or spring vacations teachers can visit historical or literary landmarks in their immediate environment. Returning to their classes they can share their experiences with their pupils, thus enriching the content of their subjects and stimulate their classes.

Membership of Professional Organisations. Teachers should become members of the professional organisations the functions of which are:

(a) To advance education ideals.

(b) To care for the welfare of children and young people.

(c) To improve teaching, supervisory, and administrative procedures.

(d) To safeguard the welfare of teachers.

(e) To improve salaries.

(f) To assure pension and tenure privileges.

(g) To secure for teachers the right to participate in educational policy-making.

In-Service Training. Refresher courses, seminars and workshops provide opportunities for the discussion of classroom problems and find out their solutions. They also come into contact with their co-workers who might have something new to say. This also enables them to keep in touch with the latest developments in the field of education.

Punctuality. A teacher must realize that coming late to school and going late to the class upsets the school work, causes indiscipline and undermines the tone of the school. A good teacher makes it a point to be punctual in every work. Following the teachers coming late, the student may also develop in himself this very habit.

Judicious Use of the Praise and Blame. Praise and blame are the two important weapons in the armoury of the teacher and these should be used very judiciously. "Praise like gold and diamond owes its value to scarcity," writes Robinson Johnson.

A word of praise or commendation will easily enhance the pupils' interest in any course of action. Praise, rightly employed, is a forceful incentive at the disposal of the teacher.

Rebukes and scoldings are also to be used very sparingly, otherwise they lose their value.

Justice and Impartiality. The teacher should not show undue favour to some. All should be equal in his eyes. Undue favour to some students will lead to frustration among others.

Patience. He has to deal with a large number of students having low and high power of understanding. He may have to repeat his lessons many a time for the sake of the less intelligent and he should not be irritated in doing so. Some students, by nature, pick up lessons very slowly and a teacher should possess the required patience to make them understand gradually. Good habits are not formed overnight. It requires time and patience to inculcate virtues in the students.

True to his Commands. Less commands should be given to the students and when given, they must be stuck to otherwise they lose their effectiveness.

Free from Religious Fanaticism. The minds of the young should not be poisoned through narrow-mindedness and bigotry. The partition of the country has shown what wrong fanaticism can do.

Free from Political Bias. The students should not be exploited for political purposes. The programmes of the various political parties must be placed before them in their true perspective.

Sense of Patriotism. If a teacher does not possess a sense of patriotism, he would not be successful in his attempts to develop love for the country in the students.

Always Alive to the Aims of Education. Never for a moment should the teacher forget that the aim of education is not to prepare child for Matriculation or any other examination but to inculcate in him the quality of head, heart, hand and health.

Regarding this Dr. E.A. Pires writes, "He has to concern himself with the total development of the child and not only with one or two aspects, must be friend to him and help him in his emotional and social developments, he must be a philosopher illumining the way of his intellectual and spiritual progress, he must be his guide in his moral and aesthetic advancement. In fact, he must be 'all things' to all his pupils, a physician concerned about their physical health, a mental hygienist leading them carefully to sound mental health, a philosopher guiding them painstakingly in their search for truth, a moralist assisting and encouraging them to acquire goodness, an artist helping them to find beauty. In fact he must be minister ministering to their every need, such a ministry calls for dedicated service."

Interest in Co-curricular Activities. It is needless to stress the importance of co-curricular activities in the present system of education. They are perhaps more important than the traditional subject. And as such a teacher can hardly afford to be indifferent to this aspect of school life.

Missionary. Dr. E. A. Pires opines that the great teacher has the zeal of a missionary. There is a certain aptness in the analogy between a missionary and a teacher, for every true missionary is first and last a teacher.

S. Balakrishna Joshi feels, "Without a band of devoted teachers who are inspired by a holy-zeal, an institution with the paraphernalia of modern convenience will be like a beautiful corpse without spark of life, a carcass without soul." According to the same author teaching is a divinely ordained mission.

Teacher as a Guide. Child being the 'Hero in the drama of education' must be allowed to play an active role in the process of education. "The teacher is a guide and director, he steers the boat but the energy that propels it must come from those who are learning," remarks Dewey. Similarly, Shri Aurobindo writes, "The first principle of true teaching is that nothing can be taught. The teacher is not an instructor or a task master, he is a helper and a guide. His business is to suggest and not to impose. He does not actually train the pupil's mind, he shows him how to perfect his instruments of knowledge and helps and encourages him in the process. He does not impart knowledge to him; he shows him how to acquire knowledge for himself. He does not call forth the knowledge that is within; he only shows him where it lies and how it can be habituated to rise to the surface."

According to J. Payne, "The teacher's part in the process of instruction is that of guide, director or superintendent of the operation by which the pupil teaches himself."

Prayer of Unknown Teacher. Henry Van Dyke writes, "I sing the praise of the unknown teacher. Great generals win campaigns but it is the unknown soldier who wins the war. Famous educators plan new systems of pedagogy, but it is the unknown teacher who directs and guides the young. He lives in obscurity and contends with hardship. For him no trumpets blare, no chariots wait, no golden decorations are decreed. He keeps the watch along the borders of darkness and makes the attack on the trenches of ignorance and folly. Patient in his daily life, he strives to conquer the evil powers which are the enemies of youth. He awakens sleeping spirits. He quickens the indolent, encourages the eager, and steadies the unstable. He communicates his own joy in learning and shares with boys and girls the best treasures of his mind. He lights many candies, which in later years will shine back to cheer him. This is his reward. Knowledge may be gained from books, but the law of knowledge is transmitted only by personal contact. No one has ever deserved better of republic than the unknown teacher. No one is more worthy to be enrolled in a democratic aristocracy, "King of himself and servant of mankind."

Mutual Relationships

Relation with Pupils. 1. Respects the individuality of the

2. Recognises individual differences.
3. Works for the welfare of all.
4. Shows impartial treatment with all.
5. Refrains from tutoring for remuneration.
6. Refrains from imposing his religious or political convictions upon his pupils.

Relation with Associates. 1. Believes in mutual help and co-operation.

2. Gives due credit for assistance received and achievement accomplished.
3. Refrains from interfering in the affairs of his colleagues unless official duties warrant.
4. Refrains from criticising his fellow teachers.

5. Organises properly and leaving for his successor such information, data and records as may be required in beginning the next year's work.
6. Refrains from shifting, responsibility to others which should be borne by himself.
7. Helps his colleagues with helpful ideas and constructive advice.

Relation with the Profession. 1. Shows a personal pride in the teaching profession.

2. Helps in raising standards of entrance to the profession.
3. Broadens his educational equipment for teaching after entering the profession.
4. Shows an open mind towards all forms of professional conduct.
5. Becomes an active member of the professional organisations.
6. Works for material conditions necessary for a high degree of professional service.
7. Refrains from getting unearned favours from publishers.
8. Honours any contract entered into.
9. Extends full cooperation to authorities.

Tips for Teachers

Teaching Procedures and Methods. 1. Prepare your lesson thoroughly.

2. Plan your work systematically.
3. Have everything ready to start class work and be sure you get the attention of every member of the class.
4. Use a variety of teaching aids.
5. Make assignments definite and clear.
6. Word questions clearly so that the students know what you are asking from them.

7. Teach the whole class and not a few students sitting on the front benches.
8. Distribute questions evenly.
9. Put questions to inattentive students also.
10. Do not often repeat your questions.
11. Do not put questions hurriedly.
12. Allow reasonable time to the students to answer your questions.
13. Encourage students to answer questions rather than having you do all the talking.
14. Encourage students to report on anything of current interest to them and the class, which pertains to the course.
15. Provide opportunities for all students to participate.
16. Avoid being side tracked.
17. Check the written work of the students carefully.
18. Make necessary explanations about corrected assignments.
19. Avoid difficult assignments when you first begin.
20. Allow supervised study time.
21. Vary methods of teaching and learning; use dramas, panel discussion, debate, etc.
22. Make your black-board writing legible.
23. Keep the students always busy in doing some worth-while work.
24. Make every pupil feel that he is essential to the success of the lesson.
25. Make a judicious use of praise, and blame to the class as a whole and to individual members.
26. Make every effort to avoid all suggestions of criticism or anger before group.

27. Explain errors to student individually rather than before a whole class, when an individual is concerned.
28. Provide problem situations by putting thought provoking questions.

Classroom Routine: 1. Tell your name carefully and accurately.

2. Learn the names of the students quickly.
3. Learn carefully the seating plan of students.
4. Keep an accurate record of absentees and tardiness.
5. Maintain a neat room.
6. Keep room well-ventilated and lighted.
7. Take the roll-call and enquire about the absentees.
8. Acquaint yourself with procedures and forms of school.
9. Insist on correct postures.
10. Be always punctual.
11. Stand throughout the great part of the class period.
12. Impress upon the students the importance of respect for school property.
13. Have a definite system for collecting and distributing materials to avoid confusion.
14. Collect materials and books as soon as the period is over.
15. Do not leave anything in disorder when you leave the class.
16. Rub off the black-board when you leave the classroom.
17. Train your students to keep themselves busy when you are not in the classroom.
18. Do not embarrass pupils before other pupils.
19. Show consideration for bashful pupils.

Guidance and Counselling. 1. Be acquainted with the home conditions of the child.

2. Study health records, test scores, anecdotal records, etc., of each student.
3. Recognise individual differences.
4. Develop feeling of friendliness so that every pupil feels free to ask your assistance in personal and school problems.
5. Be available for student conferences.
6. Maintain up-to-date cumulative records.
7. Evince continued interest in assisting students to solve their problems.
8. Share your knowledge and understanding of students with other teachers.
9. Cooperate with other guidance workers for finding satisfactory solutions.
10. Take interest in testing programmes.

Class Discipline. 1. Base your discipline on do's rather than don'ts.

2. Use the standards of the group as a foundation of your disciplinary measures.
3. Do not allow students to wander around.
4. Insist on good conduct or manners and high standards of work.
5. Be sympathetic and understanding in your dealings with students.
6. Be firm and consistent in your dealing with students.
7. Maintain a certain reserve and be friendly rather than achummy'.
8. Try to adopt and extend this philosophy, "I like you even though, I do not like what you do."
9. Be just and fair.
10. Avoid telling the class to keep order.

11. Avoid abusive language.
12. Avoid sarcastic remarks.
13. Avoid threats.
14. Attend to minor problems before they become major ones.
15. Encourage respect and honesty.
16. Make every effort to solve your own disciplinary problems.
17. Refer cases of indiscipline to the higher authorities when you must.
18. Do not discuss your family problems in the classroom.
19. Do not discuss your colleagues with the students.
20. Do not narrate your experiences too often.
21. Do not waste time in gossips.

Personality Traits. 1. Be punctual in your programmes.

2. Do not use loud voice.
3. Avoid mannerism.
4. Be always cheerful.
5. Handle controversial topics skilfully.
6. Be humorous.
7. Use polite and proper language.
8. Avoid sarcastic remarks.
9. Be well-mannered.
10. Show sincere interest in students, school activities and coworkers.
11. Be frank to admit "Don't know all the answers."
12. Cultivate initiative and resourcefulness.
13. Be true to the ethics of the teaching profession.

To play his role effectively and efficiently, a teacher is expected to understand the significance of the following and act accordingly:

Who is to Teach. The teacher is to teach and he must know his strengths and weaknesses and should strive to present reasonably good models before his students.

Whom to Teach? The teacher should understand his pupils thoroughly, their aptitudes, abilities, habits, manners and temperaments and accordingly cater to their needs.

Why to Teach? He should always remember that the aim of education is to develop harmonious personalities, who are culturally refined, emotionally stable, ethically sound, mentally alert, morally upright, physically strong, socially efficient and spiritually enlightened. He should not forget even for a moment that the traditional 3 R's have been replaced by 7 R's, i.e. Reading, Writing, Arithmetic, Recreation, Rights, Responsibilities and Relationships.

Where to Teach? He ought not to think that school is not merely a place of imparting information but a place where men of tomorrow are trained to take up their proper place in the society and contribute to national development.

What to Teach? He must know his subject well.

How to Teach? He must make use of new technology in the teaching learning process.

When to Teach? He should develop motivation among his students to make his teaching effective and inspirational.

8

Position of the Teacher

K.G. Saiyidain, the former Educational Adviser to the Government of India, observes, "The financial prospects offered by the profession are still so poor that persons with ambition and intelligence are not attracted to it barring perhaps, a few who have genuine call for it." Dr. K.L. Shrimali writes, "A general survey of the teaching profession will reveal that a large majority of teachers do not enter this profession by choice but are forced into it by circumstances. It will also be found that people who go into the teaching profession come mostly from families belonging to lower middle and lower income groups of the community. The children of administrators or of professional men such as doctors, engineers, big businessmen or landlords rarely join the teaching profession but children of farmers, small businessmen and clerks are found in abundance. Students who can afford to pay for their higher education go up to the University and try for jobs which will bring money and prestige. Those who have received higher education at Universities as regular students rarely think of becoming teachers in a school. It is only when they have failed to secure more lucrative jobs in other professions that they become teachers. They are always on the look out for better jobs elsewhere and as soon as they get an opportunity, leave teaching profession." An eminent educationist referring to the teaching profession states, "The teaching profession has been compared to a submissive wife but I am afraid she has been kept too long in an old and tattered saree." Teaching profession should not be allowed to suffer from poverty, neglect, indifference and insecurity. A frustrated teacher is bound to produce frustrated personalities. It is an irony that the builder of a nation is unable to build even a small cottage for himself. In any system of national reconstruction top priority must be given to the various problems connected with the teachers, their social status, salaries and general service conditions. A UNESCO Seminar on the Education and Training of Teachers suggested the following points to raise the prestige both of teachers themselves and of teaching as a profession :

(1) The financial rewards of the teacher must be improved.

(2) The conditions under which they work should be made attractive.

(3) Teacher's living conditions should be conducive to a satisfying life.

(4) Publicity given to the work of schools should be increased and improved.

(5) The public relations programme of individual schools or school system should be a genuine two-way process.

(6) The satisfaction resulting from teaching should be conveyed, both to adolescents making a vocational choice and to the adults whose advice strongly affects the choice.

(7) Preparation for teaching should not be inferior to preparation for other professions.

(8) The atmosphere in which teachers work should be one in which initiative and creative effort can work.

(9) Classroom teachers can themselves play a major role through the quality of their own day-to-day work.

(10) Active teacher participation in professional organisations can help to improve public attitude towards teachers and teaching.

(11) Adequate financial assistance to students in training would help to attract suitable recruits.

Recommendations of the Commission

Status of Teacher. Intensive and continuous efforts are necessary to raise the economic, social and professional status of teachers and to feed back talented young persons into the profession.

Remuneration. The most urgent need is to upgrade the remuneration of teachers substantially, particularly at the school stage.

Minimum Scales. The Government of India should lay down, for the school stage, minimum scales of pay for teachers and assist the States a Union Territories to adopt equivalent or higher scales to suit their conditions :

(a) Scale of pay of school teachers belonging to the same category but working under different managements such as government, local bodies or private managements should be the same.

(b) The principle of parity should be adopted as a State policy forthwith in each State but its full implementation may, if necessary, be phased over a programme of five years.

(c) The introduction of these scales of pay should be linked with improvement in the qualifications of teachers and improvements in the selection procedures for their appointment. This should be done on the lines of recommendations of the Committee on Model Act for Universities.

(d) Three main scales of pay should be recognised for school teachers :

   (i) for teachers who have completed the secondary school stage and are trained;

   (ii) for trained graduates;

   (iii) for teachers with postgraduate qualifications.

(e) The practice of creating posts in lower scales of pay and recruiting to these, teachers with lower qualifications when qualified teachers are available or recruiting qualified teachers into these posts and paying them at lower scales should be abandoned.

(f) Scales of pay of secondary school teachers should be related to scales of college and university teachers on the one hand and to those of primary teachers on the other.

(g) Scales of pay for headmasters of lower and higher secondary schools should have a definite relationship with those of teachers in affiliated colleges or even universities. Depending upon the size, function, and quality of schools, the proportion of teachers with postgraduate qualifications should vary from 10-30 per cent in secondary and higher secondary schools; teachers with first and second class in B.A./B.Sc. or M.A./M.Sc. should be given advance increments in the scale. Professional training should be obligatory for all secondary school teachers.

Qualifications and Recruitment. State Board of School Education and the Education Department should prescribe qualifications of teachers and lay down proper procedures for selection not only for Government schools but for those conducted by local authorities and private managements as well; local authority schools would largely come under the District School Boards : every private school recognised and aided by State Education Departments should be required to have a managing committee with representatives from the Department; the Department should prescribe the qualifications for teachers similar to those in Government institutions; every post to be filled should be adequately advertised and interviews held by duly constituted selection committee; no grant-in-aid should be paid for the salary of a teacher appointed outside the rules or the above machinery.

Promotional Prospects. (a) Qualified and trained teachers in primary schools should be considered for promotion as headmasters or inspectors of schools.

(b) Trained graduate teachers in secondary schools who have done outstanding work would be eligible for promotion to posts carrying salaries for postgraduate qualifications.

(c) Secondary school teachers with the necessary aptitude and competence could be appointed as university and college teachers.

(d) Advance increments for teachers doing outstanding work should be made possible.

Relating Salaries to Costs of Living. All teacher salaries should be reviewed every five years and the dearness allowance paid to teachers should be related to that paid to government servants.

Welfare Services. A general programme of welfare services for all school teachers should be organised in each State and Union Territory, the funds being contributed by both teachers and the State on a matching basis. The fund should be administered by joint committees of representatives of teachers and government.

Need for Central Assistance. The proposals for the improvement of salaries of school teachers should be given effect to immediately, generous Central assistance being made available to State Governments for this purpose.

Retirement Benefits. (a) The system of retirement benefits to teachers should be treated on the basis of the principles of uniformity and parity.

(b) As an interim measure, the triple-benefit scheme should be more widely adopted both for teachers in Government schools as well as the University and college teachers.

(c) The normal retirement age for teachers in schools, colleges and universities should be made 60 years with provision for extension upto 65 years.

(d) A more equitable system of investing provident fund amount should be devised.

Conditions of Work and Service. (a) The conditions of work in educational institutions should be such as to enable teachers to function at their highest level of efficiency.

(b) The minimum facilities required for efficient work should be provided to all educational institutions. Adequate facilities for professional advancement should be provided.

(c) In fixing the hours of work not only actual classroom teaching but all other work a teacher has to do should be taken into consideration.

(d) A scheme should also be drawn up under which every teacher will get a concessional railway pass to any part of India once in five years.

(e) New conduct and discipline rules suitable for the teaching profession should be framed for teachers in government service.

(f) In private schools the principle of parity should be adopted and terms and conditions of service of teachers in these should be the same as for government schools.

(g) Every effort should be made to increase residential accommodation for teachers in rural areas. A programme of building construction and grant of adequate house rent allowance in all big cities should be adopted; co-operative housing schemes for teachers should be encouraged and loans on favourable terms for construction of houses should be made available.

(h) The target to be reached over the next 15 years in universities and colleges should be to provide residential accommodation to about 50 per cent teachers in the university and 20 per cent in all affiliated colleges.

(i) Special coaching for children who need it, should be provided on an institutional basis and the teachers concerned adequately remunerated.

(j) At the University stage, part-time consultancy or additional work, such as research by teachers in higher education should be permitted; and no payment should be required to be made to the institution if the earnings do not exceed 50 per cent of the salary.

Civil Rights of Teachers. Teachers should be free to exercise all civic rights and should be eligible for public office at the local, district, state or national level. No legal restriction should be placed on their participation in elections, but when they do so, they should be expected to proceed on leave.

Women Teachers. The employment of women teachers should be encouraged at all stages and in all sectors of education, opportunities for part-time employment be provided on a large scale.

Residential Accommodation. Provision should be made for residential accommodation particularly in rural areas.

Correspondence Courses. Increasing facilities be provided for correspondence courses.

Special Allowances. Wherever necessary, special allowances should be given to women teachers working in rural areas.

Teachers for Tribal Areas. Teachers for tribal areas should be given special allowances, assistance for the education of their children and residential accommodation. Provision should be made for special training of teachers going to work in rural areas.

Teachers' Organisations. Professional organisations of teachers which carry out work for the improvement of the profession and of education should be recognised by the Central and State Governments and consulted on matters relating to school education, general and professional education of teachers and their salaries and conditions of work.

Joint Teachers Councils. Joint Teachers Councils should be constituted in each State and Union Territory to discuss all matters relating to teachers' salaries, conditions of work and service and welfare service.

National Awards. The Ministry of Education should consider the suggestions :

(a) to increase the number of national awards;

(b) to strengthen the selection committee;

(c) to give travelling allowance to the awardees as for Class I Officers of Government.

Status and Role

The Teacher in India by Prof R.P. Singh describes the diminutive role of the teacher in these words : "The present-day teacher in India is a by-product of the emergence of the middle class in the latter half of the 19th century. In spite of some of the remnants of the glory of the past that are attached to his calling to this day, it is difficult to maintain that he is a direct linear descendant of his illustrious forbear. Two major considerations as regards his diminutive role are; (a) The dignity of a teacher in the past, especially under Aryan rule, was not merely because of his learning but also because of his high caste; and (b) Teaching was an inalienable part of the priestly obligation monopolized by the Brahmin community, although technically speaking (until Manu) people from other communities could also become teachers ...."

He further says, "The halo and power of a teacher of pre-printing days is gone. A teacher has diminishing teaching value; and in keeping kids busy elsewhere, he is a very helpful tool. Beyond that he has no power no control and therefore no status."

It is further observed, "The outstanding features of the teacher during the ancient and medieval periods, therefore, constituted his priestly character, restricted purpose, and an uneventful life in a more or less stable society. With the appearance of the British on the Indian scene in the early 17th century the Indian teacher, both Hindu and Muslim......... mullahs or pandits in their diminutive and considerably mutilated role, held their sway supreme at social functions but otherwise they could be conveniently forgotten.

The 'new' teacher according to Prof. Singh, who formed a segment of the newly created middle class by the British had "no mooring in the typical Indian soil. The major distinctions between the 'new' and 'old' profession he (1) in their secular character, (2) in the systems of payments, and (3) in their outlook towards the jobs they do."

Prof. Singh draws a parallel between the situation in the United States and India and remarks, "... In the case of teachers in the urban centres of this country also the same dynamics of hire and sale is observable as it is in the case of certain other transactable commodities. The equilibrium of rural society is also being disturbed because similar strains of business are becoming gradually noticeable."

According to him, "the Indian teacher other than university teachers who regard them as a distinct group is almost the residual layer of the available intelligentsia."

"As a representative of the intellectual class also, his status has been appreciably eroded by the higher standards of proficiency required in other professions. Whereas the standard and variety of accomplishments now being expected in other walks of professional life have been gradually risen, in teaching they have either remained stationary or slid down for want of challenge."

Even during the Mughal period the teacher had lost much of his glory. Aurangzeb is said to have expressed his resentment over the teaching of his teacher, Mullah Shah (Mulla Sale as referred to by Bernier) when the latter, sometimes after his retirement came to seek favour from his pupil (Emperor Aurangzeb). "...Pray what is your pleasure with me? Do you pretend that I ought to exhalt you to the first honours of the State? Let us then examine your title to any mark of distinction. I do not deny you would possess such a title if you had filled my young mind with suitable instruction.

But what was the knowledge I derived under your tuition? ... I have a perfect remembrance of your having, during several years, harmed my brain with idle and foolish propositions... If you had taught me that philosophy which adapts the minds to reason ... If you had inculcated lessons which elevate the soul and fortify it against the assault of fortune ... ; if you had made me acquainted with the nature of man; ... and given me a sublime and adequate conception of the universe... If such had been the nature of philosophy imbibed under your tuition, I should be more indebted to you than Alexander was to Aristotle, and should consider it my duty to bestow a very different award on you than Aristotle received from the Prince. Answer me sycophant..."

Special Status

D.C. Lortie in 'School Teacher : A Sociological Study' (1975) views teachers as having a "Special but shadowed" prestige position. On the one hand, their work is seen as having the aura of a "special mission" but on the other, teachers have largely lost whatever autonomy they once had to manage pedagogical theory and their classrooms because they have become functionaries in hierarchical organisations. Whatever be the reason, teachers clearly do not attract as much do the other more secure profession..."

In the views of the National Commission on Teachers (1983-85), high salary and service conditions, lack of recognition by the government, lack of devotion to work, integrity and sense of pride are the main factors for the deterioration of the status of teachers.

Challenge of Education (1985) observes; "... so much is expected of the teacher, yet teaching has become the last choice in the job market. We, therefore, face a paradox of having better books and research but progressively more indifferent teacher.

Programme of Action (1986) states that the status of teachers had a direct bearing on the quality of education and many of the ills of the latter can be ascribed to the indifferent manner in which society have looked upto the teacher and the manner in which many teachers have performed their functions.

B. J. Biddle in an article in The Encyclopaedia of Teaching and Teacher Education (1987) lists these reasons for the relatively low prestige of teachers : Prevalence of women in the teaching profession, lack of specificity in the role expected of teachers, the fact that teachers work primarily with the young, devaluation of the knowledge deemed necessary to teach well, the large number of persons presently employed or available for employment as teachers and others.

Two important factors regarding the role and status of a teacher are generally missed today. First, a teacher in earlier times combined the functions of the 'guru' or preceptor and the teacher. He guided his students in spiritual matters also. Secondly, an individual received his education from one or a few teachers only. Nowadays, an individual before getting his M.A. degree gets his education from more than two dozen teachers. Naturally, therefore, a modern teacher proportionately gets reduced respect.

New Policies

National Policy on Education 1986

1. The status of the teacher reflects the socio-cultural ethos of a society; it is said that no people can rise above the level of its teachers. The Government and the community should endeavour to create conditions which will help motivate and inspire teachers on constructive and creative

lines. Teachers should have the freedom to innovate, to devise appropriate methods of communication and activities relevant to the needs and capabilities of and the concerns of the community.

2. The methods of recruiting teachers will be reorganised to ensure merit, objectivity and conformity with spatial and functional requirements. The pay and service conditions of teachers have to be commensurate with their social and professional responsibilities and with the need to attract talent to the profession. Efforts will be made to reach the desirable objective of uniform emoluments, service conditions and grievance-removal mechanisms for teachers throughout the country. Guidelines will be formulated to ensure objectivity in the postings and transfers of teachers. A system of teacher evaluation—open, participative and data-based will be created and reasonable opportunities of promotion to higher grades provided. Norms of accountability will be laid down with incentives for good performance and disincentives for non-performance. Teachers will continue to play crucial role in the formulation and implementation of educational programmes.

3. Teachers' associations must play a significant role in upholding professional integrity, enhancing the dignity of the teacher and in curbing professional misconduct. National level associations of teachers could prepare a Code of Professional Ethics for Teachers and see to its observance.

Commission for Teachers

Status of the Teacher. The basic problems from the nation's point of view is that unless the status is reasonably high, the teaching profession in this country will not be able to attract and retain persons of ability.

Because of low teacher status a growing number of teachers and parents are turning away from the idea of accepting teaching as an attractive career for their wards.

Status by reason of a title or position will become increasingly difficult to come by, we feel. Status on the other words, will have to be earned, by the teacher, as by any other professional worker.

The closer the teacher is able to link himself and his vocation with the mission of the nation the more relevant he will become and the more revered by students, parents and society.

1. The academic and professional requirements for entry into the profession.
2. The financial and other economic benefits.
3. The professional responsibilities assumed.
4. The freedom of teachers to take part in public affairs and
5. The degree of public recognition.

The Remuneration

As a matter of national policy, the existing pay-scales of teachers and educational administrators in a state should be replaced by a single running scale as early as possible. Such a step will go a long way in giving to the school teachers a status which is not lacking and without which he is not in a position to perform his functions effectively. A diagramatic representation of the illustrative model is given here.

Teachers have to play a crucial role in the process of social transformation. They have to shoulder complex tasks as active participants in national development. It is in this context that the social status of teachers, the national conditions of their life and the environment of their work have significance. However, increase in material benefits is not sufficient. Unless the level of professional competence does not rise along with betterment of material conditions, the status of teachers will not improve. Pursuit of excellence and establishment of reputation as a teacher go a long way in giving high status to teachers even if material benefits are not at par with other professions.

9

Moral Factors

Commitment to the Teaching Profession

The concept of professional ethics may be described in the words of Laurie as, "If a teacher has not an ideal aim he had better to take to shopkeeping at once, he will there doubtless find an ideal within his capacity." The Secondary Education Commission 1952-53 has stated in this connection as, "They (teachers) will not look upon their work as an unpalatable means of carrying a scanty living but as an avenue through which they are rendering significant social services as well as finding some measure of self-fulfilment and self-expression."

The teacher should feel the importance of his profession. He would be showing a dishonesty of purpose if once having entered it he is engaged in other pursuits. Without an exclusive attention to his job he would fail in bringing forth a fine harvest of young men and women who are able to contribute their best for the welfare of mankind. If a teacher takes to his work just to make his living because nothing else is available, he will lack the essential zeal required by the teaching profession. He must be a teacher first and the teacher last.

The professional ethics demands that a teacher does not try to exploit school influence for private gains. He realizes that if he does it, he signs his moral death-warrant. The result is that no amount of pressure can wean him from the path of duty and justice. Authority cannot coerce him, nor can temptation reduce him into any course of conduct, not conducive to the highest interests of the school.

He fights all temptations to pad his purse with money to which he is not entitled. He does not indulge in tuitions. He does not prescribe or recommend books on some consideration.

A teacher is expected :

1. To keep abreast of the developments in the teaching profession.

2. To maintain membership in some professional organizations relevant to his subject or area of speciality.

3. To manifest ethical behaviour in relations with fellow teachers and educational associates.

4. To keep abreast of subject-matter through study of books, periodicals, newspapers and other sources concerning development in his field.

5. To utilise films, filmstrips, T.V. and radio as a means of keeping abreast of new and advanced knowledge in his field.

6. To attend conferences, workshops, seminars and meetings; to take field trips which tend to broaden knowledge.

7. To exercise professional direction in his relations with parents and the community.

8. To attend to the all-round development of the learners under his charge.

A Man of Confidence. The teachers must have an unlimited confidence and faith in himself. It is essential that a teacher should be not only a man of high character but also that he be a man of confidence; confidence in his vocation, confidence in his pupils, confidence in human nature and confidence in his colleagues.

Respect for Each Other

1. A teacher should be adept in establishing good human relationships with his colleagues.
2. He should give due regard to their personality.
3. He should not indulge in forming cliques or groups.
4. He should never criticise any of his colleagues before the students, their parents and others.
5. He should not backbite his colleagues to the head of the institution or others.

Rapport with the Administration

1. He should give due regard to the head, the members of the managing committee and the personnel working in the Education Department.
2. He should be loyal to the institution.
3. He should appreciate the difficulties and limitations of the head of the institution.
4. He should not indulge in loose talk.
5. He should submit timely reports and records to the appropriate authority through the head of the institution.

Rapport with the Community

1. Participating in parent-teacher and similar activities.

2. Participating in community affairs.
3. Making himself available to parents at scheduled times to discuss pupil progress and behaviour.
4. Evincing a helpful, sympathetic and understanding attitude towards parents and their children's schooling problems.
5. Assuring through personal behaviour in the community that the school-staff image in the community is favourable.
6. Showing due courtesy to the members of the community and especially when they visit the school.

Rapport with the Students

1. Students should have free access to the teacher
2. The teacher should give due regard to the individuality of the students.
3. The teacher should take interest in the welfare of the students.
4. The teacher should attend to their individual needs.
5. The teacher should share responsibility with the students.
6. The teacher should be fair and just with the students.
7. The teacher should have faith in the students.

Knowledge about the State Education Code

An Education Code includes rules and regulations governing various aspects of education. It is divided broadly into five categories:

1. Rules regarding recognition of schools.

2. Rules regarding instructional issues, e.g. age of admission to a school, admission procedure, fees and funds, prescription of teaching material, school discipline, examination and evaluation etc.
3. Rules regarding school inspections.
4. Rules regarding service conditions and welfare of the staff.
5. School community relations.

It is very important to remember that the entire teaching-learning process is carried on in accordance with the provisions of the Education Code. Any deviation from it is likely to land the teachers into trouble.

General Attitude

A teacher is a member of the society. He lives and works in the society. In view of his special responsibilities and role, he is expected to rise above the average member of the society. His general attitude in the society should be of enthusiasm and optimism. He should be a man of cooperative attitude. He should be sensitive to the needs of the society. He should be guided by the ideals of democracy, secularism and socialism. He should be sufficiently appreciative of the needs and problems of the society.

Morality at Work

Since he ceaselessly strives to be a model to others, he regards no aspect of his work as trivial or insignificant which can conveniently be passed on to others to be done well or ill. He is too well aware of the truth of that wise statement, "Trifles make perfection and perfection is no trifle." Hence every item - be it the folding of a sheet or the writing of a circular - is done with meticulous care as if it were a religious act.

It is rightly said, "Dignity consists in being helpful and doing the right thing in the right manner and at the right time." A teacher would do well to prepare his lessons daily. Bagley has rightly said, "However able and experienced the teacher he could do never without his preliminary preparation." Efforts should be made to ensure that all the work done is neat and clean, systematic and in time.

10

Teacher under Review

What they Say ?

1. The teacher is a maker of man.

   -Adams, John (Second U. S. President, 1735 -1826)

2. A teacher affects eternity; he can never tell where his influence.

-Adams, Henry Brooks (American Man of Letters 1838-1918)

3. None can teach admirably if not loving his task.

   - Alcott, Amos Bronson (American Educator, 1799-1888)

4. The true teacher inspires self-trust.

   -Alcott, Amos Bronson

5. The true teacher defends his pupils from his personal influence.

   -Alcott, Amos Bronson

6. I am indebted to my father for living, but to my teacher for living well. Alexander (The Great Conqueror, 356-3 23 B. C.)

7. To know how to suggest is the great art of teaching.

   -Amiel, Henri Federic (Swiss Philosopher, 1828-1881)

8. Teachers who educate children, deserve more honour than parents who merely give them birth.

-Aristotle (Greek Philosopher, 384-322 B.C.)

9. And through thee I believe
In the noble and great who are gone;
Pure souls honour'd and blest
By former ages, who else
Such, so soulless, so poor,
In the race of men whom I see
Seem'd but a dream of the heart,
Seem'd but a cry of desire.
Yes; I believe that there lived
Others like there in the past
Not like the men of the crowd
Who all round me to-day
Bluster of cringe, and make life
Hideous, and arid, and vile;
But souls temper'd with fire,
Fervent, heroic, and good,
Helpers and friends of mankind ......

-Arnold, Mathew (English Educator, 1822-1888)

10. The first principle of true teaching is that nothing can be taught. The teacher is not an instructor or task-master, he is a helper and a guide. His business is to suggest and not to impose. He does not actually train the pupil's mind, he only shows him how to perfect his instruments of knowledge and helps and encourages him in the process. He does not impart knowledge to him, he shows him how to acquire knowledge for himself. He does not call forth the knowledge that is within, he only shows him where it lies and how it can be habituated to rise to the

surface. The distinction that reserves this principle for the teaching of adolescent and adult minds and denies its application to the child, is a conservative and unintelligent doctrine. Child or man, girl or boy, there is only one sound principle of good teaching. Difference of age only serves to diminish or increase the amount of help and guidance necessary; it does not change its nature.

-Aurobindo, Sri (Indian Philosopher, 1872-1950)

11. A schoolmaster should have an atmosphere of awe, and walk wonderingly, as if he was amazed at being himself.

- Bagehot, Walter (English Journalist, 1826-1877)

12. However able and experienced the teacher he could do never without his preliminary preparation.

- Bagley, William Chundler (American Teacher, 1874-1946)

13. He is wise who can instruct us and assist us in the business of daily virtuous living.

-Carlyle, Thomas (English Essayist, 1795-1881)

14. I wish that I could persuade every teacher to be proud of his occupation. Draw yourself up to your full height, look anybody squarely in the eye and say, 'I am a teacher.'

-Carr, William G. (Secretary-General of the World Confederation of Organisations of the Teaching Profession)

15. Most commonly the authority of them that teach hinders them that would learn.

- Cicero, Marcus Tullius (Latin Philosopher, 106-43 B.C.)

16. A teacher should be sparing of his smile.

-Cowper; William (English Poet, 1731-1800)

17. The teachers should take care that they do not neglect the education of classes other than Brahmans.

- Dayananda, Swami (Indian Social Reformer, 1824-1883)

18. We loved the doctrine for the teacher's sake.

- *Defoe, Daniel (English Journalist, 1661-1731)*

19. Every teacher should realize the dignity of his calling; that he is a social servant set apart for the maintenance of proper social order and the securing of the right social growth.

In this way the teacher always is the prophet of the true God and the usherer in of the true kingdom of God.

- *Dowey, John (American Educator in 'My Pedagogic Creedy', 1859-1952)*

20. The more a teacher is aware of the past experiences of students, of their hopes, desires, chief interests, the better will he understand the forces at work that need to be directed and utilized for the formation of reflective habits.

-*Dewey (How We Think)*

21. The teacher is a guide and director, he steers the boat but the energy that propels it must come from those who are learning.

- *Dewey*

22. Of all the different factors which influence the quality of education and its contribution to national development, the quality, competence and character of teachers are undoubtedly the most significant.

-*Education Commission 1964-66, 3.01 p. 46*

23. It is the supreme art of the teacher to awaken joy in creative expression and knowledge.

-*Einstein, Albert (A Swiss Physicist, 1879-1955)*

24. The spirit can only teach.

- *Emerson, Edward Waldo (American Educator, 1844-1930)*

25. The secret of education lies in respecting the pupil.

- *Emerson, E. W.*

26. The educator must teach that tolerance is better than bullet.

    -Eisenhower, Dwight D. (American President, Address at Boston University, Jan. 31, 1946)

27. The whole art of teaching is only the art of awakening the natural curiosity of young minds for the purpose of satisfying it afterwards.

    -France, Anatole (French Novelist, 1844-1924)

28. You cannot teach a man anything; you can only help him to find it within himself.

    - Galilei, Galileo (Italian Astronomer, 1564-1642)

29. Woe to the teacher who teaches one thing with the lips and carries another in the heart.

    -Gandhi, M K (To Students, pp. 16, 1869-1948)

30. The politician may succeed in his purpose even though he lacks character, but a people's teacher cannot do without character. If he lacks he will be like salt without its savour.

    -Gandhi, MK (True Education, p. 161)

31. The exercise of the spirit entirely depended on the life and character of the teacher. The teacher had always to be mindful of his P's and Q's whether he was in the midst of his boys or not.

    - Gandhi, MK (Towards New Education, p. 19)

32. If I were to be their real teacher and guardian, I must touch their hearts. I must share their joys and sorrows, I must help them solve the problems that faced men, and I must take along the right channel, the surging aspirations of their youth.

    - Gandhi, MK (Autobiography, p. 417)

33. A cowardly teacher would never succeed in making his boys valiant as a stranger to self-restraint could never teach his pupils the value of self-restraint.

    - Gandhi, MK (Towards New Education, p. 19)

34. "I have always felt that the true text-book for the pupil is his

- Gandhi, MK (Autobiography, p. 411)

35. We must procure the best teachers for our children whatever it may cost.

- Gandhi, MK (True Education,)

36. It is possible for a teacher situated miles away to affect the spirit of the pupils by his way of living.

-Gandhi, MK (Towards New Education,)

37. The teacher is a high office and it enables him to exercise great influence upon the boys and girls in his charge. They regard what he says as gospel truth.

- Gandhi, MK (True Education,)

38. There is no school equal to decent home and no teacher equal to honest virtuous parents.

- Gandhi, MK (To Students,)

39. I have found that boys imbibe more from the teacher's own lives than they do from the books that they read to them or the lectures that they deliver to them with their lips.

- Gandhi, MK (To Students,)

40. If they (teachers) impart all the knowledge in the world to their students but inculcate not truth and purity among them, they will have betrayed them and instead of raising them set them on the downward road to prediction.

- Gandhi MK (The Task Before Indian Students,)

41. When it is remembered that the primary aim of all education is, or should be, the moulding of the character of pupils, a teacher who has a character to keep need not lose heart.

- Gandhi MK (The Task Before Indian Students,)

42. Everyone of us has good inherent in the soul, it needs to be drawn out by the teachers and only teachers can

perform this sacred function whose own character is unsullied, who are always ready to learn and to grow from perfection to perfection.

- Gandhi MK (The Task Before Indian Students,)

43. I have felt that the teachers' work lies more outside than inside the lecture room ...... Unless the teachers are prepared to give all their time outside the classroom to their students, not much can be done. Let them fashion their hearts rather than brains.

- Gandhi MK (To the Students,)

44. Every teacher, if he is to do full justice to his pupils, will have to prepare the daily lesson from the material available to him. This too, he will have to suit to the special requirements of his class.

- Gandhi MK (To the Students,)

45. The teacher leads you to the threshold of your own mind.

- Gibran Khalil (1883- 1931)

46. A teacher who can arouse a feeling for one single good action, for one single good poem, accomplishes more than he who fills our memory with rows and rows of natural objects, classified with name and form.

-Goethe, Johann Wolfgang Von (German Writer 1749-1832)

47. The same persons telling to the same people the same things about the same things.

-Greek Proverb

48. To hold my teacher—equal to my own parents.

-Hippocrates (Greek Physician, 460-400 B.C.)

49. Like torches, a light to others, waste and destruction to themselves.

-Hooker, Richard (English Theologian, 1554-1600)

50. One who makes two ideas grow where only one grew before.

- Hubbard, Elbert (American Essayist, 1859-1915)

51. The teacher is indeed the architect of our future. Society can neglect him at its own peril.

- Hussain, Zakir (Head of the National Committee on Basic Education 1937, President of India, 1967-1969, 1897-1969)

52. The three R's of our school system must be supported by three T's - teachers who are superior, techniques of instruction that are modern and thinking about education which places it first in all our plans and hopes.

-Johnson, Lyndon B. (American President, Message to Congress, Jan. 12, 1965)

53. A teacher whose soul is wrinkled and whose heart is atrophied, who is devoid of energy and enthusiasm, capacity and character and who simply marks time, his eyes fixed on the calendar, is a disgrace to the profession and a curse on society. A teacher must not regard himself as a mere wage-earner whose job begins at 10 a.m. and ends at 5 p.m. when he can shake the dust off his feet and walk out of the bread-giving factory. No, he is a spiritual alchemist charged with the sacred work of creating cultured citizens.

-Joshi, S. Balakrishna, (Recipient of National Award for Teachers, Education in Practice. 1955)

54. The teacher has therefore to instruct, inspire and illumine.

-Joshi, S. Balakrishna (Education in Practice, 1955)

55. Without good teachers, even the best of systems is bound to fail. With good teachers, even the defects of a system can be largely overcome.

- Kabir, Humayun (India Educationist, 1902-1969)

56. They are literally the arbiters of a nation's destiny. It may sound a truism, but still it needs to be stressed that the teacher is the key to any educational reconstruction.

-Kabir, Humayun

57. If you neglect the teacher, you neglect the child; and if you neglect the child, you neglect the future of that country to which that child belongs.

-Kabir, Humayun

58. If a teacher has not an ideal aim, he had better to take to shopkeeping at once, he will there, doubtless find an deal within his capacity.

- Laurie

59. The school which has good teachers needs little more and the school without good teachers is little for anything else.

- Locke, John (English Philosopher, 1632- 1704)

60. For him the teacher's chair becomes a throne.

-Longfellow, Henry Wordsworth (American Scholar, 1807- 1882).

61. The best teacher of children, in brief is one who is essentially child-like.

- Mencken, H.L. (American Journalist, 1880-1956)

62. A tutor should not be continually thundering instruction into the ears of his pupil, as if he were pouring through a funnel, but after having put the lad, like a young horse, on a trot before him, to observe his paces, and see what he is able to perform, should according to the extent of his capacity, induce him to taste, to distinguish, and to find things for himself; sometimes opening the way, at other times learning it for him to open.

- Mantaigne, Michel Eyquem De (French Philosopher, 1533 -1592)

63. I do not teach, I only tell.

- Montaigne

64. Instead of facility of speech she has to acquire the power of silence, instead of teaching she has to observe,' instead

of the proud dignity of one who claims to be infallible, she assumes the vesture of humility.

- Montessori, Maria (Italian Educator, 1870-1952)

65. Teacher partly doctor, partly scientist and wholly religious.

- Montessori

66. The broader the teachers' scientific culture and practice in experimental psychology, the sooner will come for her the marvel of unfolding life, and her interest in it.

-Montessori, Maria (The Advanced Montessori Method, Vol. 1. p. 128)

67. We underscore that the prime task of the teacher is concerned with man-making namely the making of the Indian of tomorrow.

-National Commission on School Teachers, 1983-85

68. Teacher as an agent of change.

-National Commission on Teachers for Higher Education, 1983-85

69. The status of the teacher reflects the socio-cultural ethos of a society; it is said that no people can rise above the level of teachers.

-National Policy on Education, 1986

70. A teacher does not live for himself, but for his pupil and for the truth which he imparts. His aim is to be a colourless medium through which that truth may shine on opening minds. How can be this if he is continually interposing himself and saying, "instead of looking at the truth, my children, look at me, and see how skilfully I do my work. I thought I taught you admirably today. I hope you thought so too?"

-Palmer; G.H. (American Educator in The Ideal Teacher, 1842-1933)

71. I think one of the most difficult things for a teacher to learn or to acquire - let's put it that way is to be a learner.

- Parkhurst, Helen H. (Education in the Dalton Plan, 1922)

72. While books can teach, only personality can educate.

- Parkhurst

73. The teacher's part in the process of instruction is that of guide, director or superintendent of the operation by which the pupil teaches himself.

-Payne, Joseph (English Educator, 1808-1876)

74. It is like the art of the gardener under whose care a thousand trees blossom and grow. He contributes nothing to their actual growth; the principle of growth lies in the trees themselves. He plants and waters, but God gives the increase... So with the educator: he imparts no single power to men. He only watches lest any external force should injure or disturb. He takes care that development runs its course in accordance with its own law.

- Pestalozzi, Johann Heinrich (Swiss Educator, 1746-1827)

75. The first condition of a good teacher is that he shall be trained as a teacher and not brought to serve other profession.

- Pettison Mark

76. If a nation's teachers are C3, the nation itself cannot but be C3. And let there be no doubt about this - if we wish to be an A1 nation, our teachers will have to be A1.

- (Dr.) Pires, EA. (Indian Educator)

77. Do not train boys to learning by force and hardness; but direct them to it by what amuses their minds, so that you may be better able to discover with accuracy the peculiar bent of the genius of each.

- Plato (Western Educational Philosopher, 427-347 B.C.)

78. Let such persons teach others who themselves excel.

-Pope, Alexander (English Critic, 1688-1744)

79. Their (Teachers') own character should be such that there is no difference between what they say and do. When we act upon this ideal, then alone we can be sure of a bright future for our own country.

- Rajendra Prasad (First Indian President, 1951-1962)

80. Let him have towards his pupils the benevolent disposition of a parent and consider himself as holding the place of those who have entrusted him with this charge. He must neither be vicious himself nor countenance vice; austere though not harsh; mild though not familiar; let the first generate hatred, the second contempt. Let him talk frequently of virtue. The often he advises, the seldomer he will be obliged to punish. Let him be plain and simple in his manner of teaching; patient in labour; rather punctual in making his scholars comply with their duty, than, too exact in requiring more than they can do.

-Quintilian, Marcos Fabius, Quintilianus (Roman Rhetorician) 42-118 A.D.

81. The function of the teacher is of vital importance. He must be a committed man, committed to faith in the future of man, in the future of humanity, in the future of this country and the world. He must work with this implicit confidence in the power of humanity, in the recuperative power which it has and by which it can cleanse and purify itself. Unless he has faith in that, he will never be able to advance higher.

- (Dr.) Radhakrishnan, Sarvapalli, (Indian Philosopher, President of India, 1888-1975, (Speeches and Writings, 1965,)

82. Teachers, according to our tradition, have been sovereign over themselves and servants of the people. They maintain absolute control over their own feelings and try to help

humanity to the extent possible. That has been the tradition. The greatest teachers of our country have been those who have made our civilization live.

- (Dr) Radhakrishnan, Sarvapalli (Speeches and Writings, 1965,)

83. We in our country look upon teachers as gurus, acharyas: What do these words indicate? 'Acharya' is one whose 'achaar' or conduct is exemplary. If he is a victim of 'durachaar', then he is not an 'Acharya.' He must be an example of 'sadachaar', of good conduct. He must inspire the pupils who are entrusted to his care with love of virtue and goodness and abhorrence of cruelty and violence.

- (Dr.) Radhakrishnan, Sarvapalli

84. 'Andhakar' is not merely intellectual ignorance but spiritual blindness. He who is able to remove that kind of spiritual blindness is called a guru. Are we deserving of that noble appellation of an Aacharya' or a guru? That is the first thing that everyone of us will have to realize.

- (Dr.) Radhakrishnan, Sarvapalli (Occasional Speeches and Writings' Third Series)

85. The teacher's place in society is of vital importance. He acts as the pivot for the transmission of intellectual tradition and technical skills from generation to generation, and helps to keep the lamp of civilization burning. He not only guides the individual, but also so to say, the destiny of the nation.

- (Dr.) Radhakrishnan, Sarvapalli

86. A true teacher always goes down to the level of the taught. A teacher who can never let himself down, to the level of the taught is not a true teacher.

- Swami Ramakrishnananda (For Thinkers on Education, 1948,)

87. The true aim of everyone who aspires to be a teacher should be not to impart his own opinions, but to kindle minds.

-Robertson, Fredrik William (English Writer, 1816- 1853)

88. The teacher is like the candle which lights others in consuming itself.

-Ryburn, WM (Indian Educator)

89. The severity of the Master is more useful than the indulgence of the father.

- Sadi (Persian Scholar, A.D. Gulistan, (1258)

90. Self-analysis on the part of the teacher is a necessary equipment.

- Saiyidain, K G. (Indian Educator, 1904 -74)

91. You do not have to think hard when you talk to a teacher.

- Salinger, JD. (The Catch in the Eye)

92. We are, however, convinced that the most important factor in the contemplated educational reconstruction is the teacher—his personal qualities, his educational qualifications, his professional training and the place that he occupies in the school as well as in the community.

- Secondary Education Commission 1952-53, Third reprint, 1986

93. The reputation of a school and its influence on the life of the community invariably depend on the kind of teachers working in it.

- Secondary Education Commission

94. They will not look upon their work as an unpalatable means of earning a scanty living but as an avenue through which they are rendering significant social service as well as finding some measure of self-fulfilment and self-expression.

- Secondary Education Commission

95. The good teacher, in our reorganised school, will endeavour to win the love and confidence of his children

and establish his prestige on sincerity, integrity, hard work and a sympathetic handling of their problems.

- Secondary Education Commission

96. While we teach, we learn.

- Seneca, Lucius Annaeus (Roman Philosopher, 4 B.C.-65 A.D.)

97. Teachers should be held in the highest honour. They are the officer of legislators. They have agency in the prevention of crime, they aid in regulating the atmosphere, whose incessant action and pressure cause the life-blood to circulate, and to return pure heart of the nation.

- Signourney, Lydia Huntlay (1791-1865)

98. He that governs well, leads the blind; but he that teaches gives him eyes.

-South, Robert (English Divine; 1634-1716)

99. Whoe'er excels in what we prize,
Appears a hero in our eyes:
Each girl, when pleased with what is taught.
Will have the teacher in her thought.

- Swift, Jonathan (English Satirist, 1667-1745)

100. I have found that little children learn more quickly the attitude of the teacher than the knowledge imparted by him.

- Tagore (Jivan Smriti,)

101. Man can learn only from a man. Just as a water tank can be filled only with water and fire can be kindled only with fire, life can be inspired only with life. In our social organisation we are searching for a guru who will give peace to our life; in our educational system we are searching for a guru who will emancipate our mind from its imprisonment.

- Tagore, Rabindranath (Indian Philosopher, Poet, 1861-1941)

102. If the teacher does not himself possess learning how can he impart it to others? He is like a lamp lighting other lamps. But a lamp cannot put light into other lamps if it does not itself burn and shed light. The teacher who merely repeats bookish knowledge mechanically can never teach anything and can never inspire, and without proper inspiration independent creative faculties can never develop.

- Tagore (Siksa, 1342 B.S.)

103. In teaching, the guiding spirit should be personal love. Have more faith in the principle of life, in the sanctity of the human soul than in the mere methods of teaching?

- Tagore

104. Communication of life can only be through a living agency. And culture, which is the life of mind, can only be imparted through man to man.

- Tagore

105. The essence of the thing is that the teacher needs to be a real person with a full life of his own, a background of vivid personal experience, a conviction about the purpose of education and the kind of society which he wants to help bring about.

- Tomlinson, Henry Major (English Novelist, 1873-1958)

106. If there is any profession of paramount importance I believe it is that of the school master.

- Tyndall, John (English Natural Philosopher, 1820-1893)

107. The right kind of teacher is one who possesses a vivid awareness of his mission. He not only loves his subject, he loves also those whom he teaches.

-University Education Commission, 1948-49

108. No teacher who is not a master of the field, who is not in touch with the latest development in his subject and who

does not bring to bear upon his duties a free and untrammeled mind will never succeed in inspiring youth with the love of truth which is the principal object of all higher education.

- University Education Commission

109. Knowledge may be gained from books but the love of knowledge is transmitted only by personal contact.

- Van Dyke, Henry (American Essayist, 1852-1933)

110. Teacher as the 'Brahma', the 'Vishnu' and the 'Maheshvara'.

- Vedic Prayer

111. The true teacher is he who can immediately come down to the level of the student, and transfer his soul to the student's soul and see through and understand through his mind. Such a teacher can really teach and none else.

- Vivekananda, Swami (Indian Social Reformer, 1863-1902)

112. The teacher is the real maker of history.

- Wells, Herbert George (Historian, 1866-1946)

113. The teacher has a double function. It is for him to elicit the enthusiasm by resonance from his own personality, and to create the environment of a larger knowledge and a firmer purpose.

-Whitehead, Alfred North (Prof of Philosophy, Harvard, 1861-1947)

Various Opinions

1. The vanity of teaching often tempeth a man to forget he is block-head.

-Halifax Lord, (English Statesman, 1886-1959)

2. He is awkward and out of place, in the society of his equals. He comes like Gulliver from among his little people, and he cannot fit the stature of his understanding to yours.

- Lamb, Charles (English Essayist, 1775-1834)

3. The average schoolmaster is and always must be essentially an ass, for how can one imagine an intelligent man engaging in so purile an avocation.

   - Manckeen, H.L. (in Prejudices)

4. He who can, does. He who cannot, teaches.

   -Shaw, George Bernard (English Writer 1856-1950)

5. Everybody who is incapable of learning has taken to teaching.

   - Wilde, Oscar (Irish Dramatist, 1854-1900)

6. He is either dead or teaching school.

   - Zemobius (Greek Sophist A.D. 117-138)

Role Model

A poor teacher tells

An average teacher explains

A good teacher demonstrates

And a great teacher inspires.

11

Measurement and Evaluation

Examinations have been in existence since times immemorial. "To close down examinations would be to give the signal for educational saturnalia", observed Sir Michael Sadler. J. C. Mathur emphasises the value of examinations when he writes, "Even in the idealised picture of society portrayed in H.G. Wells' Utopia, examinations find an important place." "Nevertheless examinations and specially external examinations have a proper place in any scheme of education," writes the Secondary Education Commission. Examinations are good servants as they help to evaluate the achievements of our students. They are a great touchstone for measuring the amount of knowledge acquired or the degree of skill achieved.

The Purposes

To Evaluate the Achievement of the Students. The abilities and the achievements of the students must be evaluated. Examinations are conducted to discover whether or not the child has been able to acquire a certain amount of knowledge or skill.

To Measure Personality. They are used to test the power of clear thinking, quickness of mind, calmness and perseverance.

To Measure the Efficiency of Teachers and of the School. They provide a suitable occasion for the authorities to measure the efficiency of the teachers. The efficiency of the institution is also measured through the examinations. They provide a proper occasion to the teachers to know whether or not their methods of teaching are appropriate.

To Help in Diagnosis. They help parents to know the progress of their children. They help to discover the specific weak points of an individual or class and thus give an opportunity to the teachers as well as to the taught to remove these defects.

To Act as Incentive. Stimulation to work hard is provided to the students through the institution of examinations. Some objectives are placed before the students and for the realisation of those objectives the students develop in them the habits of constant hard work.

To Help in Prognosis. The examinations have a prognostic value also. With this device the aptitudes of the students are determined.

To Give Uniformity of Standard. The external examinations facilitate the problem of uniformity of standards attained by the students of different institutions.

To Help in Guidance. They facilitate the work of grouping individuals for the purpose of teaching by bringing those together who have more or less the same attainment.

To Measure Fitness for Admission to Higher Courses. They are designed to determine the capacity and fitness of the candidates to pursue higher courses of general or professional study or training. Examinations which serve this purpose are called Entrance or Qualifying Examinations.

To Help in Selection by Competition. The examinations are also conducted to select the best candidates for appointment to public service or for award of prizes and scholarships.

Study of Every Subject. The students study all the subjects including what are known as 'dull ones' for fear of examinations.

Parents' Point of View. Examinations provide an opportunity to the parents to know where their wards stand and whether money spent on them is being utilized properly.

Negative Aspects

First Voice against the System. A Calcutta Principal in 1871 said that because of the examinations, "Education is cramming of a large amount of ill digested knowledge" and the students were reduced to "mere machines of memory".

The Hunter Commission and the Calcutta University Commission. These Commissions have in very unambiguous terms denounced the system and pointed out its short-comings.

Sri S.N. Mukherji, Chairman, Examination Section, All-India, Educational Conference, 1944, observed : "The conclusion is irresistible that education in India dominated by external control and tutelage in the form of fragmentary and unscientific examination has resulted in the perpetuation of mediocrity and retardation of genius, facts which are necessary concomitants, if not inevitable consequences, of the prevailing system."

The University Education Commission, presided over by Dr. Radhakrishnan wrote, "For nearly half a century, the examination has been recognised as one of the worst features of Indian Education."

The Secondary Education Commission, summarizing the glaring shortcomings of our examination very aptly and emphatically stated, "External examinations are exercising a restricting influence over the entire field of education to such an extent as almost to nullify its real purpose."

W H. Ryburn strongly criticises them when he writes, "It goes without saying that examinations are the enemies of creative work, at least as they are usually conducted."

Various Opinions

1. An enemy of true education.

2. An incubus.
3. A blood sucker.
4. A bane of educational system.
5. A necessary evil.
6. A glorification of memory.
7. A begetter of rivalry and strife.
8. A dead hand of education.
9. A growing tyranny.
10. A presumptuous attempt to gauge the depth of human ignorance.
11. An obstacle to learning.

The main defects of examinations are as under:

Examinations Lack Definite Aim. Our examinations are not geared to the realization of specific objectives. The same test serves different purposes like passing a course, admission to the next course, passport to employment, discovering individual capacities, securing scholarship etc., with the result that it becomes invalid for any purpose.

Sultan Mohiyuddin writes, "Business firms wanting employees look at the results of the examination, the high schools base their admission on it, and government accepts it as a passport to all departments of service; there are no specific, mental or moral traits, and disabilities that the ordinary examination seeks to discover and measure, and there is, therefore, no definite guidance it can offer to the professions, business houses and higher educational institutions."

Element of Chance. Element of chance plays an important role and decides the fate of large number of students. It is often found that some students prepare a few selected questions and leave everything to chance. If perchance, the same questions are set in the examination, they pass with credit. The question arises, have they actually attained the requisite standards? Perhaps not! Now take the case of another student who has been regular in his work throughout the year. He might not secure as good marks as the one mentioned above. Should we conclude that the former are more intelligent than the latter?

Lowering of Educational Standard. According to the Secondary Education Commission, the examination determines not only the content of education but also the methods of teaching, in fact, the entire approach to education. The efficiency of a teacher is judged by the pass percentages of his results. The teachers adopt the trick of the trade to improve their results. 'Idea of exam,' the sole aim and 'Cram' the only method, dominate the entire educational system. The students do not feel interested in a subject unless it is included in the examination scheme. They are more interested in notes and guides rather than in text-books with the result that they ignore habits of independent study. Stress is laid on spoon feeding and pupils are encouraged to memorise facts and vomit them out in the examination.

To quote the Secondary Education Commission, "The present system of examination does not test anything except memory and a certain kind of verbal felicity."

Thomson called them, "a presumptuous attempt to gauge the depth of human ignorance."

Valentine rightly observed, "There is a grave danger of certain studies being crammed and spoilt by the prospect of an examination ahead."

P.C. Wren quotes Sir Oliver Lodge, "External examinations which have to be prepared for specially are hampering to the teacher. They tend to keep his attention directed to some artificial and rather than to the immediate object of his work, namely the drawing out and development of the minds committed to his care."

Lowering of Moral Standard. Examinations teach the students different ways of becoming dishonest. Books are smuggled in the examination centres and attempts are made on the life of the supervisors who try to catch the students who use unfair means.

Ignore Qualities of Character. They fail to provide any measure to test the originality, initiative, truthfulness, honesty, sociability of an individual and thus they fail to test real education. Sultan Mohiyuddin writes, "Training in originality and independence of thought, correctness of judgement or reasoning, responsiveness to noble ideas and sentiments and enjoyment of beautiful things—these ceases to be the aims of teacher's effort for they are not judged by the traditional examination. Examination is the sole aim and cram the sole method.

Subjectivity. Subjective attitude of examiners influence the marks of individuals and leads to a great variability in marking. Vernon points out, "The same script might receive a different mark if read after instead of before dinner."

Dr. R.K. Singh says, "Our examinations are subjectively weighed and subjectively scored and are not, therefore, dependable indices of pupils' achievements." The Harvard University Commission in England says, "Where the panel of readers (examiners) is large, where thousands of books are being rated, where physical conditions of weather and health are not always under control, and where practically all judgments are subjective, it would be indeed strange if discrepancies in ratings are not numerous, if mistakes are not frequent and costly."

Heavy Mental Strain. Most of the students are in the habit of working strenuously just near the annual examination and this severely tells upon their health, leads to mental dyspepsia and discourages the formation of healthy mental habits.

Develop Frustration. Failures in examinations lead to frustration and even to suicides in some cases.

As a matter of fact, the examinations have met with heavy criticism from all quarters. This criticism is due to the excessive development of the examination system and a large number of students subjected to it. Candidates complain against the examination system because of its mental strain; the teachers against the examination because of its harmful influence on school work; the parents denounce it because of its injurious effect on the physical and mental health of the children; the practical psychologists speak ill of it because of its unreliability and invalidity and the educational theorists attack it because of its lack of definiteness in aim and purpose.

Corrective Measures

(1) To minimise the subjective element, new type of objective tests should be introduced along with the essay type of questions.

(2) Questions put should be thought-provoking and evenly distributed over the entire course. Difficult as well as easy questions should find a place in the question paper.

(3) Due consideration should be given to the work of the students done in the class. The teacher's recommendations should be given their due importance. He should be trusted and given a fair opportunity to know and study closely the pupils in his charge.

(4) Cumulative records should be maintained in respect of all the students.

(5) The paper-setters and examiners for external examinations should be drawn from the teachers who actually teach subjects in schools.

(6) Standard of marking should be prescribed so as to minimise the variability in marking.

(7) The system of permitting private candidates to take the examination should be discouraged.

(8) The system of compartmental examinations should be introduced at the final public examination.

(9) In place of numerical marking the system of symbolic marking be adopted. Five-point scale seems to be the best type of symbolic marking scale, i.e. 'A' stands for excellent, 'B' for good, 'C' for fair and average, 'D' for poor and 'E' for very poor.

(10) Examinations should be regarded as means and not ends. They should be conducted in such a manner that they become effective instruments of education. They

should serve as stimulus to learn new facts, gain new experiences, discover weak points and estimate progress.

(11) Oral examinations should be held in addition to the written one. Some qualities like candidate's alertness, intelligence, special interests, mental outlook, his personal qualities of mind and character and his mastery of acquired knowledge can be better tested by viva voce tests than by written examinations.

(12) An examination should have only one definite aim before it and that aim must be clearly known to the teacher and the examinee.

(13) A well-conducted examination should test both the actual attainment and capacity for future achievements. A combination of the traditional examination and carefully constructed intelligence test, therefore, supplies a more reliable means of selecting candidates for higher courses of study than the traditional examination alone.

Question Papers

This is a common form of questions and is properly known as Essay Form Questions. This type of question is used for purposes like :

(i) Selective recall of information.

(ii) Comparison and contrast.

(iii) Establishing relationships.

(iv) Interpretation and application.

(v) Creative thinking and problem solving.

The following points may be kept in view while framing right kind of essay form questions :

1. Sufficient time must be devoted by the teacher on the framing of questions. The question should be worded in such a way that content of the answer will be

according to the expectations of the teacher in the case of all students.

2. The questions should not be too general, vague and comprehensive. They should define the task for the candidate and indicate clearly the scope of the answer.
3. A large number of short and more specific questions requiring short or limited answers should find a prominent place in the paper and be preferred to a few long and general questions.
4. The time allowed for the examinations should be carefully considered in relation to the amount of writing required on the part of the students. The examination should be so timed that the students are usefully engaged for the whole duration.
5. The questions may be arranged in order of difficulty, i.e. from the easier to the more difficult.
6. Clear instructions to the students regarding the number of questions to be attempted, marks given to each question, or part thereof, and marks reserved for any special purpose, such as diagrams, neatness, etc., may be given in the beginning of the question paper.
7. As far as possible, equal marks may be alloted to each question.
8. Choice may not be provided in a question paper. However, if provided, it should be within a section, in which case one of the alternatives provided in the question has to be attempted and the pupil cannot leave out the question altogether.
9. Question paper may be reviewed before it is handed over to the person concerned. Quite a few points may strike the paper setter on this second reading. A paper setter should safeguard his reputation as a setter by taking all the care that is possible at the beginning.

Fresh Ideas

Evaluation is a Continuous Process. The Education Commission 1964-66 observed ' "It is now agreed that evaluation is a continuous process, forms and integral part of the total system of education, and is intimately related to educational objectives. It exercises a great influence on the pupil's study, habits and the teacher's methods of instruction, and thus hopes not only to measure educational achievement but also to improve it. The techniques of evaluation are means of collecting evidence, about, the student's development, in desirable directions. These techniques should, therefore, be valid, reliable, objective and practicable."

Academic and Non-academic Subjects. One of the best definitions of evaluation is given by Clara M. Brown, "Evaluation is essential in the never ending cycle of formulating goals, measuring progress towards them and determining the new goals which emerge as a result of new warnings. Evaluation involves measurement which means objective qualitative evidence. But it is broader than measurement and implies that considerations have been given to certain values, standards and that interpretation of the evidence has been made in the light of the particular situation."

Evaluation in its broader concept includes examination of academic and non-academic aspects of education. The term 'evaluation' is a newly introduced term. According to Wrightstone, "Evaluation is a relatively new technical term, introduced to design a more comprehensive concept of measurement than is implied in conventional tests and examinations—evaluation involves the identification and formulation of a comprehensive range of the major objectives of a curriculum, this definition is in terms of pupil's behaviour, and the selection or construction of valid, reliable and practical instruments for appraising and specified phases of pupil behaviour." In examination and measurement the emphasis is upon the academic subjects only whereas evaluation includes all the changes that take place in the development of a balanced personality and measures the qualities of head, hand, health and heart of an individual.

H.H. Remmers and N L. Gage point out, "It is the felt need that has caused the shift from the term 'measurement' – implying mathematically precise mensuration of knowledge to the term 'evaluation' which widens the areas to be studied to include subjective opinions and qualitative changes as well as objective and quantitative changes to include changes in attitudes, appreciations and understanding as well as acquisition of knowledge and skills."

Evaluation is a process by means of which changes in behaviour of children are studied and guided towards goals sought by a school.

Procedure for Improving the Product. Wiles defines evaluation as, "Evaluation is a process of making judgments that are to be used as a basis for planning. It consists of establishing goals, collecting evidence concerning growth or lack of growth towards goals, making judgment about the evidence, and revising procedure and goals in the light of the judgments. It is a procedure for improving the product, the process, and even the goals themselves."

Designing Learning Experiences. Chester T. McNernly observes, "The purpose of any programme of evaluation is to discover the needs of the individuals being evaluated and then to design learning experiences that will solve these needs.... Evaluation is an important and delicate process not only from the standpoint of determining the needs and growth of programmes and individuals but also from the standpoint of what it does to the individuals being evaluated. An evaluation cannot adequately be made by using a single check-list, an isolated anecdotal record, or a battery of examinations; a complete evaluation will require the use of many techniques."

Evaluation in Terms of Purposes. Thomas H. Briggs and Joseph Justman write that evaluation is "a process by which the values of an enterprise are ascertained." Further they write, "Evaluation should be conceived primarily in terms of educational purposes which the programme of supervision is intended to serve."

(i) If the purpose is to stimulate teachers to improve their techniques of classroom instruction, evaluation must concern itself with ascertaining the extent which such improvement is being affected.

(ii) If the purpose is to enrich and vitalize the course of study, evaluation must seek to determine whether the pupils are really deriving greater educational value from the "enriched" and vitalized programme than they did formerly.

(iii) If the purpose is to re-establish faculty 'esprit de corps' and school morale, the objectives of evaluation will be to assess in various ways the degree of improvement in personal and professional attitudes in human relations, and ultimately, therefore, ill efficiency of teaching and learning.

(iv) If all important purpose of the supervisory programme is to promote greater educational attention to individual needs of pupils, evaluation will necessarily concern itself with estimating the success with which guidance procedures, differentiated programme of study, courses and units of learning experience,, individualised teaching and learning procedures, and other educational measures designed to achieve greater satisfaction of individual needs are operating.

Shane and McSwam conceive evaluation, "as a process of inquiry, based upon criteria cooperatively prepared and concerned with the study, interpretation, and guidance of socially desirable changes in the developmental behaviour of children. It is a process within the child as a result of which he responds to the psychological interpretations, he makes of his school-community environment."

Correlation between the Educational System and the System of Evaluation. Evaluation cannot be done in a vacuum. It is always with reference to the objectives of a particular system of education. Evaluation has, to be very comprehensive in a system of education which aims at the many-sided development of the personality of a child.. "The school of today concerns itself not only with the intellectual pursuits but also with the emotional and social development of the child, his physical and mental health, his social adjustment and their equally important aspects of his life in a word, with an all-round development of his personality," writes the Secondary Education Commission. In the light of these objectives of the system of education, a comprehensive programme of evaluation would include:

1. Evaluation of the academic subjects.
2. Evaluation of the skills.
3. Evaluation of the physical development.
4. Evaluation of the moral development.
5. Evaluation of the social development.

The Objectives

1. Evaluation, appraises the status of and changes in pupil's behaviour.
2. Evaluation discloses pupil's needs and possibilities.
3. Evaluation aids pupil-teacher planning.
4. Evaluation expands the concept of worthwhile goals beyond pure achievement.
5. Evaluation serves as a means of improving school-community relation.
6. Evaluation familiarizes the teacher with the nature of pupil learning, development and progress.
7. Evaluation relates measurement to the goals of the instructional programme.
8. Evaluation facilitates the selection and improvement.
9. Evaluation appraises the teacher's competence.
10. Evaluation appraises the supervisor's competence.
11. Evaluation serves as a method of self-improvement.

12. Evaluation serves as a guiding principle for the selection of supervisory techniques.

New Techniques

Fairly exhaustive methods have been designed by educationists to evaluate the various aspects of child's growth. Following are the commonly used techniques :

1. Intelligence Tests.
2. Achievement Tests.
3. Aptitude Tests.
4. Personality Tests.
5. Tests of Attitude and Behaviour.
6. Rating Scales.
7. Questionnaires and Check Lists.
8. Interview.
9. Anecdotal Records.
10. Autobiographical Method.
11. Pupil's Diary.
12. Case History.
13. Sociometric Techniques.
14. Projective Techniques.

Evaluation. 1. Evaluation must be comprehensive in scope. It is concerned with all aspects of the growth of the child.

2. Evaluation must be comprehensive in method. It employs different procedures and seeks many kinds of evidences.
3. Evaluation keeps in view the objectives of the instructional programme.
4. Evaluation is cooperative. Teachers, administrators, pupils and parents should be involved at different levels of participation in the formulation of definitions of goals and values and in the collection and interpretation of evidence.

5. The testing programme should become an integral part of the curricula and should not be treated as separate department.
6. Greater reliance and insistence are necessary on teacher made

The Suggestions

Evaluation at the Lower Primary Stage. The Education Commission 1964-66 stated, "One of the main purposes of evaluation at the primary stage is to help the pupils to improve their achievement in the basic skills and to develop the right habits and attitudes with reference to the objectives of primary education. These objectives and their implication for evaluation should be made clear to the teachers."

The lower primary stage covering Classes I to IV should be treated as an ungraded unit, because this would help the children coming from different backgrounds to advance at their pace. As the conditions in most primary schools, however, are not favourable to the general adoption of this procedure, it has recommended that the experiment should be tried out in the beginning in Classes I and II, which should be regarded as a single ungraded unit. The two year block may be divided into two groups, one for slow learners and the other for fast learners to enable different pupils to proceed at the level of their ability and move from one unit to another. Such a division, however, will be practicable only in a large sized school with more than one section in each class.

Advantages Claimed. This will put an end in the existing practice of detentions in Class I and to the drop-outs and wastage resulting therefrom, and will also provide for continuity and flexibility in the educational programme of the first two classes. If the experiment regarding the upgraded unit succeeds in Classes I and II, it may be extended to the remaining classes of the lower primary stage.

Preparation of the Teachers. Teachers should be prepared for the upgraded system through the regular training courses and orientation programmes and should be helped with a supply of diagnostic tests and remedial material. The orientation may be given by the State Institutes of Education. Observation techniques, which are more reliable for assessing the pupil's growth at this stage than more formal techniques of evaluation, should be used by teachers in a planned and systematic manner.

Evaluation at the Higher Primary Stage. Due importance should be given here also to oral tests, which should form a part of the internal assessment.

The teacher should be helped in such assessment with a rich supply of evaluation materials prepared by the State Evaluation Organizations, including standardised achievement tests.

Diagnostic testing is necessary here and indeed throughout the school stage. In most cases, such testing will be through simple teacher-made diagnostic tests.

Cumulative record cards play a vital role in indicating the growth and development of the pupil at each stage, his academic and emotional problems, and his difficulties of adjustment, if any, and the directions in which remedial action is to be taken to solve his problems or difficulties. In the first instance, the cards should be introduced from Class IV onwards in about 10 per cent of the selected schools as an experimental measure; but once the majority of teachers are trained in evaluating certain important aspects of the child's personality and the proper maintenance of the records, the use of the cards may be gradually extended to all the higher primary and, as a next step, even to lower primary schools.

Primary External Examination. An external examination was necessary for (1) maintaining certain uniform standards at the end of the stage; (2) providing a basis for choice of courses at the secondary stage; and (3) creating incentives for better teaching and learning. But all these arguments do not establish a case for an external examination of the formal type to be compulsorily taken by all the pupils in Class VII or VIII.

The Commission has advanced two arguments against external examinations :

(1) It is not necessary or desirable to prescribe a rigidly uniform level of attainment for all the primary school pupils in a State or even a district, through an external examination.

(2) Instead of creating incentives for better teaching, the external examination intended for all will saddle teachers with standardized programmes and encourage the process for rote memorization, which is the besetting evil of teaching and learning methods in our schools today.

(3) Again, since full-time education at the lower secondary stage will provide, by and large, general education without any streaming, the argument regarding the choice of courses does not hold good; and for the diversion of pupils to full-time vocational courses to be made available at this stage, an examination which will test merely intellectual ability and academic attainment will not be of much help.

Level of Achievement. While not in favour of a compulsory external examination, the Commission believes that for the proper maintenance of standards, periodic surveys of the level of achievement of primary schools is necessary. The Commission recommends that such surveys should be conducted by the district educational authorities to assess the standard of performance of the schools in a given area by means of standardized or highly refined tests prepared by specialists in the State Evaluation Organisations.

Advantages Claimed. (1) This procedure will enable the education officers to pick out the weaker schools and help them to improve their performance.

(2) It will also assist the schools in finding out the weakness of their pupils for purposes of remedial work.

Common Internal Examination. The Commission recommends that by making use of the standardised or refined test material referred to above, the district educational authorities may, if they so desire, arrange for a common examination to be taken by the pupils of all the schools in a district at the end of the primary stage. Though the question paper will be set by the district educational authorities or by special paper-setters appointed by the State Evaluation Organization, the assessment of the pupils of each participating school will be done by the teachers of the school themselves, and not by any external examiners.

Advantages of Such a Common Examination. (1) As the question papers will contain standardized tests and highly refined and professional tests items, the evaluation will be more valid and reliable than what is possible through the kind of annual and final examinations conducted in the ordinary primary school.

(2) Through such a common test inter-school comparability with regard to levels of performance in the district can be obtained, and this would be helpful, as shown above, both to the education officers and to the schools.

Question Papers of Short Duration. Question papers in the different subjects at this common examination should be of short duration, each of not more than one hour or one hour and a half, so that the entire examination should be completed in two or three days.

This proposal aims at reforming the existing examination by making it less formal, reducing its burden on the pupils' minds, and increasing its validity as a measure of educational attainment. The certificate regarding the completion of the course should be given by the school and not by any external agency, and this certificate should be accompanied by a statement showing the results of the common final examination, if any, together with the results of the internal assessment made by the school of the pupils' performance throughout the year, as shown in his cumulative records.

Examinations for Scholarship. In addition to the common examination, the Commission recommends that special tests may be held at the end of the primary course for the award of scholarships or certificates of merit and for the purpose of identifying talent and pupils may appear for these tests on a voluntary basis. The evaluation of the pupil's performance in these tests will be done by external examiners.

Improvement in External Examinations. (a) The technical competence of paper-setters should be raised through an intensive training programme sponsored by the State Boards; (b) the question paper setters should be oriented to testing not merely the acquisition of knowledge but the ability to apply knowledge and the development of problem-solving abilities; and (c) the nature of the questions asked should be improved. (d) It is essential that scientific scoring procedures should be devised so that there may be optimum reliability in the assessment of the candidate's performance. (e) With the ever-increasing number of students appearing for the Board examinations, the task of getting the answer scripts properly valued and processing the results efficiently within a given time is becoming more and more difficult. It is necessary that this process should be mechanized so as to make it more accurate and expeditious.

Large Incidence of Failure. The Commission observes, "the matter about which the public at large is most deeply concerned is not the irrationality of the scoring procedures, or the inefficiency of the administrative processes, but the large incidence of failures in the external examination at the end of the school stage. An analysis of the results of the different Board examinations for the last five years show that about 55 per cent of the candidates appearing for the high school examination and about 40 per cent of those appearing for the higher secondary school examination fail regularly every year. In the case of the private candidates the percentage soars up to 70% or even more. Failure often has a demoralizing effect on the unsuccessful candidates. The failure of such large numbers of students, particularly after they have been screened year after year by means of annual and other school examinations, is a sad reflection on our methods of education as well as on our system of examination."

"We also believe that with the proposed improvement in the Curriculum, instructional materials and methods of teaching, and the reorientation in the training of teachers, the incidence of examination failures will be reduced. But we do not think that a student should be branded as a total failure, if he passes in certain subjects but is unable to make the grade in others. There is no reason why he should carry with him the stigma of being declared as unsuccessful candidate if he has partially succeeded in his educational effort."

Certificates Given by the Board. The Commission recommends that the certificate issued by the Board on the basis of the results of the external examination at the end of the lower or higher secondary stage, should give the candidate's performance only in those subjects in which he has passed but there should be no remark to the effect that he has passed or failed in the whole examination. The Board, however, should issue a statement along with the certificate showing his marks or grades in all the subjects.

Permission to Reappear. The candidate should be permitted to appear again if he so desires, for the entire examination or for separate subjects in order to improve his performance.

Certificate from the School. On the completion of the course, at the end of the lower or higher secondary stage, the student should receive a certificate also from the school giving the record of his internal assessment as contained in his cumulative record card. This certificate may be attached to that given by the Board in connection with the external examination.

No Compulsory External Examination. External examination need not be compulsory for all the students of Class X or Class XI/XII. A student may choose to leave the school with the school certificate only without appearing for the external examination, and seek a job or even an entry into some vocational Course on the basis of the certificate and the school records. It must be recognized, however, that since admission to institutions of higher secondary education as well as of higher education will be selective, the authorities controlling such institutions will lay down their own rules of eligibility for admission. A student seeking entry into these institutions may have not only to pass the external examination in the subjects laid down and secure the prescribed grades but also submit himself, if necessary, to certain admission tests required by the institution.

Freedom to Selected Schools to Assess Students. In order to lessen the importance of the domination which the external examinations excercise over school education still further, the Commission recommends that a few selected schools should be given the right of assessing their students themselves and holding their own final examination at the end of Class X, which will be regarded as equivalent to the external examination of the State Board of School Education. The State Board will issue certificates to the successful candidates of these schools on the recommendation of the schools. A committee set up by the State Board of School Education should develop carefully worked out criteria for the selection of such schools. For the success of this experiment it is essential that the schools should not only be freed from the requirements of an external examination but should be permitted to frame their own curricular, prescribe their own text-books, and conduct their educational activities without departmental restrictions.

This suggestion is indeed a bold one in the direction of freedom of educational experimentation and it carries certain responsibilities also. The Commission, therefore, suggests that right given to the experimental schools should be reviewed periodically as institutions invested with such powers should continuously earn their privilege, The Commission envisages that after the, experiment, is, tried out successfully in a few schools, more and more schools will be released from the restrictive influence of the external examination and given the freedom to work out their own ideas in education.

Methods of Internal Assessment. This, internal assessment or evaluation conducted by individual schools is of great significance and should be given increasing importance. It should be comprehensive, evaluating all those aspects of the student's growth that are measured by the external examination and also those personality traits, interests and attitudes which cannot be assessed by it. Internal assessment should be built into a total educational programme of the school and should be used for improvement rather than for certifying the level of achievement of the student. It must be pointed out that all items of internal assessment need not follow quantified scoring procedures. Some of them may be assessed in descriptive terms and results should be kept separately and not combined artificially with other results to form aggregate scores."

The written examinations conducted in schools should be improved on the same lines as the external examination.

Methods Suggested by the Commission. (1) The results of the internal assessment and external examination should not be combined because the purposes and techniques of the two evaluations are different and because the results of the internal assessment of the different institutions are not strictly comparable. The results of the external and internal assessment should, therefore, be shown separately in the certificate(s) given at the end of the course.

(2) It should be an important point in the inspections of schools to review the internal assessment made and to examine the correlation between the internal and external assessments. Persistence in over-assessment should be regarded as a weakness in the school programmes. It should be taken due note of while classifying the schools and should also be related to grants-in-aid so that institutions which tend to over-assess their students persistently would stand to lose in status and finance. The grants-in-aid rules should also authorize the Education Departments to withdraw recognition for persistent irresponsible assessment.

Creation of a Well-organized Machinery. In the end, the Commission states, "The comprehensive programme of evaluation that we have described in the preceding paragraphs requires for its implementation a well-organized machinery both at the State and the Central levels. The Secondary Boards of School Education that now conduct external examination at the secondary stage will be converted into State Boards of School Education with enhanced powers and functions. At the Centre will be the National Board of School Education that will be responsible for evaluation programme at the national level."

Home Examination

Why Internal Assessment? The internal philosophy is interested more in what students get out of education and not just in their passing certain type of examination. Education as a whole is not only concerned with the acquisition of knowledge but also aims at developing in the pupils the desired interests, appreciation, habits, attitudes and personal qualities. Written examinations fail to assess these qualities and the teacher's observation and other informal techniques may be called for which can be used only internally.

Internal assessment mitigates another defect of the external examination. In place of basing results on the assessment at any one time, internal assessment can be as continuous as desired.

Internal assessment enables us to diagnose pupil's difficults in learning. It points out the potentialities of an individual and provides opportunities to find out the needs, goals and interests and aptitudes of an individual and shows him the way for their development. This has a motivating effect and this in turn induces him to utilise his resourcefulness which is otherwise cramped.

Since internal assessment is continuous, it builds regular study habit among students.

Internal assessment by entrusting the teacher with responsibility provides motivation to him.

By assessing both the tangible and intangible attainments of students it supplements external examinations.

The Problems. The Report of the Training Course on Evaluation mentions the following problems for the implementation of Internal Assessment programmes :

(i) How to get acceptance of the programme of internal assessment by teachers, students, public and administration etc.?

(ii) How to develop competence among the teachers to undertake internal assessment effectively?

(iii) How much of minimum facilities need to be provided in the schools for carrying out an effective programme of internal assessment?

(iv) How to coordinate standard of different schools?

(v) What sorts of machinery is required to be developed so as to keep up and progressively improve the standard of internal assessment?

(vi) How to relate the external and internal marks?

Problem I : How to Get Acceptance of the Programme of Internal Assessment?

(a) The analysis of the examination paper, answer books and examination marks to be made and the data to be placed before the people concerned to realise a need for the development of a more adequate measure of pupil's growth.

(b) Experiments to be made in some selected schools to prove the superiority of the system of assessment which is advocated to be introduced.

(c) Developing a sound technique of internal assessment with the help of teachers and taking their full cooperation in the implementation of the scheme leading to their confidence in it.

Problem II : Competence of Teachers.

(a) In the teacher's training courses, the concept of Internal Assessment in Evaluation, its problems and techniques should be included as an integral part of the training college programme.

(b) For teachers already in schools, special refresher courses or training camps may be held by way of in-service education.

(c) Periodic conferences of teachers and the principals at least twice a year (in the beginning of each term) may be held so that the objectives of internal assessment are classified.

(d) A conference of teachers of different schools in the same region may also be held to evaluate and develop the system and form of maintaining records.

Problem III : Problem of Minimum Facilities.

(a) The curriculum should be detailed out adequately in the light of objectives of education.

(b) The curriculum should provide ample freedom to the teacher for planning his work in relation to his own environment.

(c) Any rigorous conformity to particular method of work as is generally advocated by the inspecting staff and other authorities should be avoided to be prescribed in order to allow teachers to develop their own initiative.

(d) Teacher-pupil ratio to be brought to a reasonable size of I to 30 at the maximum.

(e) Provision to be made to the standard of the class for organising class-libraries accordingly

(f) Study and research in these aspects will help in developing maximum criteria for certifying accrediting necessary in course of time.

Problem IV : The Problem of Coordinating of Standards among Different Schools and School Subjects in Internal Assessment

1. Advisory bodies of experts in different areas of knowledge may be appointed. These may issue suggestions to different institutions from time to time and also in the form of articles or books for the guidance of the teachers. A complete change in teacher's attitude will be necessary. It shall have to be brought home to them that these experts are not official supervisors but only advisers to whom they may refer their problems in time of need.
2. A common core-curriculum may be provided for all schools. It shall be sufficiently flexible leaving enough scope for the teacher's ingenuity and skill.

3. Extensive facilities for the training of teachers in the new techniques of evaluation shall have to be made available and government grants to the institutions may be regulated by the qualifications of staff and other educational facilities available in the situation.
4. Assessors to check the teacher's estimates may be appointed and their identity may be kept confidential. They may compare assessments from different schools and also check them against other criteria which they may decide upon.
5. Teacher's estimates may be scaled against the results of external examination and coordination established, if possible.

Problem V : What Sort of a Machinery is to be Developed so as to Keep up and Progressively Improve the Standard of Internal Assessment?

The State Evaluation Unit will be one good agency for the purpose but it may work in cooperation with other agencies such as Curriculum Committee, Guidance Bureau, the Inspection Department, Central Evaluation Unit and the Research Bureau for the purpose.

Inspection of school by a team of subject experts may also prove helpful in this respect.

Problem VI : How to Relate the Internal Assessment to the External Examination Marks?

(a) Internal assessment should be in relation to the various aspects of pupil's growth such as his scholastic achievements, his interests, attitudes and personality traits, etc.

(b) There should be some minimum standard of pass prescribed for both internal and external examinations in academic subjects and the result should be announced on the basis of pupil's record of achievement in both and mentioned separately.

(c) To make the result comparable it may be desirable to bring both internal assessment and external examination total marks at par so far as academic subjects are concerned.

(d) It should, however, be noted that internal assessment may be in symbols and grades or in qualitative description for assessing pupil's achievement in some fields, and therefore, external and internal results may not always be comparable.

(e) Certificates showing the achievement of students both at the external examination and internal assessment will provide better scope to the employer for making the choice.

(f) This type of certificate will provide the opportunity to carry on some studies to find out whether the internal or external result is more valid and reliable in respect of a particular school.

(g) This will also help in developing criteria for classifying and accrediting schools.

Internal Assessment as a Challenge. Internal assessment presupposes responsible teachers. It takes for granted that they will realise the sanctity of the trust reposed in them. They must discharge their responsibilities with impartiality and equity. They should rise above their prejudices and petty values. The success of the scheme depends upon their sincerity, honesty and integrity. They should have the moral courage to face the challenge of favouritism and nepotism. They should work honestly and should not cook figures. They should not create such impression that those students get high marks in the internal assessment who dance on the fingers of their teachers according to their wishes.

Internal assessment should not be used as a tool of maintaining discipline in the institution. Discipline should not be secured by threatening the students to spoil their career or ruin their markings in case they question the authority of the teachers or the Principal. other crime can be more serious than this on their part. Internal

No

assessment is likely to result in non-uniformity of standards of marking in different institutions. To mitigate this evil a general procedure of assessment and of different techniques must be laid down.

The entire staff should be associated with the different aspects of assessment of a single child. This would help in eliminating to a greater extent the subjectivity and misuse of power.

Sympathetic hearing must be given to the genuine grievances and complaints of the students. The students must be convinced of the awards. Of course, the success of this system of internal assessment depends on teachers themselves. They must justify the confidence reposed in them.

Role of the Headmaster. According to the Group Report of the Short Term Training Course for the State Administrators of Basic Education, "The Headmaster plays an important role in the assessment work of the school. The Headmaster should not only carefully observe the various records maintained by the children and the teachers but also devise his own records so that he may have a glimpse of the progress of work done in the school."

Objective Tests in New Form

Modern educators lay much stress on this type of test to supplement the traditional type of tests. These tests are of a large variety. However, only seven or eight types tests are usually used.

Significant Features

1. The number of questions in the essay or old type of tests is very small, generally five or six questions in the paper.

   There are a large number of questions in the new type tests.

2. Answers required in the old type of tests are large.

   The answers are so short in the objective tests as can be written in a word or two or at the most in a sentence.

3. Essay type questions are usually broad, general and indefinite. The examinees are at a loss to know how much they will have to write as answers.

   Objective questions are specific, narrow and definite.

4. In essay-type tests personal factors like bias, temperament, whims, etc. of the examiner influence marking.

   Scoring becomes objective in the new type of tests.

5. In the answer of the essay test there is scope for partial credit. Answers may be partially wrong and right.

   In the new tests, there is no provision for partial credit. Answers must either be right or wrong and hence full or no credit.

6. In the essay tests examinees have to devote a long time.

   Questions can be answered in a short time in the new tests.

7. In the essay tests, questions are selected at random and the entire course is not covered. Some chapters or questions are completely ignored.

   The entire course can be covered by comprehensive questions in new tests.

8. Essay tests put premium on expression. Students hardly find any time to think over the question.

   New tests put premium on thinking.

9. Pupils having linguistic skill are at an advantage in the essay tests.

   New tests are advantageous to the intellectually smart students.

10. It takes a short time to frame questions in the essay tests.

    It takes a long time to frame questions in the new tests.

11. Students find it easier to prepare essay questions. They can safely omit many portions of the subject-matter in the essay tests.

Students have to devote a longer time to prepare as they have to go through the entire course for clear conceptions.

12. Essay tests are very suitable for testing composition, skills and knowledge of the subject.

    New tests are not suitable for testing composition and skill to well as appreciation of the subject.

13. In the essay tests there is great scope for 'guessing' questions. Students prepare themselves from 'Made Easy' books.

    In the new type there is scope for guessing answers.

14. Essay tests take a longer time in examining scripts.

    Short answers take less time to examine scripts.

15. Printing cost is small in the case of essay tests.

    Since there are many questions, printing is costly in the new tests.

16. Answer scripts cost much as answers are very lengthy in the case of essay tests.

    Answers being very short and usually can be written on the question paper itself, this makes the answer scripts less costly.

17. There is less scope for adopting unfair means by the students in the examination hall.

    There is enough scope for adopting unfair means in the new tests.

Matching Test. Under column A, names of certain books and under column B, names of certain authors are given. Write down the names of right authors under column C.

A	B	C
Bhagvad Gita	Lord Krishna	–
Indica	Kalidasa	–
Buddha Charitam	Kalhan	–
Raghu Vansham	Megasthenes	–
Raj Tarangini	Ashvaghosha	–

Advantages. It makes practicable the use of a large number of responses and therefore tends to reduce the guessing element.

Disadvantages. It is not well adapted to testing for the acquisition of knowledge or understanding of and ability to use relatively complete interpretative ideas.

Rules. 1. The position of the correct answer must be chosen at random.

2. Do not include a large number of items in either of the columns to be matched 12 is the maximum.
3. In general, it is a good idea to include more responses than statements in order to avoid the selection of the last response on an elimination basis.
4. Do not mix statements or responses highly dissimilar in character.
5. This should not be used for testing small units of subject-matter.

Multiple Choice Test. Against every statement certain alternatives are given. Put tick mark against the correct one.

(a) Kalidasa was a Statesman/Dramatist/Warrior.

(b) Hieun Tsang was a Buddhist/Hindu/Muslim.

(c) Edicts were built by Kanishka/Prithvi Raj/Ashoka.

(d) During whose reign Megasthenes visited India? Chandragupta II/Harsha/Chandragupta Maurya.

True-False Test. Certain statements are given below. Against each statement are mentioned two words, i.e. True and False. Underline the correct ones.

In such a type of test a student chooses one of the two responses. This generally consists of a set of statements, approximately half of which are true.

(a) Buddha was born before Christ. True/False.

(b) The Aryans built beautiful temples. True/False.

(c) The Vedas are the religious books of the Hindus. True/False.

(d) Kanishka was a great writer. True/False.

Advantages. 1. It is easy to construct.

2. It is capable of sampling very quickly a wide range of knowledge.

3. It is well adapted to the situation in which it is impossible or extremely difficult to find enough plausible alternative response to make a multiple choice item, or in which there are only two possible answers.

Disadvantages. 1. The guessing element is more important than in any other type of test item.

2. In order to reach a reasonable standard of reliability, it needs to be much longer than other kind of objective test.

3. It can seldom be made diagnostic.

Rules. 1. Statements should be simply worded otherwise they are liable to be false.

2. The order in which the statements must appear, should be entirely at random.

3. Students should be warned of the guessing effect.

Simple Recall Test. In which states are the following situated

Ellora	—
Nalanda	—
Thaneshwar	—
Ujjain	—
Mohen-jo-Daro	—

In a simple recall test, answer is not suggested but is recalled.

Advantages. 1. It is similar to ordinary questions.

2. It is natural in its approach.

3. It is free from guessing effect.

4. It is easy to build.

5. In it recall is demanded instead of mere recognition.
6. It is well adapted to testing for acquisition of descriptive information.

Disadvantages. 1. Its scope is limited to rote knowledge or skill at simple arithmetical and scientific problems.

2. It does not measure thinking or organised ability.
3. Objectivity may often be much less than in other types of so-called 'objective' test items.
4. Grading is not quick as it is for other types of objective questions. It may call for expert judgement as answers may be different from the scoring key.

Rules. 1. Try to ask questions freely on important items of knowledge.

2. As far as possible, there should be only one right answer.
3. Keep the questions and sentences as short as possible.
4. Use direct question form as far as possible.
5. Arrange for the answers to be written in, the right-hand margin. This will facilitate scoring.

Best Answer Type. Put cross against the correct answer.

(a) Buddha went into jungles because
   (i) he was turned out by his father
   (ii) he wanted to find out the truth
   (iii) he wanted to become a Rishi

(b) Alexander did not proceed further because
   (i) he did not know the route
   (ii) his forces refused to go further
   (iii) he was defeated by some king

Completion Test. Fill in the blanks by appropriate word(s) in the following:

(a) Tibet was the original home of the Aryans according to

(b) The fourth Buddhist Council was held at ....

(c) Early invaders in India came from ....

(d) Patliputra was situated on the banks of the river ....

Principles of Construction of New Type of Tests. 1. Prepare a list of all the topics falling within the scope of the examination.

2. Keep in view the most significant items in each topic.
3. Every item should have only one correct answer.
4. Easy questions should come first and then moderate and in the end the most difficult ones.
5. Include different types of objective tests, i.e. Recognition, Recall, etc.
6. Frame definite and brief questions.
7. Give reasonable time to the students to answer the paper. Suggests the following time :

Recall Type - 4 to 8 items per minute.

True-False type - 10 to 15 items per minute.

8. Give clear instructions.

Advantages. 1. Subjective factor of marking is completely eliminated.

2. Handwriting and speed of writing, etc. do not in any way interfere with the testing of the knowledge of the students.
3. Chance element is eliminated to a considerable extent as there are many questions covering the entire field of the subject-matter.
4. Scoring becomes very easy. Less time is required for the assessment of such papers.
5. They discourage cramming.
6. Objective tests can be standardised on the basis of the results of the standardised test. The authorities of a particular school can measure the standard of their institution by comparing with other schools of the area.

Limitations. 1. They do not provide any opportunity to judge the power of expression of an individual.

2. They encourage guess work. The students have to choose simply one of the given alternatives.
3. They fail to provide any opportunity to the teachers to find out where the students make mistakes.
4. They fail to test the power of reasoning of the students.
5. Like the essay type of tests, these also fail to test the character-building aspects.

Reforming Steps

Examinations in India have been proverbially described as the bane of our educational system. Successive Commissions and Committees have stressed the need for examination reform and suggested specific measures towards this end. The University Education Commission (1948) observed, "We are convinced that if we are to suggest any single reform in university education, it would be that of examinations". The Secondary Education Commission felt, "Examinations today dictate the curriculum instead of following it, prevent any experimentation, hamper the proper treatment of subjects and sound methods of teaching, foster a dull uniformity rather than originality, encourage the average pupil to concentrate too rigidly upon too narrow a field and thus help him to develop wrong values in education."

However, very little was done in India until 1958 when the erstwhile All India Council for Secondary Education set up the Central Examination Unit to organize programmes of examination reform at the secondary stage. The Central Examination Unit developed a comprehensive programme of examination reform to meet the educational, social and psychological points of view. The main dimensions of this reform are as under:

1. Improvement of Written Examination.
2. Improvement of Practical Examination.

3. Introduction and Improvement of Oral Examination.
4. Introduction and Improvement of Internal Assessment.

This programme of examination reform has been developed through conferences, meetings, seminars and workshops conducted all over the country. The main agencies that collaborated in the development of this programme are :

1. State Boards of Secondary Education.
2. State Departments of Education.
3. State Evaluation Units.
4. State Institutes of Education.
5. Teacher's Training Colleges.
6. Extension Services Departments.

The work of examination reform in the States by and large consists of the following type of work:

(i) Training of paper setters in different subjects.
(ii) Training of examiners.
(iii) Training of resource personnel.
(iv) Conducting studies related to school evaluation.
(v) Conducting studies relating to external examination.
(vi) Publishing literature on various aspects related to evaluation.
(vii) Preparing test items in different subjects, unit tests in different subjects and question papers and diagnostic tests.

The Central Examination Unit of the NCERT was abolished in 1970 on the recommendations of the Review Committee.

12

Record of Marks

Card for Record

A cumulative record card is that card which contains the results of different assessments and judgments held from time to time during the course of study of a student. A cumulative record is an account of the child's history in the school. It begins a soon as the child enters the school and continues till he leaves the school for good. Generally it covers three consecutive years. It contains information regarding all aspects of the life of the child—his physical, mental, social, moral and psychological. It seeks to give as comprehensive a picture as possible of the personality of a child. "Periodically the significant information gathered on students through the use of various techniques—tests, inventories, questionnaires, observations, interviews, case studies, case conferences and the like - should be assembled in summary form on a cumulative record," writes Jane Warters.

In the words of W.C. Allen, "The Cumulative Record is defined as a record of information concerned with appraisal of the individual pupil - usually kept on a card - kept in one place."

Need for School Record. The modern type of cumulative record was first made available in 1928 by the American Council of Education. The need of such a record was felt in view of the inadequate information that was contained in the various forms that were available. The Secondary Education Commission has made the following observation regarding the need for school records : "Neither the external examination, singly or together, can give a correct and complete picture of a pupil's all-round progress at any particular stage of his education; yet it is important for us to assess this in order to determine his future course of study or his future vocation. For this purpose a proper system of school records should be maintained for every pupil indicating the work done by him in the school from day to day, month to month, term to term and year to year. Such a school record will present a clear and continuous statement of the attainments of the child in different intellectual pursuits throughout the successive stages of his education. It will also contain a progressive evaluation of development in other directions of less importance, such as the growth of his interests, aptitudes, and personality traits, his social adjustments, the practical and social activities in which he takes part. In other words, it will give a complete career."

The Merits

1. A good record contributes to guidance work in general in the following ways: (a) By providing a sound basis for understanding the individual, (b) By showing the significant experiences of individual, (c) By indicating his readiness for new experiences, (d) By pointing out the routes to new goals, (e) By pointing out his strengths and weaknesses.
2. It helps curriculum revision by revealing the needs of the students.
3. It helps in the improvement of the methods of teaching by revealing the needs of the students.
4. It provides a helpful basis for educational and vocational placement.

5. It is an aid in the search for talent. It assists the teacher to find out students who are gifted in abstract verbal ability, science, the arts and social relations.
6. It helps the teacher to find out the slow learners and accordingly he suggests measures.
7. It serves as a link between the teacher and the parents. The teachers find it convenient to write letters or descriptive reports to the parents on the basis of the information contained in the record.
8. The school authorities can make suitable recommendations to the prospective employers and college admission officers.
9. The cumulative records help in furnishing sufficient data for reports to the various authorities engaged in the student welfare field.
10. At the time of the transfer of a student from one school to another it helps the new school authorities to know about the child and to avoid mistake and to facilitate the adjustment of the child to the new environment.

Writing about cumulative record Jane Warters rightly says, "It aids teachers in the study of the individual by making it possible for them to understand his present through an analysis of his past, by furnishing clues regarding the cause of his behaviour difficulties and failures, and by disclosing his strengths and weaknesses."

The Indian Education Commission discusses the importance of this card as "cumulative record cards play a vital role in indicating growth and development of the pupil at each stage, his academic and emotional problems and his difficulties of adjustment if any, and the directions in which remedial action is to be taken to solve his problems and difficulties."

Maintenance of the Record. The maintenance of the cumulative record card should begin when the student enters in school and should follow the student from class to class within a school and from school to school as he continues his progress.

The class teacher will maintain the cumulative record. In view of the fact that he spends much time with the students he will be in a better position to judge the child from different aspects. He will maintain a diary or note-book in which he will note down from time to time his observations about his students. At the end of the year he will make the necessary entries in the cumulative record card. It is very desirable that he consults his colleagues who also know the pupils. These entries should be made after careful consideration. All teachers should share in the work of collecting and reporting information on students.

Methods of Popularising this System. The use of the cumulative record in our educational institutions is still in its infancy. It cannot be imposed upon the teachers. The teachers must be familiarized with the advantages of this system. Talks and refresher courses should be organised for this purpose. Faculty meetings should be organised to discuss the nature of the information that these cards should contain. It must be remembered that the maintenance of cumulative records is a cooperative affair in which administrators, counsellors, teachers, clerical staff, students and their parents must participate and all of these must be convinced of the importance of such records. Teachers and counsellors must be provided with time to make necessary entries. The records should be placed at a place where all may use them easily.

Forms of Cumulative Record Card. It is used in various forms such as card sheet, printed folders, cards or sheets contained in an envelope, booklet or some combination of these forms.

Contents of the Cumulative Record. The card usually contains the following sections

1. Personal Data.
2. Home Circumstances.
3. Health Information.
4. Psychological Report.
5. Scholastic Achievement.
6. Performance in Co-curricular Activities.
7. Educational and Vocational Plans.

8. Personality Characteristics.

9. General Overall Remarks.

Cumulative Record Card

Name of the Pupil ....

Name of the Father ....

Occupation of Parent/Guardian ....

Address of Parent/Guardian ....

Date of Birth ....

Schools Attended

Name of School	Month and year of enrolment	Class in which enrolled	Month and year of leaving	Reasons for leaving

Home Circumstances

1. Economic status of the family ....
2. Child's position in the family (whether only child, eldest or youngest child) ....
3. Type of family (whether joint or unitary) ....
   ....
4. Education of the Parent/Guardian ....
5. Special circumstances of ....

Attendance

Year	Possible	Actual	Nature of Long absence, if any

Scholastic Achievement

(Average percentage of marks or corresponding letter grades based on the results of periodical and annual tests

Group	Subject Marks/Grade	Class .... 20 .... Marks/Grade	Class .... 20 .... Marks/Grade	Class .... 20 ....
Language and Literature				
General Science and Science				
Social Studies and Social Sciences				
Any other Group				
Craft/Work Experience				

Physical Data

Year	Height	Weight	Any serious illness or physical disability

Report of the Medical Officer

20...
20...
20...

Psychological Report (if any)

20...
20...
20...

Performance in Co-curricular Activities (Average Grade of the Child)

Activities	Class 20	Class 20	Class .... 20........
1. Sports and Athletics			
2. Personal Hygiene			
3. Literary (debating etc.)			
4. Dramatics			
5. Community service (sanitation drive, literacy, campaigns etc.)			
6. Any other activity			

Notable Proficiency and skill in different fields or special merit obtained or position of responsibility held, if any

Years and Class	In Scholastic Achievement	In Bal Sabha	In Scouts Troop	In Sports	In Social Service	Any other
20 .... Class						
20 .... Class						
20 .... Class						

Personality Characteristics

Nature	20	20	20 ......
1. Honesty			
2. Punctuality			
3. Courtesy			
4. Habits of work			
5. Cooperativeness			
6. Sociability			
7. Self-confidence			
8. Emotional Stability			
9. Leadership			
10. Initiative			

General Remarks

Year	Signature of the Class Teacher	Signature or Stamp of the Head
20		
20		
20		

Significant Features

Validity. The facts recorded must be authentic. It is better not to write any information than to give untrue information.

Comprehensiveness. A cumulative record should contain information as complete and comprehensive as possible.

Accuracy. The information in the card should be accurately recorded from the original source. If instead of 105 one writes 150 as score of an individual in English let us say, one can imagine the difference in the educational guidance of that student.

Objectivity. Personal opinion and judgements should be reduced to the minimum.

Economy of Space. The criterion of a good cumulative record form is that the maximum possible information is contained in the space available.

Recency. Any piece of information should be recorded as soon as it is obtained.

Outcome of a Cooperative Enterprise. It should be the result of group thinking.

Evaluation. It should be evaluated every year so as to know how far it serves the purpose.

The Difficulties

Problems may be classified under the following heads

(1) Who should maintain the records?

(2) Where to keep them?

(3) When to fill up these cards?

(4) How to check the maintenance?

(5) What should be the design of these records?

(6) How to tackle the problem of new admissions and migrations?

(7) How to help the teachers in discharging this function?

Who Should Maintain the Records?

Functions of the Class Teacher. The records may be kept by the class teacher and he should be responsible for getting the necessary entries made. Class teacher's responsibility is greater as he will not only ensure correct and up-to-date entries but also act as a liaison between the pupil and the subject teacher, and between the pupil and the parent.

Function of Special Teachers and Teacher Incharge of Various Activities. This function is to assess the child's attainment from time to time to record the same and to pass it to the class teacher.

Where to Keep Them? This is a very formidable problem. Arrangement will have to be made 'So that it is easily accessible to the teachers. If possible it may be kept by the class teacher in his safe custody otherwise it may be kept in the Principal's Office. However, in either case, its contents should remain confidential.

When to Till up These Records? Entries in the card should be made at the time of a particular event or test. It is advisable that every teacher should have a small note book to record his observations at the time of the incident about a particular pupil. He may record the significant entries according to his convenience. As a rule, other teachers may not record the entries on the card itself. They would pass on the entries to the class teacher. This would enable the class teacher lo maintain the records neatly and scientifically. Too many hands may spoil the beauty and the neatness of the card.

How to Check the Maintenance? The Principal should check after every three months that the entries are regularly made and the records are kept up-to-date. He may assign this work to one of his colleagues but must sign the record card himself.

What Should be the Design of Record Cards? Usually three types of cards are being maintained in schools.

(a) Folder type, (b) File type, (c) Envelope type.

The Problem of New Admissions and Migrations. The record should move with the student in case he is transferred from one school to another. It should go with the pupil from class to class and from school to school.

How to Help the Teacher in Discharging the Function?

(i) Teachers should be trained in the maintenance of these records.

(ii) The state authorities should get the model forms of records prepared for the schools.

(iii) This work should be done by the teachers on the last working day of the month. There may not be any teaching work on that day. If we do not give adequate time to the teachers to fill up these cards, they will fill up these mechanically.

(iv) Adequate provision should be made for the safe custody of these cards.

(v) The supervisor should inspect the maintenance of these records at the time of the annual inspection of the school.

13

Process of Planning

Realizing the need for institutional planning the Education Commission 1964- 66 observed:

"No comprehensive programme of educational development can ever be put across unless it involves every educational institution and tall the human factors connected with it—its teachers, students and the local community - and unless it provides the necessary inducements to make them put in their best efforts."

What is an Institutional Plan? Mr. M.B. Buch describes it as a programme of development and improvement prepared by an educational institution on the basis of its felt needs and the resources available or likely to be available with a view to improve the school programme and school practices. The plan may be for a longer duration or a shorter duration. It is based on the principle of optimum utilisation of the resources available in the school and community.

Significant Features

1. The plan is prepared on the needs of the school as identified by the school staff.

2. It is based on the principle of optimum utilisation of resources available within the school and the community.
3. It is a cooperative venture of the community, management, school staff and the students.
4. It is goal-oriented.
5. It is specific for an institution. There cannot be a single plan for all the institutions.
6. It results into establishment of democratic procedures within the school.
7. An important outcome of institutional planning is the establishment of a better rapport with the community.
8. It aims at school improvement as well as school development.
9. It forms the basis of the District Plan for educational development and improvement.
10. It is continuously developing. An institutional plan cannot be rigid not admitting changes.
11. It results into improvement—motivation on the part of teachers, students, community and the managements.

Main Stress on Motivating the Human Agencies. The Education Commission felt:

"In our opinion therefore the emphasis in this movement should be not so much on physical resources as on motivating the human agencies concerned to make their best efforts in a coordinated manner for the improvement of education and thereby offset the shortcomings in the physical resources."

Programmes Based on Human Effort and not Physical Effort. The Commission suggested the following programmes:

1. Reduction in stagnation and wastage.
2. Improvement of teaching methods.
3. Assistance to retarded students.
4. Special assistance to gifted students.

5. Trying out new techniques of work.
6. Improved methods of organizing programme of the school.
7. Increasing the professional competence of teachers through programmes of self-study.

Positive Aspects

Institutional planning is required to make the educational planning into the country more realistic. It reverses the normal trend followed today where the direction of the planning is from top to bottom. Institutional planning will give the right direction to the educational planning in the country, i.e. the upward direction from bottom to top.

Institutional planning is a recognition of the role of practitioners of education in the process of planning education in the country.

Institutional planning introduces a scientific approach to the improvement and development of education within a country.

The Importance

Mr. J T Naik explains the significance of institutional planning as : "It is hardly worthwhile to discuss whether this idea is old or new. The more important question is whether it is relevant to our present situation. My humble submission is that it is. In this process of magnifying the scope of educational planning we have unfortunately lost sight of the individual institution and of its uniqueness, which necessitates planning at that level. It is to correct this mistake that we propose to develop this programme of institutional planning in which we want to pay adequate attention to the macrocosm, the individual institution, without forgetting the wider horizon, the macrocosm of State and national planning."

Spirit of Institutional Planning. Dr. Shib K. Mitra outlines the spirit of institutional plan as: "I think the whole notion of institutional planning is based on this idea that at every stage right from the school to this topmost level in the field of education constant effort has to be made in order that we do not have new ideas for the sake of new ideas but in order that we can do a better job with whatever resources we have at our command."

Institutional Planning as a Basic Link in the Planning Process. Dr. B.D. Nag Chaudhari explains it as, "I would like to reiterate that planning for each institution provides an important and basic link in the planning process. To derive the benefits of such detailed planning at the micro-operational level, it has to be linked appropriately with the planning at the District, State and Central levels. We can then formulate an integrated National Educational Policy which will be responsive to the changes of the situation and incorporate within it the seeds of gradual improvement. While the planning at the State and national levels deals with the formulation of national goals, priorities and weaning out disparities, the implementation of programmes, the evolution of new programmes, experimentation on new techniques, discovery of talents and guidance are major task at the institutional level. Since the implementation of the plans and programmes is as important and vital as plan formulation, institutional planning has a special contribution to make in national development. Planning for each school and college has an advantage that it brings to the plan formulation process a realism, an appreciation of the felt needs of the community and an awareness of the difficulties and problems at the operational level."

How to Prepare a School Plan ? The major steps in preparing a plan of improvement and development for a school are :

(i) Undertaking a survey of the needs of the school.

(ii) Undertaking a survey of the resources available in the school as well as community.

(iii) Preparing plans of improvement programmes, and

(iv) Evaluating improvement programmes.

Institutional Improvement Plans at the District Level. The District Educational Officer will receive the institutional plans from the different schools within his jurisdiction. This will give him a detailed picture of the improvement projects undertaken by the schools in the district. This will also give him an idea of the in-service training needs of the teachers in his district. A useful analysis and consolidation of the various institutional plans at the district level will tell the D. E.O. the following:

1. Type of improvement projects going on in the school.
2. The way he will try to bring about coordination between similar projects going on in different schools.
3. The overall in-service education needs of the teachers in his district and how he will obtain the services of the nearby Extension Services Department for organising the courses in different subjects for the teachers of his district.
4. The financial requirements over the period of next 5 years if the minimum essential developments are to be financed.

The D.E.O. will keep institutional plans with him while going out for usual inspection. He will be in a position to study the progress of various improvement projects and also he will be in a position to disseminate the successful programmes of different schools to all the schools in the District.

A seminar on Institutional Planning was organised jointly by the National Council of Educational Research and Training and the Ministry of Education, Government of India in November, 1968. The seminar held at the Regional College of Education, Bhopal, provided an opportunity to the participants, among whom were Inspecting Officers, staff members of Training Colleges and heads of Secondary Schools deputed by some State Governments to discuss the concept and methodology of institutional planning with several experts in the field.

School Principals and Institutional Planning. Improvement means change. It is necessary for a principal to know that the school does not consist of furniture and equipment only. The Principal should realize that the school has a social system and to bring about a change in a social system has its own complexities. As a social system the school has various aspects like goals, established procedures, different subject groups, relationship among the various subject groups and its own norms. An attempt to change one aspect of the school life will influence and disturb the overall school equilibrium.

The first job of the Principal should be to look at the whole school system, assess the strengths and weaknesses of his staff members and carefully create the ground work for various changes. He will have to proceed in a planned manner.

Various Steps

Individual and Group Conferences. The first step might be a series of individual conferences with the staff followed by group conference. After this there might be a staff meeting in which the Principal and outside experts may explain the whole purpose and the needs for preparing an institutional plan. The Principal shall take a close look as to how the suggestions in the staff meetings are received by the teachers. In other words, he will evaluate the result of the first staff meeting.

Discussions with Teachers and Experts. The second step will be a discussion about undertaking a survey of the needs of improvement and development of the school. This will be a longer process as most teachers find it difficult to identify the real problems. Experts from outside, senior teachers and the Principal himself will have to work with individual teachers and subject teachers groups to have the survey of the real needs felt by the school staff for improvement in various areas. It will be necessary for the Principal to list the areas requiring improvement in a proper sequence from the view point of available resources and the nature of difficulties involved in implementing the programmes. The Principal will always encourage teachers to take up such programmes as can be completed by the teachers without much difficulty. It is the success in the initial programmes that will inspire confidence for undertaking major improvement programmes.

Survey of Resources. The third step will be a survey of the resources available in the school and the community. Here again greater stress will be laid on knowing, what already exists in the school.

Preparation of Improvement Programmes. The fourth step will be preparation of improvement programmes. Here adequate reading material, reference materials, expert guidance shall have to be provided to teachers planning improvement programmes. Each improvement programme will take the form of a project and guidelines of preparing projects will be supplied to the teachers by the Principal.

Evaluation of the Programme. The fifth step will be the evaluation of the programmes after they have been implemented and completed. In fact the Principal will carry on periodical evaluation of the various programmes and staff consultative surveys of the teachers to modify the procedures if need is felt for it.

The Scope

Academic Programmes : Here improvement of instructional programmes and enrichment of curriculum should be included to improve the school results both in the home examinations as well as in external examination by reducing wastage and stagnation, improving the attendance ratio, improving ways of home assignment etc.

Co-curricular Area : Here a programme of school beautification, creating an environment which can stimulate learning by pupils, physical education programmes, co-curricular programmes etc. should be included.

In-service Programmes and Professional Growth of Teachers : This is an important area for planning. A plan for the professional growth of individual teacher should be prepared. Programmes for the in-service education of teachers and group programmes for the in-service education of the entire school faculty should be prepared in a planned way. Stress should be laid on the in-service needs of the individual teachers.

School Services : There is an urgent need to prepare a planned programme for the improvement and utilisation of library service, laboratory service and guidance services, etc. Other services which directly concern the students welfare like the mid-day meal, drinking water, sanitation and hygiene should also be planned for improvement.

Maximum Utilisation of School Resources : This is an area which is the most important for any programme of institutional planning. There are schools which have surplus teachers without adequate work. There are schools which have teachers not fitting into the curriculum offerings. There are schools which have shortage of teachers. The institutional planning should aim at maximum utilization of all available teacher resources. The planning should also aim at utilizing the unutilized teaching aids, the building facilities, the playgrounds, etc. A good institutional plan should study this area of human and physical resources and their maximum utilization for the improvement of the school.

Educational Leadership

Planning Stage

1. The first step for the District Educational Officer is to create an awareness amongst the Heads of Institutions for institutional planning and its importance by calling a meeting of the heads of schools at the district level.
2. The heads of institutions will be asked to prepare improvement and development plans on the basis of felt needs and availability of resources in consultation with the teachers, students and the local community and fix priorities. Every school will, however, be required to put up a minimum action plan.
3. The plan will be phased according to the extent, need and resources, which should be normally for one academic session, which may be the duration of the plan.
4. The District Educational Officer will have the advisory role to play with regard to the institutional plans and he will be helped by an academic cell which may be created in his office. This cell will consist of subject experts, specialists in guiding research workers, who will be associated with the plan at all stages. The cell will provide expert advice from time to time according to the needs of the school.

5. The autonomy of the schools in institutional planning, implementation and to a certain extent in evaluation is a must at all stages, it being their own plan.
6. The District Educational Officer will extend help and guidance to the schools promptly when the schools ask for it.
7. The District Educational Officer will ensure recognition of good work at different levels. The Directorate will also encourage good workers.

Practical Aspects

1. D.E.O. will arrange publicity of the state and national plans as far as they relate to and affect the schools and the teachers.
2. He will use his influence and good offices in tapping local resources, different agencies and enlisting community help for the implementation of the plans.
3. He will provide resource personnel from the district, extension services and from outside.
4. He would arrange for in-service training of teachers in areas of institutional planning.
5. He will encourage inter-school visits for exchange of ideas and provide T.A. and D.A. facilities.
6. He being a very important link between the schools and the department, will secure financial aid for the schools wherever needed to encourage good work and if the requirements of the plan so demand.
7. He will help in getting the pupils' fund rules liberalised to facilitate utilisation of funds by the head of the institution with the help of the school committee set up for the purpose.
8. Due publicity will be arranged for good plans and significant individual work, through school and district bulletins, departmental journals, conferences and seminars.

Self-evaluation. The school community will make appraisal of the entire plan programme chalked out, targets achieved, difficulties experienced. This will be done frequently and modifications made to make it more practicable and useful.

Supervision and Inspection. The D.E.O. and the panel inspection team comprising of experienced headmasters (including retired personnel) will evaluate the programme at least once a year or more if possible.

The evaluation will be done by the team in terms of the extent of contribution of creative ideas in planning, resourcefulness shown in implementation - the depth of their qualities as well as the number of people involved in making their contribution. This should be helpful in judging as to how far the plan has been successful. A scrutiny will be made by examining the process and the produce.

Conclusion. The success of institutional planning, implementation and proper evaluation will depend on the dynamic leadership, initiative and personality of the D.E.O. He will be instrumental in encouraging good work by securing special development grants for the schools on the basis of the performance.

Aims and Objectives

Shri J.P. Naik observes, "to give a motto to institutional planning which is different from what we use at present. Our usual motto is: not failure but low aim is crime. This is a good idea. But we use this idea in a wrong way. We choose a high aim and when we fail, we justify it philosophically as inherent in the high aim itself. This is a bad policy in all matters and especially in institutional planning. For institutional plan, therefore, our motto should be : 'Not high aim but failure is crime. I do not mind how small a plan a teacher prepares'. Let somebody say 'I want to improve the handwriting of my children'. I will be quite happy; what we decide to do is immaterial. But once you decide to do something, I will not accept any excuse for a failure. This is what we have to insist upon : doing things with dignity, with pride in oneself and with success. If we can follow this up, the institutional plan can be put successfully on the ground."

14

Management of Time

"Well arranged time is the surest mark of a well arranged mind."

Spark Plug of the School. Dr. Jaswant Singh writes about the importance of time-table thus : "The schedule is the spark plug of the school which sets into motion its various activities and programmes."

Time Table as a Mirror. It is a mirror that reflects the entire educational programme followed in the school.

Definition of Time-Table. In the words of H.G. Stead, "It is the time-table that supplies the framework within which the work of the school proceeds. It is the instrument through which the purpose of the school is to function." The school time-table is a chart which indicates all the activities undertaken in a school. It shows the hours of work in the school, kind of work or subjects, the teachers at work and at rest, the rooms being used in a certain period, recreational time, time of roll call, time of morning assembly, time of drill, games and other co-curricular activities and time of interval.

The Time-Table

Eliminates Wastage of Time and Energy. Undoubtedly all planned programmes eliminate wastage of time and energy and it is equally true in the case of a school time-table. The work is more or less equitably distributed among the members of the staff. It directs the teacher's energy and attention to one thing at a time by placing proper persons at their proper places at the proper time and in the proper manner.

Ensures Due Attention to Every Subject or Activity. In framing the time-table, due attention is given to every subject. Periods are allotted to different subjects according to their importance and their fatiguing nature.

Develops Moral Values. It helps to develop qualities like punctuality and regularity both in the teachers and the taught by placing before them a set programme of activities.

Brings System in the School Life. It provides work for the students and keeps them busy. It brings system in the school life and thereby helps in maintaining discipline. In the absence of any time-table there is bound to be chaos and confusion in the school.

Ensures Regular and Even Progress. Regular and even progress is ensured because time-table prevents laxity and shortages.

Psychological Value. It has got a psychological value leading to the removal of fatigue which may occur due to prolonged hours of teaching and learning.

It Ensures Equitable Distribution of Time to Different Subjects and Activities. Time-Table helps in avoiding the allotment of too much or too less work to one teacher.

Develops Good Habits. It helps in developing regular habits of work.

Advance Planning by the Teachers and Students. Time-Table helps in chalking out plans in a systematic manner.

Form of a Time-Table. The form of a time-table depends upon the nature of activities carried on in a school. The more the number and variety of activities, the more types of time-tables. In an ordinary school four forms of time-table, i.e. consolidated time-table of the school, class time-table, teachers' vacant period time-table and teachers' time-table will serve the purpose. Time-table for Co-curricular activities is coming into vogue in view of their importance in the field of education; similarly in schools where games are properly organised, the need for games' time-table can hardly be stressed. The progressive schools maintain special room time-table. Time-table for home-work is also maintained by some schools.

Ideally speaking there should be seven types of time-table :

1. Master time-table indicating the entire programme of the School.
2. Class time-table.
3. Teachers time-table.
4. Vacant period time-table.
5. Games time-table.
6. Co-curricular activities time-table.
7. Home work time-table.

One copy of the class time-table should be kept in the classroom concerned. A copy of the teachers' time-table should be put in the staff-room. One copy of each time-table should be kept in the Headmaster's office so that he may know at a glance what work a particular class or teacher is doing at a given time, and which of the teachers is having leisure, so that he may be sent for by the Headmaster for consultation or for any other work, if necessary.

General Considerations Underlying Time-Table Construction. The construction of time-table makes large demands on the ingenuity and skill of the Headmaster. Framing of a time-table is time-absorbing task. Some of the chief factors which determine the construction of a time-table are :

Types of School. Whether school is a boys' school or girls' school, urban or rural, infant school or school for girls, public or ordinary, will determine the nature of activities of the school and accordingly time-table will be framed. The double shift will call for shortening the duration of the school hours. Similarly, co-educational schools will necessitate numerous changes so as to meet the specific needs of both the boys and the girls. In the higher grades of schools the duration of the periods will be longer than in the lower grades of schools.

Amount of Time Available. The amount of time to be given to each subject or activity is determined by the total amount of time available at school. Generally speaking, the higher the grade of the school, the longer the school day. There are certain departmental regulations concerning school timings which have got to be obeyed.

Suggestions for Improvement

(1) The working hours per day should vary from four hours at the pre-primary stage to about six hours at the higher secondary stage.

(2) The total period does not include the time for co-curricular activities.

(3) The period includes the time for library period or the guided studies.

(4) At the lower primary stage the hours of instruction should be about 900 and at the higher primary and secondary stages they should be not less than 1,000 and preferably raised to 1,100 or even 1,200 if conditions are favourable.

Relative Importance and Difficulty of Subjects. There are certain social and economic considerations that determine the importance of a subject in the school curriculum and accordingly time is allotted to each subject in the school time-table. Subjects like English and Mathematics which are considered to be important and difficult are allotted more time. In a rural school, more time is given to gardening and nature study.

Incidence of Fatigue. The element of fatigue influences the construction of the school time-table in a number of ways. Subjects requiring more brain-work are placed on the time-table when the brains of the students are quite fresh and when they are capable of doing hard and difficult work. Each part of the morning is better than the corresponding part of the afternoon. In other words, the middle of the morning is better than the middle of the afternoon although the middle of the afternoon is better than the end of the morning and the end of the morning is better than the end of the afternoon. It is a common feeling to think that mental freshness is the greatest in the morning. The fact is that it gradually increases until it reaches its maximum about the middle of the morning. That is the case after recess. Mental freshness is greater not just after recess but in the second period after recess. The best periods for fatiguing subjects are, therefore, the second and third periods in the morning and second period after recess. The order of subjects causing fatigue is as follows : Mathematics, English, Indian Languages, Science, Nature Study, Science practicals, Drawing, Crafts, Music, etc. The second and the third periods in the morning and the second in the afternoon are considered to be the best periods for the fatiguing subjects. English and Mathematics should, therefore, be placed as far as possible in these periods. The worst period is the last period in the afternoon and it may be used for manual work, science practical, physical exercises, etc.

The 'fatigue principle' is true of the days of the week also, Tuesday and Wednesday are considered to be the best days in which maximum work could be done. The end of the week is like the end of the day and fatigue is the greatest.

The younger are quickly fatigued, and therefore, the duration of the period in the lower classes should not exceed thirty minutes and in the higher classes it should not exceed forty minutes. In the summer season, the duration of the period should be reduced.

Various Principles

Principle of Justice. Work among the members of the staff should be equitably distributed. Unequal distribution of work causes frustration among them and hampers progress. Similarly, time should be allotted for different activities according to their importance in the school curriculum.

Principle of Variety. It should always be remembered that to keep the children sitting the whole day long is in no way a wise procedure. As often as possible and convenient, the classes should change place and posture. It has been stated 'Change of room, of seat, of posture is an antidote against weariness." Change of occupation is one of the best forms of rest. This applies to both students and teachers. The children should not be kept at the same subject or type of subjects or at subjects which are more fatiguing for too long a stretch. Variety can be introduced in the following manner :

(a) No subject except in case of science practicals should be kept for two consecutive periods as it is likely to cause monotony in the class.

(b) Variation in the subjects should be aimed at in order to avoid boredom, e.g. English History should not be followed by Indian History.

(c) The same class should not, as far as possible, sit in the same room for the whole day.

(d) The same-teacher should not have consecutive periods in the same class, as far as possible, except in the primary classes.

(e) If a subject is taught only two or three times a week, the periods should follow at intervals.

(f) The drill period, science practicals and craft work, all provide for a change of the nature just referred to above.

Free Periods for Teachers. Free periods for the teachers should be provided so as to increase their efficiency and also for correction work. These free periods of the teachers should be scattered all over the week as far as possible. The language teachers should be given more free periods as they have to do a lot of correction work. In the period immediately preceding the science and other practical period, the teachers concerned should be kept free to enable them to make the necessary preparation for the work to be undertaken in the coming period. On an average, the teachers should be allowed two vacant periods daily.

Principle of Play and Recreation. Careful attention is to be given to provide for rest and recreation. The children should not be deprived of play. It affords them a good opportunity for enjoying fresh air outside and mixing freely with each other besides giving them time to have something and replenishing their energy. The recess period provides for rest and recreation and it should not be less than half an hour.

Provision for Radio Broadcasts should also exist wherever possible. This also serves the purpose of breaking the monotony and provides rest. Provision for various co-curricular activities should also be made in the time-table.

School Building and Equipment. The number of students in a school, the number of teachers for various subjects, the number of rooms, laboratory (arrangement and furniture etc.), also affect the framing of the school time-table. The time-table of a single teacher school will be quite different from that of other schools having many teachers. Sometimes, due to paucity of rooms, two classes are held in the same room. Time-table should in such cases be arranged in such a manner that when one class is busy at writing work, the other should be doing reading work and the like.

Principle of Elasticity. The time-table should not be kept rigid but flexible and fluid. In view of the various difficulties that are likely to crop up, a fluid time-table is always desirable. Sometimes specific needs of many children have got to be met and it becomes inevitable to make some variations. The transfer of teachers also necessitates to bring about variation in the time-table. It is not necessary that the time-table should show the time allowed for the sub-branches of a subject. If we allot 12 periods to English, it should be left to the teacher to decide how many periods he shall give to grammar, translation and composition and how many to text.

We should always remember that the time-table is a tool and not the master and as such it should never be allowed to dictate procedures and methods.

Modern Protests against Time-Tables. Modern Psychologists and educationists think of the curriculum in terms of activities instead of subjects. They advocate the abolition of the time-table and want to liberate the child from its limitations. They think that a useful activity is the centre round which the study of all subjects should come spontaneously.

According to modern psychology, each individual is unique in certain respects. Each child has his own tastes, his own preferences and his own rate and speed of working. When he is left to himself, he continues what he starts. He leaves it only when he loses interest or feels fatigued. If he is interested in his work, he is alert and active. This interest gives him psychological satisfaction. But when work is regulated by a rigid time-table, a child might have to stop at the time when he has begun to take interest in a subject due to the ringing of the bell or the other way that is to feel fatigued with the subject before the period is over. But because the period is meant for that fixed subject he has to continue even though he is disgusted. It is for this reason that some educational reformers would like to abolish time-table altogether. If a child is left to himself, he would give more time to those subjects in which he is interested and give up those in which he is not interested to come back at a more favourable time.

The modern educationists do not prescribe any collective time-table as they think that education must cater to the individual needs of the students. The very fact that no two individuals are alike necessitates that to meet the specific needs of many children, different methods will have to be devised and accordingly a new conception of time-table will serve the required purpose.

Usually the modern protest is due to the following defects in the rigid time-table :

1. The co-curricular programme hardly finds any mention in the time-table.
2. By dividing the school day into uniform chunks of 35 to 45 minutes, allocating certain hours per week to the study of individual, subjects, the time-table places students and teachers in a kind of 'lock-up'.
3. A rigid time-table militates against the integration of various experiences.
4. A rigid time-table is a great hindrance in the total growth of the pupil's learning experiences.
5. In the conventional time-table there is hardly any coordination of the efforts of teachers.
6. The conventional time-table does not provide time for teacher pupil conferences.

The present emphasis is on methods like the Dalton Plan, the Project Method and the like which are a great departure from the time-honour'd time-table. 'Contracts' is the important feature of the Dalton Plan. Class as a unit of organisation remains but as a unit of instruction vanishes. Child promises to do the given work in specific period which is usually a fortnight and works according to his intellectual attainments. This is because no collective time-tables are formed in such methods of education. During this time, the child is free to work in whatever subjects he wishes, when he wishes and as long as he wishes. The only condition is that he must complete all the work in his various subjects before another contract can be undertaken. In this way, each child can progress through the school at his own rate.

Many programmes have been evolved in progressive schools and the common features are :

Firstly, the instructional material is organised into larger meaningful units built round the needs and interests of the students.

Secondly, there is provision for some long periods for practical activities.

Thirdly, there are certain "unassigned" periods in which the students may indulge in any hobby.

Finally, there is no rigidity and the teachers are at liberty to alter the daily programme according to the special circumstances connected with the needs and interests of the students.

15

Checks and Balances

It is generally recognised that principals and teachers without continuous expert guidance face numerous problems in every programme of educational expansion. Our country is passing through a crucial stage in educational development. We have set ambitious targets, both qualitative and quantitative in education. No educational plan, however, excellent, can be effectively implemented, if the school inspectorate with the tradition practices and lack of 'know how' stands between the educational plans and the schools for which the plans are meant.

Prof. A.C. Deve Gowda feels, "There is general feeling in the country that the present inspection and supervision of the secondary schools need improvement. It is also realised that this improvement in inspection and supervision may also be helpful in raising the standard of education at the secondary level."

'Education in Eighteen Years of Freedom' reads as, "Before 1947, inspection was a device to ensure that an institution receiving grant-in-aid from the Government utilised money correctly. Another function of the inspector was to extend recognition to privately managed schools on the basis of certain criteria. The concept of inspection has now changed, and inspection tends to promote the professional growth of teaching personnel. The role of inspector is that of a senior colleague to teachers. The re-designation of 'inspector' as 'education officer' in many States marks this shift in the emphasis of duties."

Prof. S.N. Mukherji thinks, "It is also generally admitted that if the system of public education in India is to improve, the department of education should be strong. It needs an adequate staff, both in number and quality. The members of the State Department of Education ...... can assume leadership of the educational enterprise."

A.S. Barr and others express their views as : "Supervision as expert service on the consultancy basis is an accepted principle in all difficult and complex human undertakings in any line of endeavour."

Supervision in the sense of leadership will contribute to unity (not uniformity) of purpose and coordination of effort.

The present tendency among educationists seems to 'expel' the word 'Inspector' from the educational vocabulary in favour of 'Supervisor', or 'Education Officer'.

The Secondary Education Commission observed, "In our view the true role of an inspector - for whom we would prefer the term Educational Adviser - is to study the problems of each school, to take a comprehensive view of all its functions and to help the teachers to carry out his advice and recommendations."

A UNESCO publication entitled School Inspection describes the position as, "The officials or civil servants composing this staff are usually known as "Inspectors" less frequently as "Councillors" (German Federal Republic, U.S.A.), "Superintendents" (Australia, Canada, Philippines etc.) or "Superintendents" (Cuba, Dominican Republic etc.) and "Supervisors" or "Supervisors" (Canada, Panama, Philippines, United States, etc.).... In some instances different designations are used in one and the same country."

William T. Melchoir states in Institutional Supervisor, "Supervision" means, essentially, "Superior vision". The author is not inclined to abandon these words, for no others connote quite so well the challenge of instructional leadership."

Prof. L. Mukherjee thinks, "Perhaps much can be gained, if the very term 'Inspector' which seems to have a bad connotation being associated with Police Inspectors be changed into 'School Advisers' or 'School Visitors'. But more effective remedy would be to separate the administrative functions of the inspectorate from inspection work and entrust the same to two different agencies."

What matters is not what is, what people are called, but what functions they perform and more especially in what spirit they perform them. It is firmly held that supervision stands for a complex of attitudes and activities all directed towards the improvement of what goes in schools, and that in their varied degrees all who work in and for schools have supervisory responsibilities. Whether there should be special categories of people called 'Supervisors' or advisers or officers, or organisers, or consultants or resource persons or counsellors or by other current catch phrase, or whether inspectors should be left to enjoy their traditional title, matters little.

Two things do matter everywhere : that the people should do the jobs whatever they are, and in the right way; and that these jobs should be clearly understood.

Aims and Objectives

Different views have been put forward by various educationists regarding the aims and purposes of supervision and inspection. These may be summed up as follows :

1. To provide professional leadership to educational institutions so as to improve their work and put them on right direction and path.
2. To set suitable goals for the educational institutions.
3. To appraise the work of the educational institutions and to give suitable criticism of work being carried on.

4. To offer technical service to teachers in the form of instructional aids, specific suggestions for the improvement of instruction and assistance in pupils diagnosis and measurement.
5. To develop in teachers a growing recognition of the factors that affect learning.
6. To help teachers to define and use the purposes of education as dynamic force in their work with pupils.
7. To promote the professional growth of all teachers by providing them in-service training.

The motto of the Inspectors should not be 'check your teachers, frighten your teachers, weaken your teachers and examine them' but its variant, 'train your teachers, inspire your teachers and trust them', writes an educationist.

Supervision or Instructional Work. The Supervisor or the Inspector supervises the effectiveness of the methods of teaching used in a particular institution, the audio-visual aids employed to make teaching interesting and effective, the time-table enforced to carry out the instructional work, distribution of work among the members of the staff, distribution of the prescribed curriculum in suitable terms in the school year, written work done by the students and experiments conducted etc. In fact he is concerned with the entire planning of the institutional work. He inspects the teachers' diaries also.

Supervision of Co-curricular Activities. As the present education is not concerned with the mere teaching of three 'R's, the supervisors also supervise the work carried on in the co-curricular field. They are concerned with scouting, games and sports, clubs, school government, school magazine, library service, hobbies, school museum, school exhibition and the like.

Supervision of School Environment. The supervisors are concerned with the discipline of the students, their personal habits, their general behaviour, etc. They look up into the cleanliness of students, cleanliness of the school surroundings, beautification of the school, hygienic conditions of the school canteen, proper drinking water arrangements, cleanliness of urinals and latrines. They evaluate the steps taken by the school authorities for the welfare and the safety of the students.

Supervision of School Registers. The inspecting staff examines all sorts of school records and registers. They scrutinise all accounts and boys' funds. They see whether or not proper use of school funds is being made. They examine the school apparatus and equipment also.

Supervision of Development Aspects. The supervisors try to assess whether the school is justifying its existence or not. They examine the various steps taken by the school to serve the locality in which it is situated. They report about the school's participation in the social, cultural and recreational programmes of the community.

Supervision of Pupil's Growth. The supervisors are also concerned with the many sided development of the children.

Supervisory Procedures. A capable supervisor will not limit his supervisory procedures to the traditional classroom visits and the teachers' meeting. He will render assistance to teachers through such procedures as the following :

Guidance. The supervisor or the inspector is expected to help the individual teacher or group of teachers to plan and carry forward out-of-class projects which have a direct bearing on the improvement of learning conditions. These projects are :

(i) Planning, testing programmes and constructing tests.

(ii) Analysing test results and planning remedial procedures.

(iii) Collecting supplementary materials.

(iv) Undertaking special projects in the use of audio-visual aids.

(v) Planning and initiating instructional devices suiting individual students.

(vi) Conducting workshops for the study of special problems.

(vii) Utilising community resources for enriching classroom teaching.

School and Classroom Visits : The procedures and techniques of visits are :

(i) Observation of the work of teachers with a view to discovering opportunities for improvement.

(ii) Rating the teacher with some special device for diagnostic purposes.

(iii) Taking up demonstration lessons.

(iv) Making suggestions to teachers regarding new devices and methods, supplementary aids, economy of time, pupil control, adapting methods to pupil differences, and so on.

Teachers' Meeting and Conferences. This point may be illustrated under two headings :

Holding Conferences with the Individual Teacher. Such conferences will be held as a result of the classroom visits and observations and will involve consideration of teacher's weak and strong points and opportunities for improvement.

Holding Teachers' Meeting for Consideration of Major Instructional Problems. Points of common interests, some difficulties and certain policies are discussed and suggestions made to improve school work.

Management. The inspectors send circulars and directions to improve school work.

New Conceptions

Today supervision is greatly affected by the increasing insight into the aims of education, the relation of education to the society in which it exists, by the scientific method, and by the democratic philosophy. Supervision is becoming participatory and cooperative, that is democratic; is increasingly oriented toward the fundamental aims of education and of society.

Beginning slowly in the twenties, developing rapidly in the thirties and forties, was the concept of cooperative supervision and democratic leadership, the supervisor being regarded as an individual who served to assist the staff, as consultant and friend, rather than as inspector and critic. Democratic supervision demands respect for personality. It makes ample provision for self-direction on the part of teachers, and participation to a great extent and in-service growth.

Different Aspects

Corrective Type. This is also known as 'fault-finding' expedition. In this case the Inspector visits a school to pick holes here and there and is always in the look out of bringing out inconsistencies and gaps to the notice of the head of the institution. Such an inspection does not serve any useful purpose. It simply makes the teachers unhappy. An Inspector must remember that progress depends upon a judicious combination of encouragement to good work and removal of defects.

Preventive Type. This type of supervision helps the teachers to anticipate new situations and to find ways and means to remove them. It is obvious that this type of inspection is helpful to teachers.

Creative Supervision. According to Fred C. Ayer : "Creative supervision should encourage the discovery of all kinds of better ways of learning, teaching and community improvement not merely those which relate to self-expression and problem solving."

Barr, Burton and Bruecker think : "Creative leadership in the long run is vitally necessary to the success of democratic life."

Creativeness has been linked closely with such words as self-expression, inventiveness, initiative, originality, experimentation and improvement.

Supervision seeks for latent talents. It provides opportunity for the exercise of originality and for the development of unique contributions.

William T. Melchior stresses the following points as being characteristic of creative supervision :

(a) Creative supervision encourages teachers to feel free to think for themselves in matters pertaining to objectives, curriculum, organisation and content, methods of teaching and methods of evaluation ;

(b) It encourages teachers to share voluntarily with the supervisor and co-workers that which they think;

(c) It never stifles the inclination of a teacher to experiment with his own ideas, though the dangers of experimentation are kept in mind; and

(d) It does more than encourage, it inspires teachers to be themselves and to do for themselves, it imbues them with self-confidence and the power of self-evaluation.

Democratic Supervision. Democratic supervision eliminates the feeling that the supervisor is a superior being and the teacher an inferior worker. Democratic supervision tends to be a cooperative endeavour for the common good. Democratic supervision recognises the dignity and worth of the individual.

Democratic supervision encourages freedom while furnishing direction, advice and suggestion.

Inspirational Supervision. It inspires teachers, lifts them above themselves, reinvigorates their flogging spirits. True inspirational supervision must strive to broaden the base of leadership by utilizing the full potential of teachers. It will nurture qualities like initiative, originality, creativity, sincerity and honesty. It will discourage rigidity and sameness in teaching. It will meet the needs of teachers sufficiently to serve as the foundation for a good programme of supervision.

Inspirational supervision allows the freedom so necessary for real growth.

Autocratic Supervisor	*Democratic Supervisor*
1. Thinks he can see all angles of a problem.	Realises the potential power in thirty or fifty brains.
2. Does not know how to use the experience of others.	Knows how to utilise that power.
3. Cannot bear to let any of the string of management slip from his fingers.	Knows how to delegate duties.
4. Is so tied to routine details that he seldom tackles his larger job.	Frees himself from routine details in order to turn his energy to creative leadership.
5. Is jealous of ideas, reacts in one of several ways when someone else makes a proposal. (a) Assumes that a suggestion implies a criticism and is offended. (b) Kills a suggestion which does not at once strike him as excellent with a withering or sarcastic remark. (c) While seeming to reject it neatly captures the idea and restates as his own giving no credit to the originator of the idea.	Is quick to recognise and praise an idea that comes from someone else.
6. Makes decision that should have been made by the group.	Refers to the group all matters that concern the group.
7. Adopts a paternalistic attitude towards the group : 'I know best'.	Maintains the position of friendly helpful adviser both on personal and professional matters.
8. Expects hero-worship, giggles of delight at his attempts at humour, and so forth.	Wishes to be respected as a fair and just individual as he respects others.
9. Does not admit even to himself that he is autocratic.	Consciously practices democratic techniques.
10. Sacrifices everything, teachers, students, progress, to the end of a smooth running system.	Is more concerned with the growth of individuals involved than with freedom from annoyances.
11. Is greedy for publicity.	Pushes others into the fore-ground so that they may taste success.
12. Gives to others as few opportunities for leadership as possible. Makes committee assignments, then outlines all duties and performs many of them himself.	Believes that as many individuals as possible should have opportunities to take responsibility and exercise leadership.

Authoritarian Supervision. Authoritarian supervision is based upon practices like 'I told him to do this'. This kills the creative ability and initiative of the teachers and is hindrance in improving instruction.

Authoritarian supervision forces and prescribes methods.

Authoritarian supervision implies that the supervisor is a master, or super teacher, who can walk in, take over the class and get the desired results.

An interesting specific analysis of two types of leadership was made by a classroom teacher and quoted by Koopman, Miel and Misner.

Human Vigilance

The educational supervisor should develop the 'we feeling' and when a solution to a particular problem is sought it should be 'our solution.' The combined pressure of a group has the effect of bringing about more unanimous action.

In order to improve human relationship the educational supervisor will bear in mind the following factors :

Increased Respect for Human Personality. Superiors should have respect for their subordinates and vice versa;

Sense of High Purpose which Over-rides Material Self-Interest. The individual should be willing to make personal sacrifices for the good of the group;

Free and Responsible Participation. People give of their best when they do things voluntarily;

Appreciation for Leadership. A group should show its appreciation for the ability and good work of its leader;

Respect for Authority. This is necessary in any group except where autocratic power prevails.

Conclusion. The nature of inspection has undergone a great change with the new conception of education which stresses the all round development of the child. Modern supervision is getting democratic and creative supervision; as now understood, it is not only concerned with the evaluation of the instructional work but also with work of making up of its deficiencies. It is to aid, inspire and lead schools. It is to provide guidance and counselling to schools. The supervisors have undertaken the role of consultants or friends and guides. They are to provide democratic leadership to schools to help improve their work.

The methods employed by the present-day supervisors are not confined only to old visits and inspections but also include demonstration lessons, seminars, refresher courses, individual or joint meetings to help the teachers in improving their instructional skill and efficiency in the organisation of co-curricular activities. In short, the inspectors are to serve as 'teachers of teachers'. Supervision should mean personal cooperation and help offered by one who knows more to a less experienced or less resourceful colleague.

Supervisor's Merits

Brilly suggests that the motto of an Inspector should not be "check your teachers, frighten your teachers, weaken your teachers and examine them," but its variant. "Train your teachers, inspire your teachers, encourage your teachers and trust them." His important qualities are :

Man of Educational Vision. He should be aware of new trends in education, latest techniques in education, recent problems in the field and their solutions. He should not merely assess the academic achievements of the schools but also the all-round progress of the school should occupy his attention.

Man of Faith. There is no use of being impatient, for growth and improvement always take time. The inspector must have a far-reaching programme, but putting through it, he should proceed item by item.

Man of Experiments. He must be an experimenter. An able inspector will select forward looking, schools where the teachers and the Headmasters have a progressive outlook on education and are imbued with the spirit of experimentation and will turn these schools nurseries wherein the seeds of educational reform and progress are sown, cared for and their progress carefully watched and the message carried to other schools.

Man of Planning. The inspector should plan his work thoroughly and should not undertake it at random.

Man of Sympathy. He should always show respect for the teacher's personality. A good inspector is one who can inspire and enthuse the teachers without dominating over them like a harsh task master. He should place the teachers on a footing of human equality. He should be cooperative, sympathetic and affectionate.

Constructive Mind. An inspector should possess constructive mind rather than a destructive one. He should never undertake a visit to school with the pure object of fault-finding. An inspector who fails to praise when commendation is deserved, is failing as much in his duties as one who fails to criticise when criticism is deserved. He should have a problem-solving attitude and should help teachers in tackling the problems with which they are faced.

Organising Capacity. As he is to serve as 'teacher of teachers', he should have the capacity to organise refresher courses, meetings, seminars and discussions.

Expert in Various Subjects. An inspector should be a specialist in many languages and subjects. This is particularly important in our schools where different media of instruction are followed.

Liaison Officer. The inspector should be a friendly liaison officer between the Department and the field workers, a mediator linking up scattered educational experiences and experiments. Dr. Hart of the California University, a specialist in school administration had enumerated seven abilities which every administrator and supervisor should possess in ample degree to discharge his duties well. The first is the ability to recognise the especially worthwhile things that are taking place in the school system. The second is to organise the school system so that essentially worthwhile things discovered are spread throughout the system. The third is to overcome the inefficiencies of others without losing their goodwill. The fourth is to set goals that are within the reach of an individual. The fifth ability is that of making everyone in the school system feel worth whileness of his job. The sixth is that of helping everyone in the system to grow professionally and grow in service to society. And the seventh is to make those who work for or with the administrator or supervisor personally happy.

To sum up the qualities of an inspector, it may be stated that he should be a man of learning, faith, pulsating with life and energy and imbuded with a spirit of progress and experimentation and above prejudices of all sorts and petty personal affiliation.

Inspectors for Jobs

In view of the multifarious functions, an inspector is expected to perform, it is very essential that sufficient care is taken in the selection of the inspecting personnel. It is suggested by Secondary Education Commission that a person to be chosen as an Inspector, should possess high academic qualifications (an Honours or Master's degree with teacher's training) and should have had teaching experience in schools at least for ten years or should have been a Headmaster of a High School for a minimum period of three years. In addition to direct recruitment, the Inspectors should also be drawn from :

(i) Teachers of ten years experience.

(ii) Experienced Headmasters of High Schools.

(iii) Qualified staff of Training Colleges.

The Commission further recommends that suitable persons from any of these categories may be appointed as inspectors for a period of three to five years after which they may revert to their original posts. This will enable them to appreciate the position of the Inspector and to approach the problems of the schools with greater appreciation of the realities from their own experience.

Better Conditions

Defects in Existing System of Inspection. The main defects as noticed by the Mudaliar Commission in the present day system of inspection are :

(i) Inspections are perfunctory.

(ii) Time spent by the inspector is insufficient and greater part of the same is taken up with routine work pertaining to checking of accounts, time-table, curriculum, etc.

(iii) Enough time is not devoted to the academic side.

(iv) Contacts between the teachers and inspectors are casual.

(v) The number of schools entrusted to the care of an inspector is too large and the range too wide for him to be able to acquaint himself with their work and appreciate their problems; nor he is in a position to advise and guide the teaching staff in improving the work of the school.

(vi) The inspector instead of being "the friend, philosopher and guide" of the school, behaves in such a critical and unsympathetic way that his visit is looked upon with some degree of apprehension, if not of resentment. In the words of W.M. Ryburn, "The inspector holds an extremely autocratic position, where, if his will is not exactly law, it is so near to it that for all practical intents and purposes, the teacher and the headmaster regard it as such."

To quote G.S. Shukla, "Till now responsibility of inspectorate in education was considered synonymous with unquestionable authority and superiority demanding unqualified obedience and respect from the teaching profession." He further calls the Inspector of Schools as an educational policeman.

(vii) There are no arrangements for experts in such subjects as Domestic Science, Arts and Crafts, Music, etc. with the result that these subjects remain unsupervised.

Principles of Good Inspection. Inspection, in order to be effective and fruitful, should be conducted according to certain principles which may be listed as :

1. Inspection should contribute to the general efficiency of the school and to the professional growth of the teacher. H.M. Nutt observes, "That the supervisor exists for the sake of the teachers who work under his direction, and for the sake of pupils who work under the direction of the teachers, may be stated as the first principle of supervision."
2. Inspection should be done very sympathetically. An inspector should carry with him an abundance of sympathy.

3. Inspection implies the impartial observation of facts. The inspector must maintain a scientific and critical attitude and should be free from prejudices.
4. Inspection should be very comprehensive and thorough. It should not merely be concerned with financial aspect of school management and administrative details but should cover all aspects of school work.
5. Inspectors should try to assess the spirit of a school in addition to its instructional work. The spirit of school may be gauged from the records of staff meetings, co-curricular activities and any experimental work done in educational methods. The standard of discipline on the playing field and outside the class is a sure index of the spirit of a school.
6. The individuality of the teachers' method should be respected. The inspector should not insist on "deadly uniformity". He should try to understand the methods employed by the teachers and appreciate the good points they contain.
7. The inspectors should not be 'misers' in giving praise when it is deserved.
8. Inspection should not be cursory in character. At least two or three days should be devoted. The work of the teacher should not be judged in a few minutes. More careful and longer supervision is necessary. Doing is always better than telling. Demonstration lessons by an inspector are more useful than pages of suggestions. However, it must be stressed that it is a wrong policy to give a demonstration lesson then and there when an inspector finds a class weak in a subject or finds unsatisfactory methods being used by the teacher. Such a step is likely to lower the prestige of the teacher in the eyes of the students.
9. The inspection staff should not expect impossibilities. They should understand the local conditions perfectly well and then decide for themselves what progress may reasonably be expected.

10. The written work of the students should be carefully assessed. In the case of subjects with practical work such as science, agriculture and drawing, the inspector should always get practical work done by the students.
11. Inspection should not be confined to the four walls of the school. As the school is to serve the community and is intimately connected with it, the inspector should help the school to develop proper contacts with the community and to improve its relations with the people.
12. Inspections must be planned in advance. They should not be a hit-or-miss affair. A good planned inspection will have a set of clearly stated objectives and will contain an outline of the devices, means and procedures which are to be used in the attainment of these objectives. It will also include clear-cut lines of the criteria, checks or tests which are to be used to test the results of inspection in order to determine the success or failure of the programmes.
13. The academic work of the school should be thoroughly checked by a panel of experts with the inspector as chairman.

Checking List for Supervision of Instruction

Teacher...................... Date ....

Subject .... Class ....

Note. Check in one of these three columns A,B,C. If a given feature does not appear, check in the column "No".

Classroom Management	*No.*	*A*	*B*	*C*
1. Was sufficient attention given to lighting and ventilation?				
2. Was the equipment of the rooms (for example, desks, black boards etc.) in order?				
3. Were there sufficient audio-visual aids? (for example, maps and charts).				
4. Were supplementary materials effectively arranged?				

Contd.

Classroom Management	*No.*	*A*	*B*	*C*
5. Was the teacher's voice pleasing and his enunciation, clear?				
6. Was the teacher's dress suitable?				
7. Were the teacher's manners suitable?				
8. Did the teacher show evidence of possession of the following qualities?				
(a) Self-control				
(b) Tact				
(c) Resourcefulness				
(d) Sympathy				
(e) Fair-mindedness				
(f) Enthusiasm				
(g) Decisiveness				
9. Did the lesson begin and end in time?				
10. Did the teacher handle laboratory material efficiently?				
11. Were the students with defective sight or hearing seated on front desks?				
12. Did students enter, leave and move about the room in an appropriate manner?				
13. Were the postures of the students good?				
14. Were pupils' responses well directed and expressed?				
15. Was the attention of the entire class keen and continuous?				
16. Was the group characterised by an attitude of courtesy and cooperation towards all its members?				

Arrangement of the Subject-Matter

Classroom Management	No.	A	B	C
1. Was the time effectively divided between (1) testing and drilling upon previous assignment (2) Assignment and new material.				
2. Did the assignment involve activity of the group?				

Teaching Devices

Classroom Management	No.	A	B	C
1. Were all pupils kept busy throughout the entire period?				
2. Was there proper balance between teacher activity and pupil activity?				
3. Was emphasis placed upon the formation of good habits rather than the acquisition of facts?				
4. Was sufficient drill given to secure mastery of necessary skills and facts?				
5. Did all the students participate in drill?				
6. Were the questions suitable?				
7. Were the questions well distributed among the members of the group?				
8. Did the pupils ask questions spontaneously?				
9. Was there any evidence to show that the pupils had been taught how to attack and solve a problem?				

Aim

Classroom Management	*No.*	*A*	*B*	*C*
1. Did the teacher have a clear and worthy aim of the lesson?				
2. Was the aim attained?				

Strengthening of the Supervisory Staff. A major part of the time of the Education Officer is being spent on administrative activities with the result that adequate time is not left with the Education Officer to discharge his supervisory activities. Keeping in view the present situation it is not advisable to separate the administrative and supervisory work. However, it is extremely important that the supervisory staff should be strengthened.

More Clerical Staff is Needed. More clerical staff is needed to cope with the routine type of work of supervision and inspection. In many cases supervisory remarks remain untyped for months because of the shortage of typists and other clerical staff with the result that schools fail to derive immediate benefit from the supervisory remarks.

In-service Training to Education Officers. The importance of in-service training to the Education Officers can hardly be minimised. They must orient themselves with new thoughts and techniques in teaching-learning process. Like all others in the field of education, the education officers also need constant in-service refresher courses, workshops and seminars.

Frequency of Inspections and Follow-up work. With regard to frequency of inspections, it is suggested that there should be at least two in one year, one of them may be informal visit and the other regular annual visit. More visits are desirable specially in the case of those schools which in the view of the Education Officer require special measures to become educationally sound. Needs of each school should be ascertained and remedial measures adopted.

The remarks and suggestions of the Education Officer should be sent to schools within one week of the visit of the supervisor so that these may be considered by school personnel without delay.

School inspections without any regular follow-up programme do not prove to be effective. Planning of follow-up programme is as essential as regular inspection.

Preparation for Classroom Visitation. The supervisor should prepare himself adequately for a classroom visit. A wise supervisor will secure as much information as possible concerning the professional background and abilities of the teacher.

Class visitation may be announced or un-announced. Announced visitation offers the teacher an opportunity to prepare the best work of which he is capable.

Unannounced visitation enables the supervisor to observe the normal classroom work. Such visitation is favoured by most of the principals and teachers.

The advantages and disadvantages of the two types of visitation suggest that no one type should be used exclusively. There should be a judicious combination of both.

Changes in the Techniques of Supervision. Since environmental conditions vary from time to time, teacher to teacher, subject to subject, and group to group, supervisory techniques cannot be wedded to any set theory and practice, and therefore, the Education Officer should have a plan ready in hand as to 'what', 'where', 'when' and 'how' to observe and revise the plans periodically.

Behaviour of the Supervisor. The supervisor should greet the teacher in a friendly and courteous manner. Usually he should seat himself at the rear of the room. Generally speaking he should not interrupt the work of the class or take over any part of the instruction. He should record his observations as objectively as possible.

Encouraging Professional Growth. Very little is done by the Education Officer for the professional growth of teachers.

A number of teachers may be asked to demonstrate the techniques in which they are most successful. Discussion should always follow immediately after the demonstration. Observers should be given an opportunity to ask whatever question they wish. All suggestions should be made and accepted like an ideal sportsman.

Motion pictures and film strips may be used wherever possible.

The demonstrator should explain the application of principles in his procedure after the demonstration is over.

Adequate preparation should be made by the supervisor while giving a demonstration lesson as this is likely to serve as a model for teachers. It should be well thought-out and well planned and efficiently executed.

In-service Training for Principals and Teachers. Refresher courses, seminars, workshops, study circles etc., should be organised for the benefit of principals and teachers. These will enable them to be in touch with the day-to-day changes in the field of education.

Inter-school Visitation. In many cases teachers can offer valuable assistance or guidance to one another by mutually visiting their classes. For this it is very essential that a cooperative attitude may be developed among the teachers and the practice of inter visiting of this type encouraged.

Dissemination of Educational Literature. Supervisor may issue a bulletin at regular intervals for encouraging professional growth among teachers. Following types of material may be included in the bulletin :

(i) Abstracts or brief quotations from books, articles or speeches;

(ii) References to articles appearing in current educational periodicals to which the teachers have access;

(iii) News items of what various schools or teachers are doing;

(iv) News items of achievements in the Zone or Circle itself;

(v) Results of research, reports etc., which have come to the attention of the supervisors;

(vi) Brief reviews of the latest educational literature;

(vii) Articles from teachers and other educationists on different aspects of education;

(viii) Bibliographies of good references upon selected topics considered of immediate interest to teachers.

The Inspectorate of Education may take up the publication of an educational journal.

Strengthening Teachers' Reference Libraries. Teachers may be stimulated to read literature on professional and general topics. This is possible only when reading material is easily available. Professional magazines and books may be placed in the reading room. Central teachers' libraries and reading rooms may be established.

Supervisor's Meetings with Teachers. There are three chief types of teachers' meetings which should be held :

(1) Meetings for routine administrative purposes;

(2) Meetings for social purposes;

(3) Meetings that deal with the improvement of instruction.

These meetings should help in stimulating a desire to learn among school personnel for solving their own problems.

Contact with the Public. School in a democratic society is the source and centre of all development. Hence it is very necessary that the supervisory staff should maintain contacts with local people. At present such contacts are extremely negligible.

Need for Research and its Relation to Supervision. Action research seems to be completely missing in our educational institutions. The present day requires research in the field of education on account of the growing emphasis on the democratic way of living. J.P. Naik feels, "in its absence, policies continue to be framed on the basis of subjective opinion of individuals and very often, the same few individuals and this generally leads to sectorial prejudices and the riding of hobby-horses rather than to comprehensive studies and radical reorganisation."

The Education Officer must acquire a certain amount of knowledge and the skill in the field of educational research so that he can guide the teachers in conducting experiments with regard to the major and minor problems of the school.

Comprehensive Supervision. Supervision of the work of the teachers should be fairly comprehensive.

Administrative Wing and Supervisor's Recommendations. The inspection reports generally do not receive their due attention at the hands of the administrative wing.

More importance should be given to the recommendations of the supervisory staff by the administrative wing as regards provisions of school furniture and equipment. Every recommendation must be given its due weight.

Spotting out Talented Teachers-State Awards. Education Officers should spot out talents among the school personnel. Subject experts in various fields from amongst the teachers may be requested to give demonstration lessons from time to time.

Informal Contacts with School Staff. The supervisory staff should establish contacts with the Principals and teachers and discuss their problems, difficulties and plans. Such meetings should be of an informal nature and be confined to small groups. After the regular classroom inspection it is desirable that the Education Officer convenes a meeting of the staff to discuss the problems and difficulties and give them fruitful suggestions. This helps the teachers to come in contact with the inspecting staff.

Programmes like teachers' get-together may be planned periodically and cultural programmes organised on such occasions. Cultural programmes presented by teachers and for teachers prove to be useful in harnessing their energies in fruitful channels and enriching the development of their personality. Educational conferences and exhibitions may also be organised.

Change in Outlook. Attempts made in recent years to remove the barriers that exist between the supervisory staff and the school personnel should be accelerated. The supervisory staff should have a genuine desire to help the school staff and should always be prepared to cooperate with them to further the cause of education. This work is likely to be facilitated if the supervisory staff finds time to participate occasionally in some activities of the school like games, camps, social service programmes etc.

It must be remembered that when the teachers feel that the supervisor is one of them and is here to help them as a true friend, philosopher and guide, they will be able to discuss all their problems with the supervisors. All this requires that supervisors must be endowed both with the qualities of head and heart, i.e., keep themselves abreast with the growing latest pedagogical literature as well as develop in themselves the behaviour pattern that would endear themselves to the teachers. This may appear to be a pious hope but the recent studies reveal that all people in the field of education right from the pupils up to the Department feel that the supervisor is an important link that can help the growth of educational institutions in the proper direction. We may bear in mind that respect for personality is fundamental in democratic supervision. For it recognises each individual as a person in his own right and as such entitled to growth along the lines of his own social choices.

16

Necessity of Discipline

Basic Issues

In the words of the University Education Commission, "It is important that good discipline be looked upon not as student conformity to arbitrary standards of conduct, but rather as individual responsibility for behaviour."

Narrow and Broader View Regarding Discipline. The concept of discipline may be viewed from a narrow and old or from a modern and broader point of view. From the narrow point of view discipline means subjection to authority, obedience to law and order and bringing the child under control. From a broader modern point of view, by discipline we mean the training of mind, manners and attitudes, sublimation of instincts, bringing the lower impulses of the child under control, formation of right habits and in fact the development of character.

Discipline from the Point of View of an Individual. Discipline viewed from the point of view of an individual is a means of enabling him to bring under control his instinctive urges to reach a position where he willingly and spontaneously identifies himself with a right.

Discipline from the Point of View of Society. Discipline viewed from the point of view of the society is a means of developing a social sense or social conscience in an individual so that he identifies himself with the society and contributes for its betterment to which he belongs.

External and Internal Discipline. According to William A. Yeager, "Historically, it always is associated with the concept discipline, having the connotations of strict mental, moral and physical training, requiring for its achievement, submission to authority, with proper punishment meted out for disobedience in any form."

Thus it implies something 'external', that is conformity to all external stimulus or impulse. More recently, a school control has come to imply something internal, a response to an inner stimulus or impulse.

To quote T.P. Nunn, "Discipline consists in the submission of one's impulses and powers to regulation which imposes form upon chaos and brings efficiency and economy where there would otherwise be ineffectiveness and waste."

S. Bala Krishna Joshi writes, "What is discipline? To put it in a nutshell, it is decent and decorous conduct which contributes to harmony, joy and success, and exalted sense of responsibility, respect for authority, love of orderliness, eagerness to discharge duties with regularity, promptitude and efficiency, a desire to be agreeable and helpful to others by exercising, if necessary, a wholesome check on individual proclivities and a capacity to maintain equipoise in the face of the most trying circumstances—these constitute discipline."

Discipline and Freedom. Divergent and conflicting opinions have been expressed by the leading educationists from time to time on the question of 'freedom in schools'. There is the extreme view put forward by Rousseau and the persons of his way of thinking that the child should be left free to act practically whatever he likes and free not to do whatever he does not like. This is a revolt against the old conception of 'discipline' and 'freedom' which puts stem restrictions on the child and shuns completely all ideas of 'freedom' and ,self-discipline'. The protagonists of such an idea believe in the efficacy of the 'rod' as an instrument of discipline. However, the truth lies somewhere between these two extreme views. Ryburn writes, "Freedom in school should bear some relation to the freedom that is found in the world at large." It would be very harmful to leave the child at the mercy of his environment. The theory of 'Natural Consequences' or 'Laissez-Faire', "Children should never receive punishment as such - it should always come as a natural consequence of their fault, is fraught with grave consequences".

Unregulated freedom can be given only at our peril. Bagley rightly puts it as, "The pupil is immature and helpless and he must not be given a long rope with which he may hang himself " Absolute, freedom is a myth. It did not exist, does not exist, will not exist and should not exist.

Excessive Restrictions are Equally Bad. A child who is constantly loaded by many 'dos' and 'don'ts' is unlikely to develop into a well-balanced personality. He will not get sufficient opportunities to do his best. His initiative and drive will be checked. His faculties will remain stunted. His creative powers will remain unharnessed. Authority which derives its strength and sanction from 'fear' paralyses the human mind and spirit. The 'fear atmosphere' will simply create hindrances in providing a suitable environment to the child to grow and blossom. "The man whose tongue is constricted by laws or taboos against free speech, whose pen is constricted by the censorship, whose laws are constricted by an ethic which considers jealousy a better thing than by affection, whose childhood had been imprisoned in a code of manners, and whose youth has been drilled in a cruel orthodoxy, will feel against the world that hampers him with the same rage that is felt by the infant whose arms and legs are held motionless. In his rage he will turn to destruction, becoming a revolutionary militarist, or a persecuting moralist according to temperament and opportunity," writes Russell. It is wrong to believe 'what the whip was to do to the horse, the rod was to do to the child.' 'Compulsion' kills spontaneity.

Discipline is not synonymous with 'class order.' We usually make the mistake of identifying discipline with the orderly behaviour in the classroom teaching and other forms of school activities.

School discipline cannot be conceived in terms of military discipline which is based on :

There is not a reason why

There is not to make reply

There is but to do and die.

Various Steps

Dr. Adams has marked three distinct stages in the development of ideas of discipline.

First Stage -'Flogging' was the order of the day in the first stage. Rod was the chief instrument to educate the educant. Fear atmosphere prevailed in the school. The student had to abide by certain rigid rules and regulations and any branch of these meant penalties. The rod and instruction were deemed inseparable. Discipline was enforced from above and known as 'external discipline.'

Second Stage - "Impression rather than Repression" The second stage was when teachers believed that 'impression' rather than 'repression' should be the basis of discipline. They did not support the Flogging Theory. There was a scope for light corporal punishment. According to Ross, "The compelling power of the educator's personality takes the place of punishment; it is his personal influence and that of the school system which he plans and governs that are effective in ensuring that desirable modes of behaviour are followed. There is a reign of respect and love rather than one of terror."

Third Stage of Laissez Faire : The doctrine of Laissez Faire or Free Discipline which constitutes the third stage is the outcome of the teachings of educationists and psychologists like Rousseau, Froebel, Montessori, Dewey, Neill and others. 'Save the child' is the slogan of these educationists.

Repression is Dangerous. Some masterminds contend that the repressive measures only help splitting up the personality of the child into two, i.e. the outer one orderly and obedient and the inner one frustrated and rebellious.

Discipline and Order. J.E. Brown writes that discipline like honour and peace has almost as many different meanings as it has uses. He defines order as, "an outward semblance of good behaviour not in itself to be despised, since it permits work to be carried on smoothly." To achieve order nothing is needed but an authoritative presence with a voice to match, failing which a strong arm is effective.

By discipline he means, "a cooperative mental attitude in which each member of the class freely gives of his best because he feels himself a member of a corporate body whose aims are recognised as worthy; and misbehaviour on the part of any member is condemned by the whole body because it is recognised not only or even chiefly as a crime against the whole 'Community.' The aim of such discipline is to produce self-control led men and women who will work without supervision. This is the ideal stage and known as constructive discipline. Constructive discipline is the outcome of the activities and experiences that inculcate in the individual virtues of self-control based on reason and not on force. It is the outcome of persuasion and not of compulsion. It comes out of doing rather than of talking. Like religion it cannot be taught but can only be caught and practised."

Importance of Discipline. P.C. Wren states, "As in the army, the navy, or the State, so in the school, the pre-requisite, the very condition of existence is discipline." Discipline gives the real power and self-control by which potentialities can find their full development. Discipline enables an individual to undertake and discharge his share of responsibilities worthily.

Discipline and Democracy. Discipline is the essence of democracy. In democracy it is not forced from above. It grows from within. It is based on the realization by the individual of the worth of all other individuals. It is the result of "training of conscience which consists in the cultivation of good will and the development of moral insight."

To quote- the Secondary Education Commission. "Discipline is the fruit, the valuable by-product of cooperative work willingly and efficiently undertaken."

Positive Aspect of School Discipline. An eminent educationist has suggested, "The discipline employed in our classrooms should be designed to place upon the child more and more responsibility for his own choices, purposes and behaviour as he grows in the ability to shoulder such responsibility. Such 'discipline' instead of being repressive and utilising punishment and repraisal for missteps will plan with the children the purposes to be achieved and through the social control of group approval will teach the child to discharge creditably the responsibilities assigned to him by the groups."

Discipline is the fruit of cooperative work willingly undertaken and efficiently completed. Discipline from without is always temporisation.

Discipline through the Influence of Social Group. Discipline in the school will not be a matter of arbitrary rules and regulations enforced through the authority of the teachers, helped by the lures of rewards or the fear of punishment. The students will be given full freedom to organise functions, to conduct many of the school activities through their own committees and even to deal with certain types of disciplinary cases. In this way, discipline be maintained through the influence of the social group and it will gradually lead to the development of self-discipline.

Self-control

It is very erroneous to think that free discipline or self-discipline or creative discipline can be had by resorting to external discipline. At the same time it must be remembered that the goal of self-discipline cannot be achieved in a day or so. It can be had only with increasing watchfulness. It requires patience of a very high order. Cooperation of the various agencies of education is absolutely essential to inculcate right types of attitudes and habits in the students. A school is said to be a cooperative society where all work for the welfare and happiness of each and each for the whole. The rules and the regulations of a cooperative society are framed to a considerable extent, by the members themselves and are not imposed from above. All the members of this society are expected to respect and honour them. Discipline is not the business of school authorities. Why? It is, as a matter of fact, the business of the whole society. The Secondary Education Commission observes, "Discipline, they say, should be a responsibility of parents, teachers, the general public and the authorities concerned."

Student Government. This is considered to be a very effective way of securing the willing cooperation of the students. By participating in various committees formed to govern themselves they realize that rules and regulations and their enforcement are very essential. They learn that no society can function smoothly if the members do not obey its rules. They get opportunities to understand and appreciate the significance of tolerance, open-mindedness, cooperation and fellow-feeling. They learn to appreciate that rights and responsibilities go together.

The Secondary Education Commission observes, "Discipline in the school will not be a matter of arbitrary rules and regulations enforced through the authority of the teachers helped by the lure of rewards or the fear of punishment. The students will be given full freedom to organise functions, to conduct many of the school activities through their own committees and even to deal with certain types of disciplinary cases. In this way, discipline be maintained through the influence of the social group and it will gradually lead to the development of self-discipline."

Games. Students learn that for the success of a team, they must cooperate with each other and also must subordinate their individual interests. Every player knows that the rules of the game must be obeyed if he wants to participate in it. Thus the students learn to discipline themselves.

The Secondary Education Commission has suggested that "Another important method of bringing home to the pupils the value of discipline is through group games. It is on the playing fields that team spirit can be cultivated. Extra-curricular activities will promote a proper spirit of discipline."

Cooperation among the Staff Members. Children are imitative and suggestive by nature. They acquire many habits simply by imitating their teachers. Lack of cooperation among the members of the staff and between the staff and the Headmaster, is bound to develop attitudes of non-cooperation in the students. This unhealthy aspect of the life of the institution has a great demoralising effect on the minds of the students.

Methods of Teaching. Good methods of teaching facilitate learning. Use of audio-visual aids, black-boards, story telling etc., brings life in the dead-matter of various subjects. Methods like Dalton Plan, Project, the Heuristic and the Basic Scheme develop habits of constant work among the students, besides sharpening their power of thinking. Learning by doing is a device which keeps the students busy. The students make mischief only when they are passive listeners. Rightly it is said that the best method of keeping the students disciplined is to fill the time with work.

Sympathetic Attitude. 'Love the child and the child will love you, hate him and he will hate you' is an old saying. A sympathetic teacher is sure to win the hearts of his pupils. Once this is done, there is no reason why they should go astray. Quite a large number of troubles arise due to the harsh and unsympathetic behaviour of the authorities towards the students.

Personal Relationship. Loss of personal relationships between the teacher and the taught is fatal for creative education. Without it, we cannot think of students developing ideals of a creative citizen.

Punishment. It has a definite place but should be used very carefully and judiciously. It must suit the nature of the offending child. 'Just rebuke' may be sufficient in some cases while in others, even corporal punishment may prove to be futile.

Co-curricular Activities. These provide them suitable channels to utilize their surplus energy. They are also very helpful in sublimating their instincts. Sultan Mohiyuddin thinks, "The various activities and pursuits will furnish their motive power, work will be done for its own sake, the mutual relations of the members of the school will be properly appreciated and the rules and laws of the school will be recognised as necessary for smooth functioning of the school as whole and for the effective participation of each individual member in the school life, and in consequence the needs of the individual and of the group will be properly adjusted."

Material Conditions of Work. Good' furniture, library, laboratory, sufficient classroom accommodation, hall, playgrounds, good arrangement for light, water, ventilation and sanitation, etc., present a congenial environment conducive to self-discipline.

Moral Education. A programme of moral education stimulates the interests of the adolescents in the social aspects of religions. It helps them to fortify their faith in the conviction that there are certain fundamental values in life which are very essential for a gracious and harmonious living. Albert L. Ayars writes, "The school programme of moral and spiritual values should not be thought as a course of division of instruction. It is an integral part of the curriculum, emphasized in all courses and activities."

Indiscipline on Rise

We can hardly minimise the gravity of the problem of indiscipline in our educational institutions., "No amount of improvement and reconstruction in education will bear much fruit if the schools themselves are undermined by indiscipline," observed the Secondary Education Commission. In the candid opinion of Prof. Humayun Kabir, "Failure to take effective steps at this stage can so aggravate the problem that it may shake the very foundations of our national life." In the absence of discipline in a school, there is bound to be chaos and confusion, waste and inefficiency. Discipline is the life-blood of an institution. An indisciplined life is like a boat without rudder tossing every now and then at the passing current.

Prof. K.G. Saiyidain attributed these causes

1. Sense of frustration among students.
2. Lack of sufficient interest in studies.
3. Overcrowding in schools and colleges.
4. Undignifying examples set by politicians.

Shri K.M. Cariappa observed on January 6th, 1966 that students were being exploited by unscrupulous politicians who encouraged them to strike and indulge in acts of rowdyism.

A number of factors are responsible for the growing sense of indiscipline in our students. The fault lies partly with the system of education, partly with the teachers of educational institutions, partly with the existing social, economic and political conditions and partly also with the conditions prevailing in our homes. Prof. Humayun Kabir in a pamphlet Student Indiscipline has described the following causes of indiscipline in our students :

(a) The loss of leadership by teachers.

(b) Growth of economic difficulties.

(c) Defects in the existing system of education.

(d) General loss of idealism.

Loss of Leadership by Teachers. Failure on the part of teachers to take active part in the struggle for freedom, sweeping criticism of the present system of education and of teachers; inadequate salaries of the teachers and frustration caused by it, entry of unqualified persons in the teaching profession, control of politicians over educational institutions and the acceptance of tuitions on an almost commercial scale by some of the teachers are considered to be some of the major factors which have led to their loss of leadership among the student community. Strained personal relations between the staff and the head have also an adverse effect on the minds of the students. The Secondary Education Commission observes: "Discipline among students can only be promoted if there is discipline among the staff both within the school and in organization connected with the teaching profession. The teacher has always to realise that all his activities are being watched by his pupils to that extent, therefore, both in his personal conduct and his general attitude to all his problems concerning the country, he has to realise that there are limitations within which he must act for the best interest of the profession."

Economic Difficulties. Another reason, though to a very limited extent, of indiscipline in some educational institutions is that some students who otherwise may be topmost are economically distressed. On the one hand they feel that they are superior to the other children in studies and on the other hand find that their economic condition is far inferior to that of some well-to-do but mediocre students. This leads to discontentment with the existing order and in the absence of any soothing influence, they gradually become bitter and indisciplined.

Defects in the Existing System of Education. It would not be unfair to say that the present system of education is rather indifferent to the development of character among pupils.

The progress of a child is judged by the results of the annual examination. The energies of the students are not properly utilized during the major part of the year and the students seek outlets in activities which are anti-social. Co-curricular activities hardly exist to canalise their energies. They are considered as sheer waste of time. Frances W. Parker writes, "The fundamental reason why children do not act is because they do not have the conditions for right action." Maulana Azad has also stressed this point : "I am convinced that if the young are at times restless and turbulent, it is not due to any intrinsic defect in them. Their restlessness is largely due to the fact that they do not have enough channels for the expression of their youthful urges."

Education not being in accordance with the age, ability and aptitude of the students, develops frustration among them.

The running of most of our educational institutions more or less on commercial lines fails to establish moral and spiritual links between the teacher and the taught.

The authoritarian attitude of the authorities in our educational system is also an important factor in the growth of unrest and indiscipline in our students.

The students have no say in majority of the cases in the disposal of Boy's Funds and it raises suspicion in their minds. Lack of imagination on the part of the authorities to understand the growing awakening among the students aggravates the problem all the more.

Classes being overcrowded, the individual needs of the students remain unattended to and the personal contact between the teachers and the students does not develop.

Too much talk of self-discipline and liberalism in the field of education has also done some harm. Loud talks of student government have sometimes led the students to believe that there are no rules for them to be obeyed.

General Loss of Idealism. There appears to be a general fall in the standard of morality in the different walks of life. It will not be wrong to say that the society is undermined by indiscipline to a greater extent. Discipline is greatly affected by the tone of the society as a whole.

Roots of Tussle

(a) Demand for removal of a teacher on the grounds of inefficiency from the point of view of students.

(b) Retention of the teacher whom the management intends to transfer or retire.

(c) Refusal of the authorities to pen-nit some students to appear in an examination owing to shortage of attendance.

(d) Demand for grant of holiday in the memory of some important personality or for the celebration of some public event.

(e) Demand for a change in the date of examination.

(f) Stiffness of the examination paper.

(g) Demand for the establishment of the students' union.

(h) Demand for the remission of fine to particular student who has been fined due to his behaviour.

(i) Demand for certain facilities (library, etc.) in the school.

(j) Enhancement of funds.

General Aspects

(i) Disrespect for authorities, i.e. rudeness.

(ii) Disrespect for school rules and regulations.

(iii) Disrespect for teachers, i.e. discourtesy.

(iv) Coming late in the class.

(v) Deliberately not doing assignment.

(vi) Unruly behaviour in the class, to be noisy and disturbing others.

(vii) Making noise in school assembly and public gatherings.

(viii) Damaging and spoiling the school property.

(ix) Using indecent and abusive language.

(x) Making uncalled for remarks to the fair sex.

(xi) Forming gangs.

(xii) Organizing strikes.

(xiii) Aggressive behaviour, e.g bullying and teasing.

(xiv) Using unfair means in the examinations.

(xv) Dishonest dealings, i.e. stealing, lying etc.

(xvi) Deliberately not paying the fee in time.

Checking Devices

A review of the causes of indiscipline shows that the problem of indiscipline is not an isolated one. Many-sided attempts will, therefore, have to be made to tackle this problem. The parents, the political leaders, the teachers and the government must fully cooperate with each other for the creation of an ideal atmosphere. The following measures should be taken to check indiscipline

(a) Restoration of the lost leadership of the teachers.

(b) Improvement in the economic lot of the students.

(c) Reform in the system of education.

(d) Revival of the sense of values.

Restoration of the Lost Leadership to the Teachers. The salaries of the teachers must be raised to ameliorate their economic lot. High salaries are bound to attract right type of persons to the teaching profession. To raise the social status of the teachers, special measures should be adopted.

Refresher courses and seminars help the teachers to know the current educational thoughts and practices.

Holiday Homes should be established so that with moderate expenditure, the teachers are in a position to enjoy their holidays.

Improvement in the Economic Lot of the Students. A large number of scholarships and stipends should be given to the meritorious students who are economically handicapped. At nominal prices the State should take steps to supply tiffin to school children belonging to poor families. There should be provision for supplying free books etc. to the students.

Reform in the System of Education. Far reaching changes in the curriculum are needed. Secondary education should be diversified to meet the varying needs of the adolescents. Youthful activities should be provided in large numbers. Programmes which offer excellent opportunities of developing character and citizen-ship should be undertaken.

"The problem of discipline must be looked at from the point of view of proper utilisation of the abundant energy of the youth. If youthful urges and energy are canalised and fields are found which will utilise all their enthusiasm and devotion, there will be little occasion to impose restrictions from above. Discipline must be achieved by giving proper direction to the energy of the youth and not by suppression," observes Maulana Azad.

Examination system should be changed radically so that the students work throughout the year. The work of a student should be assessed after taking into account the record of his achievements throughout the year.

Our methods of teaching require a great transformation. The students should be made active partners and not passive listeners.

Personal contact with the students should be established to understand and solve their individual difficulties.

Autocratic attitude on the part of the authorities should be replaced by democratic ideals. An atmosphere of love, affection and sympathy is very conducive to the development of the personality of the child. Cooperation of the students should be secured in utilising boys' funds.

Students and teachers should keep aloof from politics and the political leaders should make it a point not to exploit students for the furtherance of their political cause.

"At the time of election, members who contest election do not hesitate to utilise students for the furtherance of their objective, namely the winning of the election. The utilisation of immature minds for purposes of campaigns with or without slogans attached thereto is not calculated to promote sound discipline among students," observes the Secondary Education Commission.

New Values

If we are to revive a spirit of idealism among students, we must create a favourable social atmosphere based on higher values of life. If humanity is to survive, materialistic conception of life must give way to spiritual values. Moral education in one form or the other must form an integral part of our educational system.

Prof. Humayun Kabir stresses the importance of moral and higher values in these words, "if education trains the future citizens it also determines the shape of future society. The value of such education depends upon the character and competence of the teachers who impart it. It is no exaggeration to say that incompetent and dissatisfied teachers undermine the very foundation of society. Their incompetence and dissatisfaction infect the children and sow the seeds of revolution, disruption and decay. A band of teachers, devoted to ideals and pledged to the continued recreation of traditions, can, on the other hand, ensure conditions of unlimited progress and prosperity for mankind."

In the end we must stress with Sheviakov and Fritz Rede, "discipline is not coercion through force - discipline is a spirit, and a spirit cannot be ordered or punished into or regimented, for true discipline is based on willing co-operation which springs from knowledge, idealism and a sense of duty."

1. Come prepared to the classroom.
2. Use a variety of teaching aids, i.e. maps, charts, etc.
3. Modulate your voice.
4. Plan your daily work very systematically.
5. Make the students active participants in the classroom activities.
6. Keep the students always busy in doing some worthwhile work.

7. Be always cheerful.
8. Be humorous.
9. Make your hand-writing legible.
10. Show love, sympathy and affection to your students.
11. Make a judicious use of praise and blame.
12. Put on suitable dress.
13. Teach the whole of the class and not a few students sitting on the front benches.
14. Put thought-provoking questions.
15. Distribute your questions evenly.
16. Put questions to inattentive students.
17. Do not often repeat your questions.
18. Allow reasonable time to the students to answer your questions.
19. Do not put questions in a hurried way.
20. Use precise language in framing your questions.
21. Ask the weak students to repeat the good answers given by others.
22. Avoid sarcastic remarks.
23. Do not waste time in gossips.
24. Do not narrate your college experience too often.
25. Do not discuss your family problems in the classroom.
26. Pay attention to the seating arrangement of the students.
27. Correct the postures of the students.
28. Provide seats on the first bench to the short-sighted.
29. Pay attention to the sanitary conditions of the classroom.
30. Do not play with the piece of chalk.
31. Give reasonable home-work to the students.
32. Take keen interest in co-curricular activities.

33. Do not try to win popularity through cheap methods.
34. Learn to 'ride your eye' through the eyes of the students.
35. Do not get personal work from the students.
36. Visit the home of the sick students.
37. Do not show undue favour to some students.
38. Check the written work of the students very carefully.
39. Stand throughout the major part of the class period.
40. Do not allow yourself to be 'side tracked' by irrelevant questions.
41. Learn the names of the students very quickly.
42. Respect the personality of the child.
43. Do not use abusive language.
44. Learn as much as possible regarding the home conditions of children.
45. Be physically strong, emotionally stable, ethically sound, mentally alert and socially efficient.

17

The Consequences

"The bigs hit me, so I hit the babies; that's fair," was the reply of a boy of medium size who was ill treating a smaller boy, to Bertrand Russell.

Compulsion kills spontaneity. "Children who are forced to eat acquire a loathing for food, and children who are forced to learn acquire a loathing for knowledge," writes Russell.

Reward and Punishment

Many great educationists like Rousseau protest against all sorts of well-established system of rewards and punishments and have waged a bitter war against the theory of original sin and its repression. Their watchword is 'Freedom to the child because they think that by nature a child is innocent and noble and adult restrictions and discipline simply spoil the intellect of the child and stand in the way of his progress and happiness. They believe in the 'discipline of natural consequences' and are convinced that natural punishments are the best and leave no room for punishments in the life of the school. Sir T. Percy Nunn writes. "The conviction that punishment and the fear of punishment are the natural foundation of school government, is gradually being recognised as merely a barbarous superstition." A.S. Neill in his book The Free Child writes, "My contention is that unfree education ignores almost entirely the emotions of life, and because these emotions are dynamic, their lack of opportunity for expression must and does result in cheapness, ugliness and helplessness. Only the head is educated, but if the emotions are free, intellect will look after itself."

Herbert Spencer would like the child to suffer the unavoidable consequences of his conduct.

Rousseau harps on the same tone when he says, 'Children should never receive punishment as such - it should always come as the natural consequence of their fault."

Plato writes, "A free man ought not to be a slave in the acquisition of knowledge of any kind. Bodily exercise, when compulsory, does no harm to the body, but knowledge which is acquired under compulsion, obtains no hold on the mind. Then, do not use compulsion, but let early education be a sort of amusement, you will be better able to find out the natural bent."

Froebel thinks, "Control over the child was to be exercised through a knowledge of his interest and by expression of love and sympathy."

S. Balakrishna Joshi feels, "The unwritten moral code of the institution must be more binding on the members than the rules of conduct in vogue."

Ross and others state, "To impose control on the pupil wholly from without is to deny him his most essential and effective learning experiences and to nullify the educative influence of the school."

Punishments are Indispensable. There are other educationists like Bagley and Bray who think that punishments are indispensable in the life of the school. Bagley puts it, "The child is immature and helpless and he must not be given a long rope with which he may hang himself."

Bray justifies punishments with these words, "Punishment is the lesser evil applied to avoid the greater one that lives in the future." It is always seen that evil if not checked in time brings havoc ultimately. "Nip the evil in the bud" is an old saying.

P.C. Wren, though admits that punishment is an evil thing to be avoided, yet says that it is a necessary evil like the surgeon's knife.

According to H. Thring, school punishment is not vengeance. Its object is training, first of all the training to the wrong-doer; next the training to other boys by his example. Both he and others are to be deterred from committing the offence again.

The Purposes

Now the question is what kind of punishment should be given in schools. Punishment is always negative and not a stimulant. A conflict is always liable to develop between the child punished and the authority which punishes him. And what is the purpose behind the punishment? This question has been differently answered by the various authorities. Following are some of the purposes of punishment:

Retributive. This is based upon the idea that the offender must suffer as much pain as his victim. If a student has slapped another he should be given a slap by the teacher. The tendency behind this form of punishment is purely a revengeful one. This tendency has been described as low and selfish.

Offensive. Another view is that the purpose of punishment is to punish the offender because he has violated the law. Sometimes the purpose of punishment is to protect others from further wrongs and a noisy child who disturbs others is removed from the class to a lonely place so that others may work quite peacefully.

Exemplary. The third purpose of punishment is to deter the offender and also others from repeating the same kind of offence. A child may be filled for coming late to school so that he may not come late again for fear of the same punishment and example may be set for others.

Reformatory. The positive and correct view of punishment in a school is that the child should be reformed by means of punishment if at all its need arises.

Causes of Punishment

(a) Late coming.

(b) Absence without leave.

(c) Inattentiveness.

(d) Misbehaviour with other students, teachers and others who come into contact.

(e) Calling names.

(f) Bullying.

(g) Stealing.

(h) Negligence in the matter of home-task.

(i) Absence from the examination.

(j) Using unfair means in the examination.

(k) Damaging the school property.

(l) Disobeying the school laws.

(m) Running from the school.

Forms of Punishment

Reproof. Tongue is said to be the most potent weapon in the armoury of a teacher. 'A word to the wise' is an old proverb. Sometimes a mild reproof to a sensitive and intelligent student may achieve the desired results and a vulgar abuse to an obstinate student may prove to be futile. But rebukes are to be used as sparingly as possible. Mohiyuddin says, "Sarcasm, ridicule and abuse are cowardly weapons to employ and psychologically they are very unwholesome and ineffective means of correction."

Deprivation of a Privilege. The wrong-doer may be prohibited from playing any game in the school for some time; may be deprived of his position if he is holding any and may also be denied certain concessions like fee, etc., if enjoyed by him.

Fines. Absence fines, late fee fine or some other kind of fines depending on the nature of the offence may be imposed on the wrong-doers. It is true that this kind of punishment imposes a burden on the parents but occasions may necessitate the levy of fines.

Moral Punishments. Sometimes moral punishments such as apologies, public or private, are accepted from the student.

Making Good the Loss. The student who destroys some property may be asked to make good of the loss.

Loss of Marks. Sometimes marks are deducted when students use unfair means.

Isolation. In this respect the views of Russell are worth noticing when he writes, "when a child persistently interferes with other children or spoils their pleasures the obvious penalty is banishment." A child who repeatedly makes a noise in the class may be asked to sit in one corner of the room - away from the class.

Detention after School Hours. When students fail to do their home-task, they may be detained to sit after school hours and be made to do the work under the supervision of a teacher deputed for the job. To avoid hardship to teachers, teachers' time-table specifically providing for such type of job will be very helpful. But the danger, sometimes, is that pupils may not form unpleasant associations in connection with the work given to them. They will never develop a taste for that work which has been given as punishment.

Repetition of Words. The child who is inattentive in the class may be asked to repeat the lesson, i.e. may be asked to repeat lines of poetry, or the spellings of a difficult word, etc.

Corporal Punishment. Slapping, caning, hands up, kneeling down, boxing the ear etc., are some of the usually employed forms of this punishment.

Suspension and Expulsion. Sometimes there are certain incorrigible students who undermine discipline and adversely affect the morale of the students. Their presence in the institution is considered to be undesirable and as such the authorities are left with no alternative but to suspend or expel them. These are the two extreme forms of punishment. Great care should be taken to ensure that these are resorted to very cautiously and rarely.

Arguments against Punishment

1. Punishment is an animal tendency. It has no connection with human values.
2. Children are very tender by nature. They become timid from the fear of punishment.
3. The children become stubborn through punishment.
4. Sometimes from fear of punishment students leave educational institutions.
5. Punishment cannot inculcate love for discipline.

Points to be Kept in View

1. Punishment should be given only when it is assured that the desired aim would be fulfilled.
2. Punishment should be resorted to very rarely.
3. The accused student should be provided opportunity to explain his point of view before inflicting punishment.
4. Punishment should be proportionate to the degree of the offence.
5. Sarcastic remarks should not be used.
6. Punishment should be according to the nature of the child. Punishment for the same type of offence may differ from child to child.
7. Punishment should be given immediately when a wrong act has been done.
8. Punishment should not be given in anger.
9. As far as possible corporal punishment should not be given.
10. Punishment may be given in the form of making good of the loss done.
11. Expulsion or rustication should be resorted to very rarely.
12. A 'Punishment register' should be maintained and the names of the students punished should be recorded in that register. The nature of the offence and the form of punishment should be recorded.

The Punishment

Violent antagonistic views have been put forward regarding this type of punishment. In the old type of educational system, it occupied a very important place and was considered to be an indispensable weapon in the hands of a teacher to reform the child. It was believed that he who had not been chastened was not educated.

As already pointed out, most of the modern educationists consider it to be out-dated and out-moded and call it as a barbaric act. They condemn it outright. Allers points out that severity will destroy permanently a man's ability to fight the battle of life. Russell doubts very much whether punishment need ever be severe. H.G. Stead has dubbed this type of punishment as a lazy means of control.

E.B. Castle writes about corporal punishment in these words, "I find little weight in the arguments of those who support the practice of corporal punishment. For minor offences it is too harsh, for serious moral delinquency it is irrelevant and may be positively evil; as a stimulus to learning it has been proved to be in the long run a deterrent rather than encouragement."

Allers feels, "Severity and lack of sense can permanently destroy a man's ability to fight the battle of life; people emerge from such an upbringing as moral cripples."

Hobbes thinks, "The fool cannot be mended by flogging and he who flogs is the greatest fool."

Dr. Cyrill Norwood writing about the method of discipline practised by masters in English Public Schools says, "They flogged their ward through term after term with a high sense of duty accomplished, flogged if a lesson were not known, flogged for inattention, flogged for disorder, flogged for bullying, flogged for vice. Often they did not know who the boys were whom they flogged and why they flogged them."

Mohiyuddin states, "W.E. Gladstone, 'the grand old man' of England was flogged at Eton, two of his school fellows being compelled to hold him down while he was subjected to the rod; and the list of other eminent men flogged in the schools is impressive."

Dr. Arnold of Rugby brought a radical change in this direction. Following are some of the chief objections to the corporal punishment .

1. It is not in consonance with the creed of non-violence.
2. It coarses the child and the person who inflicts punishment.
3. It is a negation of cooperation.
4. It has an appeal to the brutal instincts only.
5. There is no proper standard of applying it.
6. It is negative in its effect.
7. It gives rise to permanent injuries.

Conditions and Principles to be Observed

(i) It should be given only by the head of an institution.

(ii) Neither party should be in anger.

(iii) The instrument of punishment should not be very heavy.

(iv) The child and the head both should be very clear about the cause of punishment.

(v) Its scope is limited to moral offences.

(vi) In no case it should be applied to scholars other than those between six and twelve years of age.

(vii) There should not be long interval between the time of offence and punishment.

(viii) It should not be applied to the delicate parts of the body.

(ix) It should not be administered to highly emotional and delicate children.

(x) It must be suited to individual temperament and physical and emotional development of the offender.

Departmental Regulations: The Punjab Education Code empowers the Headmaster only to inflict corporal punishment for misconduct in Upper Middle and High Departments of recognised schools for boys. The corporal punishment must take the form of strokes, not exceeding ten, with the cane on the palm of the hand. Every such punishment is to be recorded and a report sent to the parent or guardian of the boy punished. Corporal punishment has no place in Primary or Lower Middle Departments of schools.

The penalty of expulsion or rustication of a student for serious misconduct may be imposed by the Inspector or Inspectress, as the case may be, in the case of Government and Local Body schools, and in the case of privately managed schools by the Managing Body of the schools. Disciplinary action against students of privately managed schools can be taken by the Inspector or Inspectress if the case of misconduct comes to their notice at the time of their visit to the school. There is no appeal against the order of punishing authority but a copy of the orders passed by the Inspetor or Inspectress and Managing Committee shall be forwarded to the Director and Inspector or Inspectress respectively for information. The orders must state the nature of the offence committed by the student concerned.

Suitable Rewards

The view of the naturalists who dub all rewards as bribery has already been discussed. Briefly it may be stated that they think these rewards have a demoralising effect on the child because they tempt the child to work not for duty's sake but for the sake of prize.

Rewards sometimes lead to unhealthy jealousies among students. Moreover they affect only a few students and leave the group on the whole untouched.

The protagonists of the system of rewards on the other hand argue that the rewards provide incentive to the students to work hard. They contend that society as a whole is governed by a system of rewards and punishments.

Psychologically also the system of rewards and punishments can be justified if we take into account the Law of Effect as enunciated by Thorndike.

Rewards provide incentive for healthy emulation among individuals and group of individuals.

When the work of the students is given appreciation in the presence of others, they feel encouraged. This helps in infusing great confidence in them.

It gives happiness to the parents when their children get prizes. They encourage their children to put in all the more labour.

Rewards may be given for: (a) Regular and punctual attendance. (b) Good conduct. (c) Progress in studies. (d) Profi-ciency in games, sports and co-curricular activities. (e) Service rendered for a noble cause. Forms of Prizes. (a) Books, (b) Merit Certificates, (c) Praise and Commendation, (d) Scholarships, (e) Badges, (f) Position of Honour in the Honour Boards.

General Principles

1. Rewards for efforts rather than attainments should be given.
2. Group rewards should be preferred to individual rewards.
3. Rewards should be of small intrinsic value. They should not appeal to material consideration.
4. They should be given immediately to the younger students.
5. They should be a few in number.
6. Rewards should be given also for the minor virtues of school conduct such as punctuality, regularity in attendance and personal cleanliness.

The students should be made to realize that rewards are given to them as tokens of good appreciation and they are meaningful only to this extent. What is more important is the formation of good habits and hard work and this pays them most in life.

We may close the discussion on punishments and rewards with the views of Secondary Education Commission, "No school can develop into an educative community, capable of releasing the student's creative capacities, if the teachers maintain a stiff, forbidding attitude towards their pupils and try to maintain their authority through various kinds of punishment whilst the pupils on their part, stand in awe of them, and are not prepared to share their problems and difficulties with them."

18

Physical Education

Locke's famous saying 'a sound mind in a school body' is true for all ages. Regarding the importance of health Ben Johnson has stated. "O Health! Health! the blessing of the rich! the riches of the poor! Who can buy thee at too dear a rate, since there is no enjoying this world without thee." Similarly Herbert Spencer writes, "The preservation of health is a duty few seem conscious that there is a thing physical morality." The Secondary Education Commission has greatly stressed the importance of physical well-being in these words, "The physical welfare of the youth of the country should be one of the main concerns of the State, and any departure from the normal standards of physical well-being at this period of life may have serious consequences." Health education should form all integral part of education.

Aims and Objectives

(i) To make the student realise the necessity of having good health.

(ii) To give information regarding health rules.

(iii) To develop health habits among children.

(iv) To develop certain skills concerning health, e.g. training in first aid, etc.

(v) To enable students to understand the educative value of sanitation, cleanliness and healthful living.

(vi) To develop a will to listen to rules relating to health and to observe them.

(vii) To develop better human relationship in matters concerning health.

(viii) To acquaint them with the causes and remedies of general diseases.

(ix) To influence parents and other adults to better health habits and attitudes through the health programme of schools and to make the school an effective agency for the promotion of the social aspects of health education in the family and community as well as the school itself.

Meaning of School Health Programme. According to a report of the Committee on Terminology in School Health Education in America, the school health programme is defined as "the school procedures that contribute to the maintenance and improvement of the health of pupils and school personnel including health services, healthful living and health education."

Scope of Health Education. School health education is a vital part of general education. It includes all such instruction that enlightens a student about activities and functions contributing to preservation, promotion and restoration of health. By means of a health education programme the spread of diseases in the school-going children can be checked and their eradication can also be attempted. A thorough knowledge of health rules underlines the needs of the study of anatomy and also the symptoms of common diseases of children. Practical knowledge of causes and diagnosis is equally essential. School health education also includes knowledge about the environment, equipments and routine of the schools as well.

Programme for Health

1. Health Appraisal or Medical Inspection.
2. Health Counselling and Follow-up.
3. Emergency Care in Schools.
4. Communicable Disease Control.
5. Identification and Education of the Handicapped Children.
6. Health of School Personnel.

Hygiene for All

Personal hygiene teaches the individual how to keep himself in health by paying attention to his cleanliness, exercise, rest and sleep, etc. The personal habits of an individual may be either important aids to the promotion of health and prolongation of life, or they may be powerful predisposing causes of disease. It is of the greatest importance to our well-being that we should form habits that are beneficial and not which as are hurtful to us.

Personal hygiene includes: -

1. Cleanliness of the hair, the teeth, the nails, the eyes, the ears, etc.
2. Sound habits of bodily exercise.
3. Adequate rest and sleep.
4. Periodic medical check up every six or twelve months so that any disease may be detected at its very beginning and be properly treated before it has taken root.

Medical Test

Systematic medical examination in one of the most important means of taking care of the physical well-being of the students. Although this system has been in existence for many years, it has failed to achieve the desired results.

The Secondary Education Commission has observed the following defects in the prevailing system:

(i) It is done in a very superficial manner.

(ii) The remedial measures suggested are often not carried out.

(iii) Follow up work is practically absent.

(iv) Effective cooperation has not been established between the parents and the school authorities.

The Recommendations

Medical inspection to be effective should be done in the following manner:

1. It should be thorough and comprehensive and should not be treated as a mere routine. It should not merely concern itself with the height, weight and chest measurements but should also concern itself with ears, teeth, eyes, nose, heart and lungs etc. In fact no-part of the body should be left unexamined as far as possible. The first inspection should be at the time of admission of the child in a school. If it is found out that the child is suffering from some chronic disease, he may be refused admission. Child should be examined every year. The last inspection will be just prior to leaving the school which reveals the strength and weakness of the child and helps him to choose some vocation suited to his physical development also.
2. Students with serious defects should be examined more frequently.
3. Remedial measures should be taken to remove defects.
4. Three copies of the report should be prepared. One should be sent to the parents, another should be kept by the teacher-in-charge and the third one should be kept by the medical officer.

A few words may be said regarding 'follow-up' work. It has been rightly stated that medical inspection is of little or no use unless proper 'follow-up' work is undertaken. In many cases, it does not call for any extra burden. A slight care of the child brings about good results. The parents and the teachers should cooperate. Immediate action should be taken after the medical inspection is over. When the parents are unable to take remedial steps due to poverty, school should take upon itself the responsibility of looking after the health of the child. The State may arrange mobile hospital ambulances for the purpose. "In any case such remedial measures as the school medical officer may suggest should be adopted, and the school authorities should see that they are carried out," thus remarks the Secondary Education Commission.

Apart from medical inspection by the physician, daily inspection of the general cleanliness of the child should be made by the teacher. This costs nothing and can be made in a few minutes.

School Staff and Health of the Students

Personal Cleanliness. The daily morning inspection of the cleanliness of the students by the teacher is very helpful in enforcing personal cleanliness. A rapid survey of the class should be made. Competition may be introduced among the students. Cleanliness chart may be prepared and marks allotted to them.

Development of Habits Regarding Air. Stress should be laid on the need of fresh air at all times and especially while sleeping. The students should be asked not to cover their mouth at night. They should be taught to breathe through their noses.

Training in First-aid Habits. The students should be instructed to give immediate attention to cuts and bruises.

Vaccination and Inoculation. At times of epidemics, precautionary measures should be suggested to them and they should be vaccinated and inoculated.

Development of Habits of Hygienic Feeding. The students should be taught to take right type of food in a suitable quantity. They should be warned of the dangers of over-eating. They should be asked not to take sour food. The students should be made to understand the importance of drinking plenty of water.

Selection of Suitable Physical Exercises. A variety of physical activity programmes should exist in a school so that the students may choose activities to their linking.

Formation of Good Classroom Habits. A wise teacher would always pay due attention to the postures of the students. The students may be instructed to keep pens and pencils out of mouth and to use handkerchiefs when coughing. Such other matters should be attended to.

Development of Better Human Relations in Matters Concerning Health. Every child should be asked to make it a point to do his best for the betterment of the health of his friends, relatives, neighbours and the whole community.

Medical Inspection and Follow-up Work. Medical examination should be thorough and the follow-up work taken seriously.

Particular Techniques

Apart from verbal talks, a good deal of health instruction can be imparted to the students in an interesting manner through the methods as suggested below:

Health Posters. Posters depicting washing of bodies, about various diseases like plague, malaria, etc., and about food, sleep and exercise etc., can be made and pasted on the school walls. Health authorities may be requested to supply these. Each poster should illustrate one idea only. Striking headings catch our attention. Students may be asked to help in preparing simple charts and posters.

Health Projects and Weeks. Once a year, a week may be set apart for the purpose of health education. Cleanliness campaigns in the school and locality go a long way in instilling ideas about health. Various committees of the students regarding different aspects of personal cleanliness, i.e. teeth, hair, nails, etc., may be formed. One teacher may serve as an adviser to each committee. The good posture committee should arrange posture competition and the participants should be asked to show proper posture. Prizes may be awarded to the best ones. Similarly, exercise competitions etc., may be arranged. Data regarding height, weight, chest measurements etc. may be collected by respective committees. Special lectures on general hygiene may be arranged. The Panchayat Health Department or the City Health Department, as the case may be, should be requested to help.

Health Book. Each student should be asked to maintain a health book. One important health rule should be pasted on the top of each page. Pictures illustrating certain health rules may be pasted in it. It should also contain his health records.

Healthy Environment. Attempts should be made to make classrooms and the school building very attractive and conducive to health. This has a direct bearing on the child. 'As is the environment, so is the individual'.

Film and Film Strips. Well-made health films and film strips are valuable in the teaching of health education.

Excursions. 'Seeing is believing' is a true saying. Excursions to good dispensaries, water-supply centres, etc., may be planned for health educational purposes.

Health Clubs. Like literary clubs, health clubs should be organised in schools. A definite weekly or monthly programme may be chalked out in coooperation with the school Red Cross Society. Debates and declamation contests on health matters may be arranged. Plays depicting health rules be staged.

Radio. Special programmes for children relating to health should be broadcast.

We may conclude by quoting the Secondary Education Commission, "This approach to the maintenance of school children's health may appear impracticable at first sight. But a clearer appreciation of the factors involved and a better coordination of the agencies concerned with the promotion of health will show that the adopting of such measures can produce tangible results within a reasonable time."

Health Counselling and Follow-up. The main aims of this service are :

1. Giving pupils the information about their health status as revealed by appraisal or medical inspection.
2. Acquainting parents with the significance of health problems and encouraging them to obtain needed care for their children.
3. Motivating pupils to seek and accept needed treatment.
4. Promoting each pupil's acceptance of responsibility for his own health in keeping with his stage of maturity.

Teachers, nurses and parents have to play an important role in the follow-up programme as actual improvement in the health of children depends more on follow-up than on any other school health activity.

Nutrition Problems

Importance of Nutritive and Balanced Diet. The quality and quantity of food taken by a person has an important bearing on his development. In fact nutritive and balanced diet provides the body with the required energy for doing everyday work.

Balanced Diet of a Normal and Healthy Person. The diet of a normal and healthy individual should consist of edibles in the following proportion:

Food Item	*Vegetarian Diet*	*Non-vegetarian Diet*
1. Bread	14 oz.	14 oz.
2. Milk	14 oz.	10 oz.
3. Vegetables without leaves	6 oz.	6 oz.
4. Vegetables with leaves	4 oz.	4 oz.
5. Meat and fish		3 oz.
6. Eggs		1 oz.
7. Cereal	3 oz.	2 oz.
8. Sugar	2 oz.	2 oz.
9. Fruits	2 oz.	2 oz.
10. Liquids	2 oz.	2 oz.
	47	46

Changes should be made in the above list according to the profession, body build, sex, age and climatic conditions.

Report of the Secondary Education Commission points out "At no period of life does malnutrition play such a large part in causing ill-health or in promoting defects of growth as in the periods of adolescence."

Lack of Sufficient and Proper Food. When a person does not get proper food according to his age and nature of work, his health is adversely affected and malnutrition is caused.

Defective Atmosphere. Lack of fresh air, sunlight, physical exercise and unhealthy situations of school building also lead to malnutrition.

Over Work. Over work also adversely affects health.

Lack of Sleep. Lack of sleep also proves harmful for health.

Irregular Meals. Irregular and untimely eaten meals cause indigestion, dyspesia and constipation.

Physical Conditions

(i) Bad postures.

(ii) Laziness.

(iii) Easily Fatigued.

(iv) Susceptibility to disease.

(v) Pale and charmless face.

(vi) Drowsiness weight.

(vii) Under-weight

Mental Conditions

(i) Gloomy nature.

(ii) Unenthusiasm.

(iii) Forgetful memory.

(iv) Lack of concentration.

(v) Slow comprehension.

(iv) Irritability.

Why School Meals. It is now generally recognized that in the wake of under-nutrition and malnutrition of the most of the Indian children, the school must take up the responsibility to make up this deficiency. This will not only assist in improving the health and physical development of the child but also assist him in making quicker and sounder progress in his studies because a child who is better-fed and healthier makes rapid progress. It is, therefore, essential that we must develop a universal programme of school meals as an integral part of its programme of universal, free and compulsory primary education.

Free Milk. With the help of United Nations International Children's Emergency Fund (UNICEF) which gave milk powder free of charge, milk was distributed to about 7 lakh primary school children.

Contents of Mid-day meals. The School Health Committee (1960) recommended that it should be based on cheap, nutritious and locally available foods. A menu may comprise a minimum of cereals and millet 2.5 oz.; pulses - 1 oz.; non-leafy vegetable - 1 oz.; oil-¼ oz. and condiment and salt.

Subsidy by the Government. The Committee recommended that the Government should support the school meal programme besides the contribution of the community at the rate of 50 per cent of the total cost.

Storage, Preparation and Distribution Arrangement. It must be stressed that food should be prepared and served under proper -hygienic conditions. There should be adequate storage facilities and also adequate space for feeding of children.

Assistance of the Central Government. In order to assist the development of the programme, the Government of India approved a centrally sponsored scheme of grand-in-aid to State Governments in 1962-63. Under this scheme, assistance is offered to State Governments to the extent of one-third of the total expenditure incurred by them in school feeding programmes.

Supply of Gift Food. The Mid-day Meals programme known as Nutritional Support to Primary Education was launched on August 15, 1995 on a nation-wide scale.

The Gestures

We can hardly ignore the seriousness of poor postures. It affects health, physical efficiency, mental attitude and appearance of an individual. Most of our diseases are the outcome of poor postures. A teacher can do much in the classroom work and physical instruction period to prevent bad postural habits in the students. As a result of poor postures says Dr. Mosher; "constipation, diarrhoea, flatulence, disturbance of the circulation, nervous irritability and, most marked of all fatigue out of proportion to the effort expended lessen the efficiency of the individual and often make life a burden." Some of the main defects of poor postures are given below:

(i) Interfere in the normal working of respiration, circulation and digestion.

(ii) Badly affect the eyesight.

(iii) Spoil handwriting because the students will not be able to hold the pen properly.

(iv) Lead to round shoulders and drooping body.

(v) Decrease physical efficiency and develop laziness.

(vi) Develop crooked bodies which are not normal in shape, and look very unpleasant.

(vii) Result in undesirable traits, e.g. timidness, lack of courage, etc.

The Reasons

(a) Weakness of the muscles which may be due to lack of exercise.

(b) Wrong postural habits due to lack of information regarding correct position.

(c) Defective desks and seats compelling the students to stretch or cramp their bodies.

(d) Wrong writing positions.

(e) Wrong reading positions.

(f) Defective eyesight.

(g) Defective hearing.

(h) Illegible writing of the teacher on the blackboard.

(i) Wrong postures of the teachers leading to depressing effects on the students.

(j) Illness of the students.

(k) Wrong type of dress of the students.

Various Categories

(i) Standing postures.

(ii) Sitting postures.

(iii) Writing postures.

(iv) Reading postures.

(v) Walking postures.

Corrective Measures

(i) The student should be asked to take regular exercise to strengthen muscles.

(ii) Suitable furniture should be provided.

(iii) Good postural habits should be developed. The students should be told that the head, neck, trunk, thigh and legs are in a straight line in a good standing posture. While writing, the students should be asked to keep their note-books at a distance of one foot. While reading, the books should be held vertically so that the top and the bottom of the books are at an equal distance from the eyes. The distance of 12 inches is an ideal one.

(iv) Stools should be provided for smaller children so that they may learn to sit without reclining against the chair.

(v) Suitable corrective postural exercises should be recommended to the students.

(vi) Students having defective eyesight and hearing should be seated on the front benches.

(vii) Rooms should be suitably ventilated and sufficient accommodation should be provided.

(viii) Bold type books should be selected.

(ix) The aid of school medical officer should be sought.

Health Services

Causes of Infectious Diseases. These are caused by germs which are organisms that are either invisible or visible only under a very powerful microscope. They invade the body and multiply rapidly. The poisons manufactured by the germs circulate in the blood and give rise to symptoms of particular diseases. Germs are carried from one person to another and the diseases spread. Germs can be carried by flies and other insects, human beings, articles used by the infected person and public conveniences.

Prevention of Infectious Diseases. The following steps should be taken to prevent the spread of the disease.

Notification. The health officer or the municipal committee should be informed at once when a case of infectious disease occurs in the home.

Isolation. The patient should be separated from healthy individuals.

Quarantine. Neighbours and relatives of the patient and all those people who have come in contact with the patient should be separated for a specific length of time, equal to the incubation period of the disease.

Disinfection and Preventive Measures. Disinfectants are agents that destroy germs. Some of the chemical disinfectants are lysol, potassium permanganate, carbolic acid, iodine, phenyl, sulphur dioxide, formaldehyde, etc. Heat and sunlight are natural disinfectants.

Education. Public should be educated about the disease—how it is spread, how to prevent it and what steps they should take to control its spread.

Stages of Diseases. There are three distinct stages in every disease caused by germs. (i) The incubation stage. (ii) The acute stage of the disease. (iii) Convalescence.

Description of Various Diseases

Disease	Incubation period	Symptoms	Affected Age	Precaution to be taken in the School
1. Measles	One or two weeks	Cold, rise in temperature, reddish rash on the body	Usually before 10 years of age	1. Consultation of the doctor 2. Sending the child home 3. The child to be kept away from school for at least 3 weeks.
2. Mumps	14 to 28 days	Swelling from ear to ear, painful eating	Common among school children	Child to be separated from the school for about 20 days.
3. Whooping cough	6 to 18 days	Common cold	Childhood before 5	Send the child home for at least two months.
4. Diphtheria	2 to 10 days	White patches on the soft palate, tonsils and throat.	Before 2 or 3 years of age	Until the child gets cured, he should not be allowed to attend school.
5. Chicken Pox	11 to 19 days	Rashes consisting of red spots, blisters, scabs	Generally upto 12 years of age.	1. Student to be sent home 2. Student not to be allowed to attend school for about3 weeks.

Contd.

6.	Small Pox	10 to 15 days	Severe headache, backache,high fever	All ages	1. Vaccination 2. Student to be sent home.
7.	Influenza	A few hours to a few days	Pain in the head, back and limbs, shivering, rise in temperature, running of eyes and nose, sneezing and coughing.	Children and Adults	1. Students to be advised not to visit crowdy places. 2. Use of handker-chief 3. Students to be sepa-rated from the school.
8.	Cholera	A few hours to a few days	Severe pain in the abdomen, vomiting, diarrhoea.	All ages	Cleanliness of urinals and lavatories.
9.	Typhoid	12 to 15 days	Severe headache and vomiting, high temperature	All ages	1. Inoculation 2. Cleanliness and disin-fection.
10.	Malaria	7 to 21 days	High fever, shivering	All ages	1. Boiled water to be arranged. 2. Less eating.

First Aid. First Aid is the immediate and temporary care given to the victim of an accident or sudden illness. Its purpose is to preserve life, assist recovery and prevent aggravation of the condition, until the services of a doctor can be obtained, or during transport to hospital or the casualty's home.

The First Aider's responsibilities end as soon as medical aid is available; but he should stand by after making his report to the Doctor in case he can be of further assistance.

First Aid Equipments

Set of splints with metal connections	6-inch kidney basin Dressings forceps
Splint straps for securing splints in lieu of bandages	Note-book and pencil Torch, electric (with spare battery)
Triangular bandages	
1-inch roller bandages	Small size prepared sterile dressings
2-inch roller bandages	
3-inch roller bandages	Medium size prepared sterile dressings
1/2 oz. packets of cotton-wool	
1/2 oz. packets of lint or gauze, plain white	Large size prepared sterile dressings
Grey (unbleached) wool (for padding)	Glucose sweets or lump sugar Assorted adhesive wool dressings
Adhesive plaster, 1/2 inch 5 yards	Constrictive bandage (rubber)
Scissors, 5-inch, blunt pointed	Small square of mackintosh
Medicine glass, graduated, or	or plastic sheeting bake lite measure
Safety-pins (assorted, rust-proof, in box)	Sal volatile or smelling salts (the latter if no water is carried)

First Aid is definitely limited to the assistance rendered at the time of emergency with such material as may be available. It is not intended that the First Aider should take the place of the Doctor and it must be clearly understood that the redressing of injuries and other such after-treatment are outside the scope of First Aid.

The Origin. The term "First Aid" was adopted officially in England for the first time in 1879 by the St. John Ambulance Association. The expression "First Aider" was not coined till 1894 and was intended to designate any person who has received a certificate from an authorised association that he (or she) is qualified to render first hand.

The originator of First Aid was Esmarch (1823-1908). He was born in Schleswing Holstein, became a distinguished surgeon and was appointed Surgeon General in the German Army on the outbreak of the Franco- Prussian War. Later he was appointed Consulting Surgeon to the large military hospital near Berlin and was recognised as one of the greatest authorities on hospital management and military surgery. However, no part of his work was more widely valued than his two manuals, entitled First Aid on the Battlefield and First Aid to the Injured. The triangular bandage was invented in 1831 by Dr. Mayor of Lausanne, Switzerland, but was later popularised by Esmarch.

Management of the Case

1. Respond quickly to calls for assistance.
2. Give artificial respiration if breathing has stopped - every second counts.
3. Stop any bleeding.
4. Guard against or treat for shock by moving the casualty as little as possible and handling him gently.
5. Do not attempt too much – do the minimum that is essential to save life and prevent the condition from worsening.
6. Reassure the casualty and those around and so help to lessen anxiety.
7. Do not allow people to crowd round as fresh air is essential.
8. Do not remove clothes unnecessarily.
9. Arrange for the removal of the casualty to the care of a Doctor or hospital as soon as possible.

Every school should establish a school clinic to look after the health of the pupils and for the treatment of minor diseases. Several schools in a town may combine and set up a dispensary under the charge of a qualified medical officer.

Medical examination should be conducted free of charge. In case any teacher finds, a student suffering from some disease, he should report it to the doctor and ensure that the treatment at the clinic is carried out. Parents of the student should be informed accordingly.

Medical Service. An efficient school medical service is now regarded as an essential part of the public system of education in all progressive countries of the world. In India the problem has acquired all the more importance in view of the poverty of the masses and low hygienic standards.

Health Service Agencies. The health service can be provided by means of:

(i) School Medical under the charge of a school medical officer.

(ii) School Dispensary or clinic.

(iii) Red Cross units.

(iv) Physical education department.

Programme of Health Service. This will consist of:

(i) Medical inspection of the students.

(ii) Maintaining records of medical inspection and health of the pupils.

(iii) Sending notices to parents regarding the physical health of the pupils.

(iv) Clinical treatment of students who suffer from some diseases.

(v) Recording of history and defects regarding special cases.

(vi) Follow-up work regarding medical inspection.

(vii) Provision of mid-day meals.

(viii) Attending to the healthful school conditions.

Importance of Mental Health. There are laws of mental health just as there are laws of bodily health. Any disregard of these rules leads to mental disorders and conflicts which ultimately lead to misery and unhappiness. It is of paramount importance to give due recognition to mental laws which result in healthy mind.

What Constitutes a Healthy Mind?

(a) Cheerful and optimistic outlook.

(b) Well-regulated instincts or habits.

(c) Well-regulated and energetic will.

(d) Normal appetite.

(e) Normal sex-consciousness.

(f) Healthy philosophy of life.

(g) Free from prejudice.

(h) Calmness.

(i) Good temper.

(j) Receptivity to new ideas.

Mental Disorders

(a) Irritability.

(b) Depressed and pessimistic outlook.

(c) Abnormal interest in sex.

(d) Lack of courage.

(e) Full of prejudice.

(f) Easily embarrassed in the presence of others.

(g) Low intelligence.

(h) Undeveloped habits and will.

(i) Bad temper.

(j) Undue anxiety.

(k) Moodiness.

It is a matter of great relief that our educationists have begun to realise the importance of mental health. 'Feeling of insecurity' and the 'feeling of inferiority' are the two great enemies of mental health. A knowledge of mental hygiene helps us to kill these two demons. A psychological approach is needed. Our attempts should be to provide suitable emotional, physical and intellectual environments in which a child may have the 'feeling of security' and the 'feeling of equality'. He should feel that his personality is respected and is given a suitable place.

Close Pupil-Teacher Contacts. The teacher should carefully observe the child in and outside the school and should know the child and his home conditions. This will develop the feeling of 'oneness' in the mind of the child who feels that the teacher is interested in his welfare.

Favourable Home and School Environment. Unfavourable home and school environment leads to mental disorders. Parents should be guided to adopt good methods of upbringing. The child should be free from unsatisfactory family relationships and strict discipline. Treatment by the parents should be just and impartial. Too much fondling may also lead to emotional maladjustment. The treatment of the teachers should be just and fair.

Medical Examination. There should be provision for the medical examination in schools and remedial measures be adopted to safeguard the health of the child. Defective physique becomes a contributory factor of mental disorders. Cases requiring special treatment should be sent to child guidance clinics.

Intellectual Life of the School. Sound methods of teaching suited to the individual needs of the child should be adopted. Activity Method, e.g. Play-way, Project Method, etc., should be encouraged. Audio-visual aids develop interest in the lesson. Special time and attention is to be devoted to weak students.

Provision of Educational and Vocational Guidance Centres. Schools should start such centres. It is not necessary to appoint psychologists in schools. Trained teachers may be asked to undergo short educational and vocational guidance courses and the work of guidance be entrusted to them. For specially difficult cases, intelligence, aptitude cnd personality tests be conducted.

Provision of Co-curricular Activities. Properly planned activities are very helpful in providing much needed and useful training in civic sense. Sublimation of instincts is also achieved.

Freedom and Self-discipline. Unnecessary rules and regulations greatly upset the mental equilibrium of the child. A child who breathes in an atmosphere of freedom develops initiative and courage. Severe punishments result in mental retardation. Let us be wise and remember the useful words of Hobbes, "The fool cannot be mended by flogging, and he who flogs is the greatest fool." Hence the right approach would be to give freedom to the child. A.S. Neill says, "We could abolish caning by an act of Parliament, but no act of Parliament can abolish the fear of teacher or a system."

Teacher's Mental Hygiene and His Dynamic Personality. The teachers should be mentally alert to develop mental alertness in the students. They should be painstaking, sympathetic, appreciative and trusting. They should not have any prejudice which may have an adverse effect on the emotional and intellectual conditions of children. They should have always higher ideals of life before them.

Report of the School Health Committee

The School Health Committee was appointed by the Government of India in February 1960 under the chairmanship of Shrimati Renuka Ray to assess the standard of health and nutrition of school children and suggest ways and means of improving them.

Terms of Reference : (a) To examine the present position of school health programme in the country in all its aspects (excluding physical education, games and sports), e.g. prevention of diseases, medical care and follow-up service, nutrition, health, education, healthy environment, etc. of the students at all stages of education and to suggest : (i) further survey of studies if required; and (ii) how the work of various agencies such as medical, social and welfare associations can be coordinated to assist in the promotion of health of school children.

(b) To examine studies and surveys so far made to assess the nutritional standard of school children and to indicate : (i) further survey of studies needed in any specific areas; (ii) to give concrete suggestions to institute appropriate measures to improve standards of nutrition among school children recommending, inter alia, ways and means for financing and organising such a programme.

(c) To examine and recommend the possibility of entrusting Primary Health Centres and other organisations for conducting a comprehensive and realistic school health programme in association with the local education administration. The recommendation should include measures to develop an effective school medical service suitable to the country.

(d) To examine the present facilities available for promoting nutritional standards of pre-school children and to suggest practical measures to improve the present position.

School Health Services : (1) All children should be provided with school health services. However, with the limited resources available at present, school health services may be made available to primary school children, i.e. children between 6-11 years.

(2) The functions of the school health services should be the provision of health measures both preventive and curative. These should include the detection and treatment of defects and the creation and maintenance of a hygienic environment in and around the school.

(3) All newly admitted children should have medical examination first and then again after four years, as the limited facilities available at present do not permit medical examination at frequent intervals.

(4) Prevention and control of communicable diseases in schools should be the responsibility of public health authorities.

(5) Emphasis should be laid on compulsory primary and revaccination against smallpox immediately. Immunization against diphtheria, whooping cough and tetanus should be made compulsory in the immediate future.

(6) With adequate training in health education and school health services, it should be possible for the teacher to undertake certain functions connected with school health services such as : (a) observation of children with a view to spot out any deviations from normal health; (b) recording of height and weight and simple testing of vision and hearing; (c) maintaining of health records of children; and (d) giving first-aid.

(7) During the Fourth Plan period, school health services should be provided to : (a) all children in the age-group 6-11 in rural and urban areas; and (b) the children of middle and high schools in areas where facilities exist.

School Meal: (1) The primary aim of the school meal programme should be to improve health and encourage sound dietary habits among children.

(2) The school meal should be based on cheap nutritions and locally available foods. A sample menu may comprise a minimum of: cereals and millet :- 2.5 oz. : pulses 1 oz. : non-leafy vegetables 1 oz. : oil - 1/4: and condiments and salt.

(3) Every school should be provided with protected water supply and facilities for drainage; sanitary environment; facilities for storage; preparation and distribution of food; adequate space for feeding of children; and sanitary disposal of garbage.

(4) It is necessary that the Government should support the school meal programme besides the contribution of the community at the rate of 50 per cent of the total cost.

Pre-school Child : (1) A comprehensive health and welfare service for pre-school children should be introduced.

(2) Services of 'Balwadis', 'Mahila Samitis', maternity and child welfare centres, health centres, clinics and nursery schools, the pre-primary schools, pediatric centres of hospitals and social welfare and similar organisations should be utilised for the distribution of milk to pre-school children.

School Health Education : (1) Health education should be included as a part of general education in the primary, middle and secondary schools.

(2) The State Administration should take immediate steps to publish text-books on health education and to have health lessons included in other appropriate text-books.

Training, Studies and Research : (1) In teacher training programmes, health education and school health should be a required part of training. The teacher should have the knowledge of the growth and development of children, personal health, community health, school health practices and methods of health education.

(2) For the teachers who are already in service, special short term courses should be organised by the local school organisations with the technical assistance from the health personnel.

(3) Future school health and school meal policies and programmes should be developed from the results obtained through scientific surveys and studies. Studies and research are quite essential for making school health programme efficient, effective and economical.

School Environment : (1) School buildings should be simple, safe, attractive and sanitary.

(2) Every school building in urban areas, where public water supply is available, should have water supply connection and adequate number of taps. In rural areas, an independent water supply system is desirable for each school.

(3) In urban areas wherever drainage facilities exist, these should be extended to all schools. In rural areas, drains should be constructed for the removal of waste water.

(4) The sale of food by hawkers in and around the school should be prohibited.

School Health Administration : (1) At the Centre, there should be National School Health Council. Such a Council will facilitate cooperation and coordination of many individuals and groups that are concerned with the health of the children.

(2) Each State should have a State Council of School Health. The Director of Education and the Director of Health Services should alternatively be Secretary and Joint Secretary of the Council.

(3) At district level, School Health and School Meal Committees should be set up as sub-committees of the District Development Councils.

(4) The district health and education organisations should be strengthened appropriately to plan, implement and supervise this additional work.

19

Education for Health

The Significance

"The physical welfare of the youth of the country should be one of the main concerns of the State and any departure from the normal standards of physical well-being at this period of life may have serious consequences," observed the Secondary Education Commission.

Hall has very emphatically observed, "A ton of knowledge bought at the expense of an ounce of health which is the most ancient and precious form of wealth costs more than its value."

Similar views have been expressed by Carlyle when he writes, "We manufacture clever devils by the thousand because health is not the object of party politics."

Our great saint Swami Vivekananda has also stressed the importance of well-built bodies when he remarks, "What India needs today is not the Bhagwad Gita but the football field." Our Indian schools must give due importance to this aspect of education. There is a great need of a general philosophy of physical education in India, though it appears to be a very strange in a country famous for ancient Yogic system. There is no denying the fact that of late we have been ignoring this side. This has led W.M. Ryburn to remark, "We need in Indian education a general physical education – a conception of education in which physical education takes its rightful place and in which its vital importance is recognised."

Regarding the significance of physical education, H.C. Buck has observed that a properly directed physical education should result in health, happiness, efficiency and character.

Froebel says, "If we wish to develop the whole being, we must exercise the whole human being."

Rousseau states, "It is the sound constitution of the body, that makes the operation of the mind easy and certain."

Spencer is of the view, "To be a good animal is the first requisite to success in the life and to be a nation of good animals is the first condition to national prosperity."

Montague writes, "physical education does neither train up the soul, nor body but the whole man."

Meaning and Concept. In the words of C.L. Brownwell, "Physical education is concerned with strength and endurance (the principal objectives of physical training). But physical education regards these qualities as a means to an end – the means of obtaining greater satisfaction in a specific activity, and the end which represents the all-round educational development associated with participation in the activity. In short, physical education means the physical activities that have characterised the immemorial history of mankind."

According to Delbert Obertenffer, "Physical education is the sum of those experiences which come to the individual through movement."

Jesse Feiring Williams thinks, "Physical education is the sum of man's physical activities selected as to kind and conducted as to outcomes."

In the words of Jay B. Nash, "physical education is that field of education which deals with big muscle activities and their related responses."

"Physical education is an integral part of the total education process and has as its aim the development of physically, mentally, emotionally and socially fit citizens through the medium of physical activities which have been selected with a view to realizing these outcomes."

- Charles A. Bucher.

"Physical education is the social process of change in the behaviour of the human organism, originating primarily from the stimulus of social big-muscle-play and related activities."

- C.C. Cowell.

"Physical education is that phase of education which is concerned, first, with the organization and leadership of children in big muscle activities, to gain the development and adjustment inherent in the activities according to social standards, and second with the leadership of the activities so that the educational process may go on without growth handicaps."

- Clark, W. Hetherington.

"Physical education should be defined as that phase of the whole process of education which is concerned with vigorous muscular activities and related responses and with the modifications in the individual resultant from these responses."

- Nixon and Cozens.

"Physical education is that part of education which proceeds by means of, or predominantly through physical activity, it is not some separate , partially related field."

- Edward F. Voltmer, Arthur A. Esslingor.

"Physical education is but one aspect of the larger problem of education in general, and any system which divorces or tends to divorce, the physical from the moral and intellectual aspects of life, is thoroughly unsound."

The Secondary Education Commission made it clear "that unless physical education is accepted as an integral part of education, and the educational authorities recognize its need in all schools, the youth of the country, which forms its most valuable asset, will never be able to pull their full weight in national welfare". The old concept of physical education as 'mere drill or a series of regulated exercises' has been rejected. "It includes all forms of physical activities and games which promote the development of the body and mind." The Commission recommended that physical education should be comprehensive enough to include all aspects of health education; full records of physical activities should be maintained; teachers of physical education should be given the same status as other teachers of similar qualifications; and other teachers of the school along with the physical instructor should actively participate in the physical activities of students. Regarding health education, the Commission emphasized the need for a properly organized school medical service in all States, and a thorough medical examination of all pupils with follow-up and treatment where necessary.

The Education Commission (1964-66) points out: 'There has been a tendency in recent government schemes of physical education to emphasize only the physical fitness value of physical education and ignore its educational value.' The concept of physical education has been made broader, as it should contribute 'not only to physical fitness but also to physical efficiency, mental alertness and the development of certain qualities – perseverance, team spirit, leadership, obedience to rules, moderation in victory and balance in defeat.' The Commission was aware of the hard realities which one encounters while preparing programmes of physical education in schools and colleges, and, therefore, it suggested that the programmes 'should take into account not only what is useful but also what is possible in view of limitations of facilities, time and number of teachers.' It also emphasized the need for re-examining and re-designing the programmes of physical education in the light of certain basic principles of child growth and development.

From the views expressed above it will be obvious that physical education is not only concerned with helping the child to grow and develop physically but learning to fit in with his social environment and adjusting to life around, acquiring the capacity to be mentally alert to all environmental responses, expressing emotions without prejudice to others and otherwise reaching his maturity progressively.

Aims and Objectives

(i) Conservation of health.

(ii) Development of well-built bodies.

(iii) Development of qualities like endurance, self-control, courage, etc.

(iv) Development of qualities relating to society, e.g. obedience, cooperation, leadership and followership, etc.

(v) Development of regular habits of exercise and play.

(vi) Development of regular health habits.

(vii) Development of the whole man. Montague rightly remarks, "Physical education does neither train up the soul nor body, but the whole man." Froebel aptly stated, "Early education must deal directly with the physical development and influence the spiritual development through the exercise of senses."

Various Schemes

The types of activities considered essential are as under :

Developmental Activities

(i) Exercise tables, 'dands', 'baithaks' and yogic exercises.

(ii) Fundamental movements such as walking, running, throwing, jumping, climbing and balancing.

(iii) Mimetics and story plays.

(iv) Stunts, pyramids, weight and conditioning exercises.

Rhythmics

Rhythm fundamentals, rhythm games, folk dances, social dances, singing games, community singing, Indian rhythmics, 'garha', 'phugdi', 'himma', 'tipri', etc.

Games, Sports, and Athletics

(i) Major Games, such as 'kabaddi', 'kho-kho', volleyball, basketball, football, hockey, cricket etc.

(ii) Dual games such as tennis, table tennis, badminton, ring-tennis, etc.

(iii) Recreative games, minor games, relays, social games, group games, lead-up games, etc.

Sports : Cycling, canoeing, shooting, riding, skating etc.

Athletics : Running, jumping, throwing, walking and relays.

Formal Activities

Drill and marching, light apparatus, calisthenics, mass P.T. exercises.

Apparatus. Parallel bars, vaulting, beam, roman rings, ropes, pommel horse, single bar, 'malkhamb', etc.

Combatives. Wrestling, boxing, judo, lathi fight, dagger fight, farigadga, sword fight, simple contests and mass combatives based on 'attack and defence'.

Aquatics. Swimming, diving and life saving.

Self-testing Activities. All types of tests.

Camping and Outdoor Activities. Hiking, cross country, camping and mountaineering, picnics, excursions etc.

Special Activities. Demonstrations, ceremonial parades, singing the National Anthem, flag salutations, practical projects, citizenship training etc.

Basic Rules

Psychological and physiological principles form the bases of physical education and it is but obvious that physical education should include activities pertaining to these principles. Following points should be borne in mind while organising a programme of physical education :

(i) Undue emphasis should not be given to those physical activities which primarily develop strength of muscles.

(ii) Activities which are suitable for the different age groups should be provided. The children should not be judged by adult standards.

(iii) Too much emphasis shall not be laid on inter-school competitions. A large number of students should be encouraged to participate in various physical activities.

(iv) Classroom physical activities should be encouraged.

(v) Physical activities pertaining to the cleanliness of the school should be organised off and on.

Physical education is not merely to be confined to the play-ground but should pervade the classroom. Physical education in the classroom may take the following forms:

(a) Direct instruction emphasising the necessity of having a good physique.

(b) Suggestions regarding the maintenance of good health.

(c) Emphasis on right postures.

(d) Provision of good seating and lighting arrangements in the classroom, thereby impressing upon the students the importance of studying under healthy surroundings.

(e) Providing ample opportunities to the children for physical activity.

The last point requires elucidation. It should be borne in mind that physical development and mental development are inseparably allied to each other. Classroom should not be devoid of physical activity. Instruction in a play-way manner affords ample opportunities to the students to be physically active and a wise teacher would always bring this spirit of play-way in class-room work. The students should play an active role in the instruction work. They should not remain merely as passive listeners. For pre-primary classes, Kindergarten and Montessori methods afford opportunities for the physical development of the children. Basic system of education is based on the principle of learning by doing. This involves many physical activities. Project Method and the Dalton Plan are the other examples which require many activities on the part of children. Paper cutting and folding may be associated with Elementary Geometry and Arithmetic. Students may learn Nature Study and Geography with the help of clay modelling. A variety of programmes may be introduced in the classroom. Reading, writing, figuring, drawing, etc. should be profitably attempted to provide practical activities. A few minutes drill or music after every lesson of the class may introduce bodily activity among the children.

We may sum up by quoting J.F. Williams, "Of all the activities of school curriculum, none is as rich with educational outcomes as the plays, games, sports and athletics of physical education."

Physical Fitness

Gymnastics and athletics are two important forms of physical education.

The chief aim of athletics is recreation. Gymnastics on the other hand stimulate normal physical development, promote good carriage and secure general efficiency in the individual. The effect of gymnastic exercises is internal and primary. They are based on sound principles. Each exercise has its own value for a specific purpose. Gymnastic exercises are very helpful in teaching correct postures. Gymnastic exercises with apparatus (Bars, Horse, Ladder etc.) are greatly liked by the boys as these involve a great degree of skill and difficulties. Gymnastic exercises like marching, easy exercises in jumping and skipping, aesthetic dancing and folk dancing appeal to the girls.

Athletic activities include running, jumping, disc throwing, hammer throwing and weight throwing, etc.

In carrying out gymnastics, the following points should be taken into consideration :

1. Lessons and exercises should be purposive and not at random.
2. A shirt and shorts are sufficient.
3. The postures should be good.
4. The boys should not be held in a straight position for a long time.
5. The gymnastic exercises should be correlated with material and play.
6. All material should be kept in order.

Modern educationists believe in freedom of children. They dislike every sort of compulsion as they think that the element of compulsion robs the child of the enjoyment which he would otherwise derive.

A child derives immense pleasure in free play. He wants to choose games and other kinds of activities according to his interest. He does not like that any time limit should be imposed on him while he is at play. Free play has direct appeal to his natural urges and it satisfies his psychological needs. "Play is a biological and social necessity for children. It is the most fundamental thing about a child - play for the child is one of the most serious facts of life; it is a form of work for the young, and the basis for all natural education," writes Davie.

It is in the nature of the child to play. He is interested in it from the very birth. Stern defines play as "voluntary self-constrained activity". The values of play may be classified as under:

(a) Educational. (b) Intellectual. (c) Physical. (d) Social. (e) Emotional. (f) Developmental.

Physical Drill. Physical drill should be organised regularly. It should be properly graded, 'simple to complex' and 'easy to difficult' should form the basis of physical drill. Violent exercises may lead to heart strain. The duration of the period should depend upon the age and strength of the pupils. A good system of physical exercises would give beneficially exercise to all parts of the body, e.g. muscles, legs, neck, trunk etc. Following types of exercises will make the programme interesting and instructive :

(i) Preparing or warming up, running in a circle, marching, etc.

(ii) Corrective exercises.

(iii) Educative exercises.

(iv) Recreative exercises.

(v) Physiological exercises.

The playground is said to be the cradle of democracy. Various co-curricular activities and especially the games and sports contribute a lot for the development of all the major qualities needed to be an ideal citizen.

Games Teach Cooperation. Team work is the pivot round which the wheel of games revolves. If the members of the team do not work for the team but for their individual distinctions, the team is sure to go to the walls. Games and sports bring home this fact to the students that loyalty and cooperation are the important contributory factors for the honour of the team. These serve to eliminate selfishness and teach the students to subordinate their own interests for the sake of a broader aim of winning the game. This lesson is very important and every citizen is expected to follow it:

Preparation for Life Situations. The players have to play sometimes against heavy odds. Courage, patience, steadfastness and perseverance are needed to play well and effectively. The players get accustomed to face very critical situations and this stands in good stead when they enter life. We cannot think of an ideal citizen without possessing these qualities.

Providing Opportunities for Leadership. Games and sports provide opportunities for leadership of a very high order. The captain of the team has to put right players at their right places and has to bring harmony among the different members of the team. Only a man of self-confidence, imagination and enterprise can lead others.

Development of Various Senses. The games and sports call for a variety of movements—physical and mental. "School games involve a wide range of activity. Most of the senses are called into action. Comparison and judgement are needed," says William Gowers. The mind has to be kept alert to meet the changing situation to the ball. Body and mind work in harmony.

Physical Development. Games and sports promote good health, which is perhaps more important than wealth. Good health is also a sign of a good citizen.

Emphasis on Struggle. They teach the lesson that struggle is more important than success. Baron de Conbertin states, "The important thing in sports is not to win but to take part. The important thing in life is not triumph but struggle. The essential thing is not to have conquered but to have fought well. To spread these precepts is to build up a stronger and more scrupulous and more generous humanity."

Satisfaction of Various Urges of Children. Games satisfy one of the important urges of the children. Play is a biological and social necessity for the children. It is the most fundamental thing about a child - play for the child is one of the most serious facts of life; it is a form of work for the young and the basis for all education.

Development of Esprit de Corps. Tournaments develop in the minds of the students love for the school. 'We feeling' comes to the forefront. Tournaments if properly conducted help in developing the idea of corporate life in the minds of students. The players play for their respective schools and the other students of the respective schools cheer up. How thrilling it is to witness the students clapping and encouraging the players of their sides! The love for the institution is clearly manifested in the minds of the students.

Tournaments are of great help in raising the standard of sports of different institutions.

However, a few objections have been raised to the inter-school tournaments : (1) They benefit too few students, (2) They are expensive in time and money, (3) They cause physical injuries, (4) They cause emotional injuries, (5) They foster over-speciali-zation, (6) They encourage professionalism and commercialism, (7) They give rise to unsocial feelings, (8) They develop poor sportsmanship.

"To suffer defeat cheerfully and not to burst into rowdyism or even resort to discourtesy, to do one's best against odds and not to lose heart, to be fair to the opponent and not to take any mean advantage of him, to play on equal and honourable terms for the sake of play and not try to win by hook and crook, in short to love the game above the prize, this is the spirit which should prevail in these inter-school tournaments."

Profitable Use or Leisure Time. Leisure time is utilised in a very profitable way and thus these games fulfil another function of education.

Training in Character. Lastly they afford a valuable training in character. Gandhiji has stated, "What is education without character?" Similarly, we ask, "What is character without self-control, courage, steadfastness, perseverance, obedience, morality, nobility and health?" For promoting all these qualities of character, games and sports are very potent and effective.

A glance over the educative values of these games and sports is apt to lead to the conclusion that playground is another school and its function is equally important.

There is no rose without a thorn. If we are not cautious enough to pluck a rose, thorn is sure to prick us. In the same way if games and sports are not scientifically planned they may do more harm than good.

We may sum up the importance of games and sports with a quotation from Aldous Huxley. "Like every other instrument that man has invented, sport can be used either for good or evil purpose. Used well, it can teach endurance and courage, a sense of fair play and a respect for rules, coordinated effort and the subordination of personal interest to those of the group. Used badly it can encourage personal vanity and group vanity, greedy desire for victory and hatred for rivals, an intolerant 'esprit de corps' and contempt for people who are beyond a certain arbitrarily selected pole. In either case sport inculcates responsible cooperation."

Games and Sports

(a) Keeping in view the different needs of children, a variety of games should be provided.

(b) Every child should be induced to take part in one or the other game. Our motto should be 'Games for All'.

(c) Every team should consist of members having more or less the same skill.

(d) Games time-table should be framed. Regular time should be given to the games.

(e) Indian as well as western games should find a place.

(f) Supervision of games by the teachers is very essential to have their benefits. 'Unsupervised playgrounds often become hot bed of vice.'

(g) The attainments of the students in this field should be mentioned in their progress cards.

(h) The teaching periods of those teachers who conduct games should be lessened.

(i) Games fund should not be spent on a few selected stars.

(j) Tournaments should be organised off and on.

(k) Winning of trophies should not become the end and be all of activities.

Recommendations of the Secondary Education Commission

1. Physical activities should be made to suit the individual and his capacity for physical endurance.
2. All teachers below the age of 40 should actively participate in many of the physical activities of students and thus make them a lively part of the school programme.
3. Full records of physical activities of the students must be maintained.
4. The training in physical education should be comprehensive enough to include all aspects of health education.
5. The teachers of physical education should be associated with the teaching of subjects like Physiology and Hygiene and given the same status as other teachers of similar qualifications.
6. The existing facilities for training of teachers of physical education should be expanded by increasing the seats in the existing colleges, by opening new colleges where necessary and by recognising some of the institutions as All India Training Centres to which aid may be given both by the Centre and the States.

Recommendations of the All India Seminar

The All India Seminar was held at Mahabaleshwar from 16th to 30th May, 1958 under the chairmanship of Shri D.G. Wakharkar. Inter alia, the seminar made certain recommendations regarding physical education at the school level. Among the important recommendations are :

1. Physical education should be a curricular subject in the schools at all levels and should be on par with other subjects.

2. The programme of physical education and recreation should cater to the needs, interests and capacities of the pupils, and should have 'carry over' value. It should promote normal growth and development, maintenance of health, acquisition of skills and desirable social attitudes and behaviour.
3. Leadership in the field of physical education should consist of (a) qualified staff, (b) specialist coaches, and (c) student leaders.
4. Any of the following qualifications should be considered as approved qualification for a person to work as a physical education teacher in a secondary school : (a) A Degree in Physical Education; (b) A University Degree with a Diploma in Physical Education; (c) A pass in Intermediate or its equivalent with a Certificate in Physical Education; (d) A pass in Matric or S.S.L.C. or S.S.C. or S.F. Examination with a Certificate in Physical Education.
5. In primary schools, classroom teachers should teach physical education.
6. Periodical refresher courses should be organised for in-service physical education teachers.
7. Special coaching camps should be conducted for school physical education teachers at Government cost.
8. Playgrounds should be provided by schools as laid down in the National Plan of Physical Education and Recreation. Schools may, however, have playgrounds with the following minimum limits:

Category	Boys	Girls
(a) High Schools	5 acres	3 acres
(b) Middle Schools	3 acres	2 acres
(c) Primary Schools	½ to 1 acre	½ to 1 acre

9. Schools having excess open space may be required to permit the use of such open space by the neighbouring schools.

10. Each school should have an indoor gymnasium with the dimensions of 60' x 15'.

11. Schools should provide daily one period for physical education in the time table.

12. The syllabus given in the National Plan of Physical Education and Recreation should be followed in all schools with suitable modifications wherever necessary.

13. Medical inspection should be compulsory for all pupils.

Supervision of Health, Physical Education and Recreation in Schools : In order to make supervision serve its purposefully, the following staff may be provided in each state :

(i) Deputy Director of Education for Physical Education and Recreation;

(ii) Two State Physical Education Officers for men's branch and women's branch separately;

(iii) Regional or Divisional Physical Education Officers (Men's and Women's branches separately), each in charge of a unit of about four District Physical Education Officers;

(iv) District Physical Education Officers (Men's and Women's branches separately), each in charge of about 50 high schools.

Report of the Ad Hoc Enquiry Committee on Games and Sports

The Government of India, appointed a Committee in 1958 to investigate the persistence of low standard in sports in India and the performance of the Indian teams in international contests, such as Olympic and Asian Games, and to recommend measures for improvement.

1. More facilities and better opportunities for training and competition should be provided and greater administrative efficiency achieved.

2. Greater facilities should be provided in educational institutions in the form of equipment, playgrounds and funds.

3. Incentives in the form of credit for achievements in sports and games should be provided.
4. Health, power of endurance, physical well-being of young people should be developed by improvement in nutrition.
5. Sports and games should be organised in rural areas through Vyayamshalas, Vyayam Mandals, Akharas, etc. and in cooperation with the Community Projects. Sports festivals should be organised and sports events encouraged on the occasion of fairs. Indigenous sports like Kabaddi and indigenous style of wrestling should be encouraged.
6. If schools and colleges and universities have to play their part in the development of sports and games in the country, they must have the minimum requirements in respect of playgrounds and equipment. The following standards have been recommended:

A College (with a student population of 1000 to 1500)	:	10 acres for playground
A High School (with a student population of 500 to 1000)	:	5-6 acres
A Middle School (with a student population of 200 to 500)	:	3-5 acres
A Primary School	:	1 acre

7. Where separate playgrounds cannot be made available for each educational institution, a common pool for a group of institutions should be created.

Recommendations of the Education Commission 1964-66. Writing about the concept of physical education, the Education Commission 1964-66 felt, "It must be emphasized that such education contributes not only to physical fitness but also to physical efficiency, mental alertness and the development of certain qualities like perseverance, team spirit, leadership, obedience to rules, moderation in victory and balance in defeat."

Five Forms of Physical Activities According to the Commission. According to the Education Commission 1964-66, physical education should include:

(i) Development exercises.

(ii) Rhythmic activities.

(iii) Sports and games.

(iv) Outing activities.

(v) Group handling activities.

Simple and Advanced Forms. The Commission further observed that all these have simple and advanced forms. The simpler activities should be introduced in the early classes, the more advanced ones should be gradually provided as boys and girls become more and more mature.

Principles of Developing a Programme of Physical Education. The Education Commission (1964-66) suggested the following eight principles for developing a satisfactory programme of physical education :

1. The physical education programme should be planned for desirable outcomes keeping in mind the interests and capacity of the participants.
2. The traditional forms of play and physical activities that have developed in our country should receive due emphasis in the programme.
3. The activities promoted should develop in each child a sense of personal worth and pride.
4. A sense of sharing responsibility in a spirit of democratic cooperation should grow from experience on playground and also in the gymnasium.
5. The programme offered should supplement other programmes of education and not duplicate them.
6. The programme should be within our financial means.

7. The programme should reach all rather than a selected few.
8. Special instruction and coaching should be provided for students with talent and special aptitude.

National Policy on Education and Sports and Physical Education

Sports and physical education are an integral part of the learning process, and will be included in the evaluation of performance. A nationwide infrastructure for physical education, sports and games will be built into the educational edifice.

The infrastructure will consist of play fields, equipment, coaches and teachers of physical education as part of the School Improvement Programme. Available open spaces in urban areas will be reserved for playgrounds, if necessary by legislation. Efforts will be made to establish sports institutions and hostels where specialised attention will be given to sports activities and sports related studies, along with normal education. Appropriate encouragement will be given to those talented in sports and games. Due stress will be laid on indigenous traditional games. As a system which promotes an integrated development of body and mind, yoga will receive special attention. Efforts will be made to introduce yoga in all schools; to this end it will be introduced in teacher training courses.

20

Role of Students

"The council should begin with concrete activities where definite success is possible. More difficult problems may be taken up as the pupils and teachers, working through the council, gain the ability to handle them."

Origin and Development

The concept of self-government is nearly as old as education. Flato's "Academy" was partially governed by elected student "Scholarchs". Aristotle extended the field of student self-government in his "Lyceum".

The student monitor system and the school court grew out of the educational experiments of TROTZEN-DORFF in Renaissance Germany, and of Lancaster, Bell, and Hill in England and India. Rousseau, Froebel and Pestalozzi contributed much to the self-government movement through their teaching and writing.

In America, a self-government plan was established before 1800 in the Willian Pen Charter School in which the school "Assembly" was elected monthly and charged with law-making powers.

In 1941, two surveys of student participation revealed that 81% to 92% of American High Schools had some organised form of student participation. The phrase, 'student participation in school government' replaced the older phrase, 'Student government'.

Need for Student Self-government. School life is not divorced from social life. An ideal school in a democracy must present a segment of real life. Its activities must be geared to the needs of social life around and it must present an idealised epitome of the social life. Just as we cannot learn speaking or writing a language without practice, in the same way our children cannot learn how to govern themselves and to get training in the democratic way of life unless they are provided opportunities for practical training in the democratic way of life. Therefore we must make the children themselves responsible for most of the activities concerning school management. When the students plan, execute and assess various activities and projects, they learn and practise democratic ideals and practices and their sense of social and civic responsibility is awakened. It has been stated by E.B. Castle, "Edicts from above do not conduce to the best human relationships; no one man or small group of adults working in a hierarchical formation can produce the pleasantness of tone that usually results from common purposes commonly achieved. Where a hierarchy of status exists and orders are received from above, those in the lower ranks of the hierarchy are almost certain to impose good behaviour instead of attempting to evoke good feelings." The educators and others experienced in social relations feel that the greatest unity of spirit and self-discipline results when members of the group have a voice in making decisions which affect them.

The Definition

Good's Dictionary of Education defines students government as "the maintenance of order and the regulation of matters of conduct in school by elected representatives chosen from the students body by the students themselves."

H.C. McKown writes that students' self-government is not possible for two reasons :

(1) Students lack the judgement that may accompany executive, legislative and judicial power.

(2) The Principal of the school is officially charged with the responsibility for the school, its equipment and its students' welfare. The students are not so charged and cannot be.

Out of the five types of self-governments given by P.W. Terry, we shall study the possibilities of introducing any one of them.

The Informal Type. It is a temporary organisation. It is formed as occasions arise. Some senior students or other outstanding pupils are invited to cooperate with the members of the staff in helping them on certain occasions such as to receive and accommodate guests at the school function day, etc.

The Specific Service Type. Certain duties such as to mark attendance, to supervise study rooms, to maintain cleanliness, etc. are assigned to some students who are either selected by the members of the staff or elected by the students themselves.

The Simple Council Type. In this form of self-government there is a certain unit of student organisation called the students' council to deal with the different activities of the students.

The Complex Type. Under this form, there are two or more central bodies of the students. One is a small body doing executive business and the other a bigger one exercising legislative powers. The former may be compared to that of a Cabinet and the latter to a Legislative Assembly or House of Representatives.

The School City Type. The administration of the school is carried on the lines of city administration. It is an elaborate form of student government. The whole of the student population of the school is divided into wards which elect Municipal Councillors.

The Mayor, the head of the city government as president of the Municipal Council is elected by people (pupils) at large or senior class or by Municipal Councillors and so also the chief of the police. The Council is invested with legislative and judicial powers. Standing Committees are also constituted for finance, athletics, social welfare, safety, traffic and publicity, etc.

Complete government by the pupils is not possible even in well-established progressive schools in our country. Nevertheless, there are practical undertakings in the schools which provide opportunities to the students to get training for future citizenship. The simple council type of self-government seems to be the best.

To start with a school may have a school Sabha. Each class or Section should elect one representative to it. Some talented students may be nominated by the head of the school in consultation with the staff adviser. The Sabha may have six Boards under it and the members may be elected from among the elected representatives. One staff-member may act as an adviser to each Board. The following activities may be undertaken by these Boards

(a) Games and sports.

(b) Health and sanitation.

(c) Activities like debates, dramas, magazines etc

(d) Disciplinary.

(e) Social service activities like adult literacy campaigns, flood relief etc.

(f) School cooperative store.

Assembly in Action

No rigid rules can be laid down for the range of activities to be undertaken by the Sabha. Every type of activity which has some educational significance may come under its purview.

H.C. McKown has given a list of 147 activities which can be undertaken by the Sabha or the Council. Some of these activities are given here :

(1) To welcome new students. (2) To supervise and help in the maintenance of good sanitary conditions in the school.

(3) To decorate the classrooms and the school premises. (4) To visit sick students. (5) To meet and welcome the visiting teams. (6) To provide assistance to the weak and handicapped students. (7) To plan campaigns courtesy, safety, punctuality etc. (8) To organise contests and competitions. (9) To publish school magazine. (10) To organise and manage a lost and found department. (11) To promote better lunch-room and cafeteria manners. (12) To promote good manners at athletic contests. (13) To appoint library and reading-room monitors. (14) To promote good behaviour at assembly, public events, before, in and after school. (15) To arrange lectures. (16) To organise exhibitions. (17) To organise the school store. (18) To organise the school-bank. (19) To introduce students to new movements in education. (20) To promote and arrange inter-school visits. (21) To arrange inter-school sports tournaments. (22) To promote inter-home room programme exchanges. (23) To hold academic contests (24) To organise excursions and trips. (25) To provide for publicity of commendable school work. (26) To promote good dress and neat appearance. (27) To look after school bulletins. (28) To collect material for school museum. (29) To supervise ventilation. (30) To discourage smoking. (31) To discourage seeing bad pictures. (32) To look after the school garden. (33) To promote good habits. (34) To arrange medical aid for the needy. (35) To assist health and police authorities. (36) To organise health social service at various occasions. (37) To assist in community-fund drives. (38) To organise school functions. (39) To organise literacy campaigns. (40) To budget its finances. (41) To conduct campaigns to improve school spirit. (42) To plan and promote a "better manners campaign". (43) To visit other schools to gain new ideas. (44) To take school government for a day. (45) To design student awards and emblems. (46) To run campaigns for new cheers, songs for school. (47) To act as coaches. (48) To act as tutors.

Important Features

The Secondary Education Commission observes, "Nothing is more calculated to develop a proper sense of self-discipline, and proper behaviour than their enforcement not by any outside authority with any symbol of punishment but by the students themselves. They should choose their own representatives to see it that proper codes of conduct are observed, both for the sake of the individuals and for the good name of the school. It is from this point of view that we commend what is known as the house system in schools, with prefects or monitors or Student Councils, whose responsibility will be to draw up a code of conduct and to enforce its observance in the school." The Report of the "Workshoppers' seminar" held at Delhi in 1955 observes : "Student participation in the government of the school is an effective method of citizenship training and is a means of keeping the energies of the pupils canalised for useful purposes in the development of a wholesome personality through a definite, constructive, well-planned programme". The Report of the Secondary Education Workshop held at Hyderabad in April-May 1955 states that the student government gives, "opportunities to pupils to learn the skill in electing leaders and of conducting their deliberations on democratic lines, thereby giving ample scope for self-expression, evaluation and judgement."

Principles underlying Student Council Organization. H.C. McKnown has given the following principles:

(a) The school must feel a continuous need for the council.

(b) Participation should be introduced gradually.

(c) A study of objectives should precede any attempt at definite organization.

(d) The council should represent the school as a whole.

(e) The average student should feel that he is represented.

(f) Both student body and faculty should be fairly represented.

(g) The council should not be too large.

(h) The council should have definite powers and duties.

(i) The council should not be considered a dumping ground.

(j) The head of the school should retain veto power.

(k) The work of the council should be continuously evaluated.

(l) Each member of the council should assume some specific responsibility.

(m) Each committee should be held strictly accountable for its particular responsibility.

(n) Officers and committee chairman should receive specialized training.

(o) The cooperative aspects of participation should continuously be emphasized.

(p) Council meetings should be held regularly and on school time.

(q) The council should give continuous publicity to its ideals, activities and problems.

Different Problems

(a) The members of the staff and the head are hesitant to part with power. They think that their prestige is in danger when students share powers with them.

(b) The students are immature and lack power of independent and critical thinking.

(c) Good students sometimes are reluctant to hold office as they think that this will have an adverse effect on their studies.

(d) Many a time it is seen that the students fail to elect their representatives who can handle various offices satisfactorily. This leads to constant troubles between the students and the educational authorities and the standard of education deteriorates.

(e) The politicians try to use students' council as a tool to further their ends and this discourages the educational authorities to allow the formation of students' unions in educational institutions.

(f) The elections of the students' council create bad blood among the students themselves. Not unfrequently they come to blows.

(g) The students' council can function effectively under ideal conditions. At a time when most of our schools are ill-equipped and under-staffed it will not be advisable to introduce such councils.

Required Elements

Change in Teacher Attitude. For the successful working of this programme it is very essential that the teachers must confide more in their students. The sense of responsibility can only grow and flower in an atmosphere of trust and freedom. The responsibility should be really handed over to the students and there be no pretext about it. "It is useless to institute self-government in name only, i.e. to call self-government system where the Head-teacher impresses his or her views upon the prefects and they accept them and impress them on the pupils. Nor is it of any value to have a system of self-government with a master or mistress always just round the corner to exercise authority," writes H.G. Stead.

G.R. Dustin is of the opinion, "A successful scheme requires a demonstrative organisation of the teaching staff of the school. The principal must first realize the meaning of democratised education. Teachers must also democratise their teaching and classroom management. Autocracy will never cooperate to make a democratic form of government a success."

Gradual Development of the Programme. Heavy responsibilities on the shoulders of children should be placed gradually. We should not demand too much from children who are immature in their judgment. It is wrong to think that a teacher's work is reduced by the introduction of self-government or a students' participation programme. Students need constant help and guidance from the teachers. The students must be told that the efficiency of an organisation depends upon the personnel of committee for the selection of which sober judgment is required. The teachers would do well if they acquaint the students with the general principles which govern the selection of suitable representatives. This will help the students in selecting their representatives.

Constant and Intelligent Supervision. In connection with the supervision work of these activities, W.R. Smith writes, "A school, city state, students' council or any other form of student management, requires a constant and intelligent supervision in which neither dictation nor aloofness is conspicuous."

Strict supervision should be made of the financial policy of the Sabha or the Council.

Very Few Restrictions on Students. Every good system of self-government should provide opportunities for as many pupils as possible to participate in its programmes. No restrictions on council membership should be imposed as far as possible.

Regular Meetings. The meetings of the various Boards should be held regularly. Each Board, committee or sub-group should be given specific responsibility and held accountable for it.

Due Publicity. The activities of the Sabha should be continuously publicised.

Non-involvement of Students. Care should be taken to see that the Sabha does not become a tool in the hand of the politicians to grind their own axe.

Constant Evaluation. The work of the council should be continuously evaluated.

Advantages. (1) The students develop love for the school. (2) They realise the necessity of having rules and regulations for the efficient and successful working of an institution. (3) They learn to respect authority. (4) They learn to tolerate difference of opinion and develop tolerance. (5) They learn the principle of 'give' and 'take'. (6) They learn to rise above casteism and communalism. (7) They get opportunities to make decisive choices. (8) They learn to lead others and develop qualities of leadership. (9) They learn to handle public money. (10) They learn to prepare themselves for future life as enlightened citizens of a democratic country. (11) They get an idea of the actual working of the Assembly and Parliament. (12) They learn to discipline themselves. (13) They realise their rights and responsibilities as citizens. (14) They learn the mechanics and devices of government and develop true spirit of citizenship.

21

Developing Motivation

The discussion on the planning of co-curricular activities may be summed up with the views of the Secondary Education Commission : "In the planning of these activities, it is important to remember that they should be as varied as the resources of the schools permit. Academic activities like debates, discussions, dramas, school magazines, social activities like the organising of different functions for the school community as well as the local community, sports activities, manual and practical activities, social service projects, art projects, must all be woven into a rich and unified pattern, within which every child will be able to find something to suit his tastes and interests. In the actual working out of these activities, academic, social, practical and sporting the teachers will find that there are really no tight boundary walls between them. Thus by planning a coherent programme of different activities, rich in stimuli, the school will not be frittering away either the time or the energy of the pupils but will be heightening their intellectual powers also side by side while training them in other fine qualities."

Clubs. Clubs may be constituted for undertaking different co-curricular activities in the schools. Every club must have its constitution. Its specific aim must be clear. It must meet the needs of the students. Johnson and Faunce give the following objectives of the school clubs :

1. They provide opportunities to the students for learning experiences based on their interests. Students are attracted to a club because of their enthusiasm for the programme it offers.
2. They supplement the curricular work. Visits to places of historical or scientific importance, etc. can be organised by these clubs.
3. They provide opportunities for the development of pupil abilities.
4. Clubs are very helpful in furnishing a constructive use of leisure time.
5. Clubs may help in the exploration of occupational interest of the students.
6. Clubs provide opportunities for the practice of group planning and decision.

Leadership of the Sponsors or the Teacher-in-charge of the Club. They must possess the following qualities :

1. The teachers or the sponsors must associate with pupils.
2. They should enlist the cooperation of the students.
3. They must be able to offer constructive suggestions for activities of the club.
4. They must be able to guide without dictation.
5. They must have the ability to plan systematically.
6. They must be willing to give time and thought in making the work of the club as a success.
7. They must be democrats in spirit.
8. They must possess a sense of humour.
9. They must have the necessary talent and skill so that their performance is higher and better than their pupils and they look upon to them as a model.

10. They should help the clubs and societies to make a wise choice of office bearers indicating what qualifications are necessary in an office bearer but should do nothing to force their choice in favour of any individual student.
11. They should make as careful a preparation for participation in co-curricular activities as they do for their teaching work.

Stage Dramas

The importance of drama as a teaching device has been appreciated from the earliest times. Dramatics afford the students opportunities for training in team-work. Knowledge gained in the classrooms of English, Art, Science, Social Studies, Music, Mathematics and Hindi all find practical application in the performing, designing, staging, lighting, costuming, advertising and setting of a well-organised educational theatre production. Dramatics are the best revenue producers of the entire co-curricular programme. With the help of a play various institutions raise funds for charitable and other purposes. Careful presentation of well-chosen dramatic production helps to teach the students to spend their leisure time more usefully, cultivate dramatic tastes and intelligent discrimination. Dramatics possess great possibilities of motivation. A dull and inactive class may be transformed into an engaging and busy one when certain lessons are dramatized under the direction of a skilful instructor. Dramatics help in making the parents interested in school work. Knowledge of the various subjects can be imparted effectively and attractively with the help of dramatics. A systematic study of historical events has to be made when pageants of the life of great persons are prepared, i.e. pageants on the life of Buddha, Chandragupta Vikramaditya, Gandhiji, etc. Children prepare costumes suiting different ages and thus come to know about the dress of the people during different periods of history. The geographical knowledge of the students is increased. Carpentry and other mechanical arts facilitate the work of the construction of the stage. Dance and music add to the beauty of a drama.

There are many activities in a drama and as such students of diverse aptitudes and abilities get chances to choose items for which they are best-suited and satisfy their hungers.

Children should be encouraged to write their own plays. The usual participants in a drama should be given opportunities to play different roles. The same pupil as far as possible should, however, not be allowed to play the role of a villain.

The planning, arranging and setting of the stage should not be made a huge affair. The equipment should be minimised. The stress should be on the educational value rather than on any other thing.

A number of rehearsals bring grace and success to the play when it is staged.

Selection of Play. The selection of the play presents a formidable problem. A committee comprising of teachers and students may be formed to select plays. The schedule for the year may be planned and it should include a variety of types of plays. Every play must satisfy the following standards :

(a) It should have a worthwhile theme. Plays depicting evils of social customs should preferably be chosen.

(b) It should have literacy value.

(c) It should be within the capacity of the pupils to understand and appreciate.

(d) It should have entertainment value.

(e) It should be free from vulgarity and objectionable subject-matter.

Tour Programmes

Meaning. Excursions mean small journeys which are undertaken to historical, geographical, cultural, educational, industrial and agricultural places which are not very far off.

Value of Excursions. W.M. Gregory evaluates school excursion in these words, "Education has been too far removed from the basic experiences for modern life. Many schools are quite deficient in opportunities for sense perception exploration and raw experiences. They need fewer words and more activities with things, situations, conditions and relations. For useful learning, pupils require experiences with the raw materials of life. A garden, a shop, a live animal collection, a trip to a farm, a mill, a store, a park, a museum all must have a place in the modern school." Following are some of the main advantages of excursions :

They Supplement Class Work. Visits to museums, forts, temples, caves, mountains, valleys, canals and fields help in supplementing the teaching of social studies by providing first-hand information. Industrial establishments and laboratories etc. are very useful places to the students of science. Excursions to these places bring reality, clarity and vividness to the 'dead matter' of various subjects, and provide for valuable correlation of subjects.

They Introduce Variety in the School Programme. These excursions infuse a new life and vigour in the children and give them some relief from the dull and monotonous life of the classroom.

They Develop Qualities of Leadership. Excursions help in developing qualities of initiative and leadership in the students by affording them opportunities to make necessary arrangements. These also encourage a spirit of cooperation among the students.

They Acquaint the Pupils with the Environment. Excursions enable the students to know intimately their environment by putting them in direct touch with the things and persons, organisations and institutions.

They Develop Self-activity Among the Students. Excursions make pupils active agents rather than passive recipients. Students get opportunities to plan various programmes connected with excursions. Besides they get opportunities to develop keenness and accuracy of observation. All their senses are at work and they experience the joy of discovery.

They Develop the Aesthetic Sense of the Students. Excursions to natural settings and places of beauty create love for nature and develop aesthetic sense.

They Foster Emotional and National Integration. Educational tours to other states foster a spirit of unity and oneness and the students realize that, in spite of so many differences of languages and castes, their country is one.

Proper Planning of the Excursions. To achieve the maximum benefit from excursions, it is essential that these should be properly planned. The teachers and the students may work out the plan of the excursion jointly. An excursion must be wisely conceived, properly planned and well conducted. It must be a result of careful thinking. The organisers would do well to obtain sufficient information beforehand regarding the importance of place to be visited so that they may be able to give suitable replies to the various queries of the students.

The fact that the excursions are arranged for educational-cum-recreational purposes should not be lost sight of and therefore, if possible, student singers, tidbit tellers and photographers should find a place in the party so that learning and laughing should go hand in hand.

The appointment of group leaders facilitates work to a considerable extent. The group leaders should preferably be those students who have some knowledge of the locality or who know the technique of explaining things in a clear way.

The importance of maintaining discipline in an excursion can hardly be ignored and a sympathetic and resourceful teacher shall not find it difficult to do so.

Personal Hobbies

The present machine age has placed enough leisure time at the disposal of man. Every prudent man would like to make the best use of leisure time. Childhood is the best time to choose a hobby and a good selection always brings happiness and joy to an individual.

Schools should create favourable attitudes towards healthy hobbies. It would serve the problem of spending leisure hours.

Hobbies give scope to the development of the innate tendencies of children. To some these help in preparing for vocation like painting and photography.

Some of the hobbies like stamp-collecting, writing, coin-collecting, gardening, etc. supplement class work. These hobbies introduce an element of 'play' in class work.

To some, hobbies help in providing mental relief from the worries of life. Last but not the least these hobbies help in developing the aesthetic sense of the students.

The following list gives us some indication of the wide range of activities which can serve as useful hobbies.

1. Woodwork. 2. Gardening. 3. Leather Work. 4. Card-board work. 5. Smithy. 6. Clay-modelling. 7. Book-binding. 8. Soap-making. 9. Basket-making. 10. Photography. 11. Tailoring and knitting. 12. Spinning. 13. Collecting stamps, coins, feather, flowers, pen-friendship, etc.

Various Agencies

It has three main objectives :

1. Promotion of health (personal as well as of the community).
2. Service of the sick and the suffering.
3. Promotion of international friendship.

For the propagation of health rules, a Red Cross Society takes the aid of posters and charts. Health plays are also staged.

Usually Red Cross Society runs a small dispensary. A library containing books dealing with health rules, diseases, their causes and remedies is also maintained.

The members of this society render a very useful assistance to the medical officer at the time of the medical inspection of the students. Its members visit the sick students of the school and render first-aid when students receive minor injuries.

The value of military training is very great. In almost all the countries in the West, regular military training to the young has become a regular feature of the national life. In an emergency or critical situation when the security of the people is in danger, the students come forward to defend the country and lend a helping hand to the Armed Forces of a country. By joining the N.C.C. the students will be brought up in the military tradition. The N.C.C. in India is going to fulfil the long-felt military needs of the students.

The National Cadet Corps Directorate, Ministry of Defence, has enunciated the following objectives of the National Cadet Corps:

Firstly, to develop character, comradeship, the ideal of service and capacity for leadership in young men and women;

Secondly, to provide service training to young men and women so as to stimulate interest in the defence of the country; and

Thirdly, to build up a reserve of potential officers to enable the Armed Forces to expand rapidly in a national emergency.

The membership of N.C.C. is entirely voluntary and there is no liability for military service. It undertakes the training of the youth between the ages of 13 and 20. Free training is imparted to the cadets. Free uniforms are issued to them and all expenses on account of messing and amenities for them during their camps are met by the State Governments. During special parades, some refreshment is also given to them.

The Secondary Education Commission has suggested that the recruitment and the training for N.C.C. should receive greater attention from the Defence Department.

The National Cadet Corps consists of three divisions

Junior Division. In the high schools Junior Divisions have been raised. It comprises three units - Army, Navy and Air Force.

Senior Division. This unit is raised in the colleges. It also consists of three wings – the Army, the Navy and the Air Force.

Girls Division. This unit is gradually becoming popular.

Assembly of Students

Fretwell calls school assembly as "town meeting of the school." Flora J. Cook writes, "The morning assembly is a common meeting ground to which each brings his offerings - the fruits of his observations and studies or the music, literature, and art that delight him, a place where all co-operate for the pleasure and well-being of the whole." In a school assembly all the students are expected to participate.

The following advantages appear to be the most important ones of a school assembly:

As a Unifying Source. McKown puts, "Through it the many seemingly unrelated and disconnected units of the school are correlated into a complete whole by united effort for, and attention to, a common cause." A student sees, feels and knows the school as an organised group. He feels that he is a part and parcel of one community, i.e. school.

As a Source of Inspiration. Students advanced in various fields present their programmes and give inspiration to others to emulate their good examples. Assembly experiences widen and deepen student interests also.

As a Source of Worthy Use of Leisure. Programmes of music, dramatics, etc., offer rich harvest of fun besides their educative values.

As a Place of Propagation of Commendable Work. Outstanding performances and achievements of the students in curricular and co-curricular fields should be recognised before the entire school. Badges, certificates and cups, etc., should be awarded to the winners in the presence of the entire school population.

As a Place of Developing Correct Audience Habits. A well conducted assembly meeting helps in inculcating good audience habits among the students. Respect for the feeling of the other members of the assembly, courtesy towards speakers and guests, sensible applause at the proper time and appreciative attitude are some of the good audience habits to be developed through a school assembly.

As a Place of Promoting Community Interests and True Patriotism. Celebration of some of the important national and international days helps in broadening the mental horizon of the students, developing reverence for the saviours of mankind and acquainting the students with the lives of the great scientists, discoverers and statesmen.

Principles Underlying Assembly Programmes. Firstly, the assembly programmes should be educational-cum- recreational.

Secondly, a variety of programmes should be introduced. Repetition of the old stuff kills interest.

Thirdly, attempts should be made to include all recognised activities, curricular and co-curricular in the assembly programmes.

Fourthly, a maximum number of students should be encouraged to participate in assembly programmes.

Fifthly, as far as possible, outside performers should be limited.

Sixthly, good songs should be used for assembly singing.

Seventhly, cooperation of the students should be secured in organising assembly programmes.

Exhibitions for Encouragement

According to Dr. K.L. Shrimali, "School exhibitions can on the one hand serve to acquaint the public with the work of the school, and on the other appraise the students body of the important activities of the community. School exhibits are stimulating both to the students who prepare them and to those who view them. Educational exhibitions can play an important role in the task of educational reconstruction. Exhibitions if planned properly, can demonstrate to us the progress made in various educational projects undertaken by them from time to time. They can serve as training centres to picture events of new activities and the progress of established projects."

Crow and Crow write, "Another excellent learning aid is the exhibition of learning materials or of samples of the pupil's work. In every classroom a certain section should be reserved for the display of such materials. Many schools have display cabinets in their corridors, some have exhibit rooms where material of current interest or the hand-work of the pupils themselves is displayed. These are now available in many school systems (U.S.A.)—collections of pictures, objects and other interesting material that are circulated from school to school. Exhibits of the pupil's work in fields of Art, Home Economics, Science, Social Studies, and related subjects are sources of great pride to the young people, and they excite the interest of other pupils, of parents, and of other lay people."

Nature of Exhibits

(a) Albums containing collections of postage stamps, photographs, leaves, specimens of hand-writings, drawings and portraits of great personalities etc.

(b) Actual products of the students, i.e. tables, chairs, paintings and drawings, cloth-work etc.

(c) Models prepared by the students.

(d) Tools, equipments and the like.

(e) Charts throwing light on the problems of general interest.

(f) Charts showing the activities of the school.

(g) Charts throwing light on the various aspects of the school life.

How to Put up Exhibits. The collection should be as varied as possible and be classified under these heads : (1) Arts, (2) Crafts, (3) Hobbles, (4) Teaching aids, (5) Statistics, (6) Common objects, etc.

1. Every exhibit should be properly classified and labelled.
2. Articles should be contained in the cases and drawers made by the pupils.
3. Durable material should be used in the preparation of these exhibits so that it may stand the wear and tear of time and rough handling on the part of the visitors.
4. Care should be exercised to keep the articles free from dust and cleaning at suitable intervals be done.
5. Necessary graphs showing the various stages of development of the production of an article should be displayed side by side.
6. If possible, the process of making various products should also be simultaneously shown so that the visitors may appreciate the magnitude of efforts put into the preparation of these products.

7. The organisation of an exhibition should be undertaken as a cooperative enterprise between the members of the staff and the students. The Head should appoint a committee of teachers to guide the students to organise an exhibition.
8. Each department of exhibition should have a guide, i.e. a student fully conversant with the various details of the exhibits; processes involved, time and money spent etc., to guide the visitors who put many queries.
9. Special exhibitions should be organised at suitable intervals.
10. Due publicity should be given when they are organised.
11. Special invitations should be given to the parents and the guardians of the students.
12. Borrowed material should be avoided.
13. Undue emphasis on the exhibitions should not be given.
14. They should be taken not as ends in themselves but as means.

Dr. K.L. Shrimali remarks about the organisation of exhibitions, "In order that the exhibition may be convincing and people may be able to think and adopt the recommended practices in their homes or educational institutions, it is essential that the facts are presented in a striking manner. A piece of work - a painting, a chart or a model – if it is neatly done and has a pleasing appearance, not only enables the doer but also the spectator, whereas work done in a slovenly manner bears the stamp of an uncultivated mind and contaminates the whole atmosphere. Exhibitions, therefore, if properly organised can help us in raising standard of efficiency of our people and in improving their taste."

Visitor's Book. The visitors should be asked to give their comments on the exhibits they see and a book should be maintained for this purpose. Their constructive suggestions should be welcomed and attempts made to incorporate these in the preparation of the articles to be produced later on.

Sale Department. From the self-sufficiency point of view, the sales of the exhibits have an important significance. Persons incharge of this department should be in a position to advise buyers on the utility of the various products. Prices should be fixed and pasted on the tags attached to the products.

Maintenance of Records. Record of each exhibit should be maintâined. Each exhibit should be given its number. Record should be kept in such a way as it may be possible at a glance to know the name of the maker of an exhibit, time taken for its preparation, cost incurred, sale price, date of sale and profits if any.

Special Exhibitions. These exhibitions may be organised from time to time : U.N.O. Day Exhibitions, Books Exhibitions, Poster Exhibition, Science Exhibition, Agriculture Exhibition, Home Industry Exhibition, Defence Exhibition, etc.

Joint Exhibitions. Some schools of the locality may join together and organise such exhibitions.

Publications by Students

In the words of Jacobson, "The school magazine offers great opportunity for those who participate in it. It is not uncommon to find that pupils and their parents consider the editorship of the school paper most valuable experience which has come to a pupil, particularly when directed by a wise sponsor who makes it a very purposive educative experience. All pupils who serve on the editorial board secure some experience in creative writing, usually the form of their writing improves because a powerful incentive for correct form exists when the material is to be printed or memeographed for public examination."

It serves as a link between the school and the parents as it reaches them through the students.

A foundation for inter-state and international understanding can be laid by exchanging magazines with schools in other states and countries.

Classroom work is supplemented to some extent through it. The students learn to write their thoughts in an effective, clear and concise manner. Study habits are developed as the students consult some books or journals to write for their school magazine and make the best use of their leisure time.

It helps in giving publicity to the school.

Spears and Lawshe list the following functions of the school paper as an aid to the school :

1. To educate the community as to the work of the school.
2. To publish school news.
3. To create and express school opinion.
4. To capitalise the achievements of the school.
5. To act as a means of unifying the school.
6. To express the idealism and reflect the spirit of school.
7. To encourage and stimulate worth-while activities.
8. To aid in developing right standards of conduct.
9. To promote understanding of other schools.
10. To provide an outlet for student suggestions for the betterment of the school.
11. To develop better inter-school relationships.
12. To increase school spirit.
13. To promote cooperation between parents and school.

Scouts : Serving the Society

In the opinion of F.G. Pearce, following are some of the important contributions of scouting :

Sublimation of Instincts. The founder of the Boy-scout Movement seems to be a very profound psychologist who started this movement which fully satisfies the hungers and urges of children. Patrol contests and games take the place of gang fights. Contact with nature satisfies sex-instinct. Self-assertion finds its outlet in producing patrol and troop leaders. Similarly, other instincts find suitable channels.

Dignity of Labour. It is an open secret that an average student shirks work. He does not take pride in doing things for himself. This movement is the best one to provide practical opportunities to the students to throw themselves with vigour and even pleasure into work.

Good Fellowship. A good deal of the sufferings of the world is due to the absence of fellowship feeling. If humanity is to survive, a spirit of good fellowship must be developed in the students who in a few years are expected to play an important role in the world. Scouting is one of those activities which knows no barriers of caste, creed and colour and which is very helpful in promoting fellowship. Camp life, rallies and other cooperative activities are the means to develop this quality of brotherhood.

Practical Efficiency. Activities like health training, first-aid, home nursing, rescue and emergency aid, swimming, riding, etc., greatly increase the practical efficiency of the scouts.

Social Service Training. Scouts render a very useful service in the fairs and gatherings. Anti-malaria work, flood relief work, adult literacy work and cleaning campaigns are the other fields of their activities.

Love of Nature. Outdoor games, camp life and excursions bring the Students in close touch with nature and develop their aesthetic sense and engender in the minds of the students love of nature.

The Spirit of Adventure. Students are by nature restless and curious to know new things. They like to explore and face difficulties. The outdoor life provides worthwhile opportunities to satisfy their lust for enterprise and discovery. "The outdoor life is the life-blood of scouting," writes F.G. Pearce.

Prof Russell has very beautifully commended the value of scouting, "The naturalist may praise it for its success in putting the boy close to nature's heart, the moralist for its splendid code of ethics, the hygienist for its method of physical training, the parent for its ability to keep his boy out of mischief; but from the standpoint of the educator, it has marvellous potency for converting the restless, irresponsible, self-centred boy into the straight forward dependable, helpful young citizen. To the boy who will give himself to it, there is plenty of work that looks like play, standard of excellence which he can appreciate, rules of conduct which he must obey, positions of responsibility which he must occupy as soon as he qualifies himself, in a word a programme that appeals to a boy of nature."

Another writer Dr. L.D. Coffiman writes, "Scouting gives us no lecture on vocational guidance, and yet it teaches the meaning, the importance of the dignity of work; it operates no bank and yet it teaches the meaning of thrift; it contains no jails and yet it teaches the meaning of self-control; it does no preaching and yet it teaches devotion to a cause and loyalty to a purpose; it is founded upon no religion, creed or sectarian doctrine and yet it emphasizes above all things the importance of religion. It is universal in appeal, natural in its methods, progressive in its outlooks, strengthened and cemented by the bonds of fellowship and the idealism of the movement."

Essentials for the Success of a Scout Troop

1. It should be started by a person who himself possesses the spirit of service and is really interested in scouting. 'Come on', and never 'Go on' should be his watch word.
2. There should not be more than thirty-two boys in a troop. This number can easily be managed by one scoutmaster.
3. Generally speaking, a troop should not be instructed as a whole. The scouts are to be trained through patrol leaders.
4. Right types of boys should be selected for scouting.
5. Preliminary training should start with outdoor life.
6. Twice a week, an hour and a half before or after school seems adequate time for scout training.
7. Inter-patrol competitions should be held as these are very helpful in maintaining keenness and promoting efficiency.
8. Scouts should be induced to take a pride in their uniform from the very start.

9. A scout troop must have ropes, flags, bandages, compass, first-aid material, books and camping and picnicking equipment.
10. A suitable room in the school which should be known as scout room should be secured.
11. Practical opportunities should be provided to the scouts to do social service.
12. Camp fires should be organised.
13. Records of the work done by a troop should be kept.
14. Too many rallies should be avoided.
15. Scout troop should not be started merely for the purpose of show or at the time of inspection.
16. The scout-master himself should follow the scout laws.

History of Scouting. Sir Robert Baden Powell founded the Boy Scout Movement in 1908. However, in India, the movement was introduced in 1911 at Bangalore.

Some forms of social and national service should be made an integral part of education at all stages. This could be done by providing for student participation in programmes (1) of community living on the school campus, and (2) of community development of national reconstruction.

Community Living on the School Campus : Labour Weeks. There are various opportunities for community work in the classroom, on the school campus and in the school hostels.

To impart social training to the students 'Labour Weeks' may be organised in the schools and the following type of work done :

(a) Cleaning of the school building, rooms, verandahs, compounds, etc.

(b) White-washing of the school building.

(c) Decoration of the rooms, preparation of charts and pictures.

(d) Removing stones, iron nails, waste-paper, etc., from the school compound, playground.

(e) Varnishing of school furniture, doors and windows.

(f) Turfing school compound.

(g) Filling pits in the streets and lanes and cleaning roads.

(h) Teaching adults.

(i) Organising first-aid centres for the public.

(j) Carrying propaganda amongst the public regarding the importance of personal cleanliness and social sanitation in order to ward off common diseases.

Regarding this type of work during a 'Labour Week', K.G. Saiyidain writes, "I feel strongly that not only in this country but in the whole world, we have to make an earnest and concentrated effort to give a new orientation to the social ideology of our children and youth, particularly in the direction of inculcating a sense of the dignity of labour and cultivating the capacity to work together for constructive and socially worthy causes. I cannot think of any better method of doing so by bringing all school children together into a fellowship of work and service where the meanest work will be undertaken in a spirit of adventure and comradeship because it is useful and provides a healthy outlet for their energies and talents."

Participation in Community Development. The organization of programmes of community development and national reconstruction will vary from stage to stage. The primary school can emulate in this respect the example of the basic schools which have done a good deal of pioneering work in the direction of the school serving the community. A well trained and enthusiastic teacher who maintains good relations with the local community can easily find appropriate situations such as those connected with public sanitation, simple village improvement projects, care of small children and help to the old and the sick, in which the school children can help the community. At the secondary stage, the children are more mature and it is possible to organize programmes of community service at a higher level.

It is no easy task to organize an effective programme of social service for all the secondary schools in the country. Its implementation should, therefore, be carried out in stages. To begin with selected schools of high quality may organize the national service programme on a voluntary basis; and to help them, the Department should draw up model plans of social and community services. The training schools and colleges may take the lead in this regard and help to build up a suitable list of activities for the neighbouring schools. As experience is gained in executing the programme, it may be extended to cover a larger number of schools and students.

Labour and Social Service Camps. Every encouragement should be given to each secondary school to develop its own programme of social service. Labour and social service camps which will run throughout the year (except during the monsoon season when outdoor work will not be possible), should be organized in each district and each secondary school which does not have a social service programme of its own should be under an obligation to participate in such camps and provide this rich and valuable experience to its students. For this purpose, a special organization should be set up in each district under the direct control of the district education officer. It will be the responsibility of the organization (1) to select one or more specific projects on which students can work all the year round; (2) to provide the necessary community contacts; (3) to assist in providing residential arrangements, implements, utensils, etc; and (4) where possible, to provide a part of the expenditure of the entire organization of the camps. The schools will be responsible for drawing up of the programme of their participation, in consultation with this district agency, for taking the students to the camps and for guiding the students in carrying out the projects assigned to them.

Positive Side

(i) These inculcate in students the spirit of community service.

(ii) These inculcate in the students the spirit of self-sacrifice.

(iii) These give children a scope for the exercise of initiative.

(iv) They build up an attitude of cooperation and fellow-feeling.

(v) These build a cooperative atmosphere in the home and the outside world.

(vi) They train students in leadership.

(vii) They give children training in citizenship and in the art of self-government.

(viii) They develop wider outlook.

(ix) The activities help in the many-sided development of the pupil—physical, mental, moral, religious and social.

(x) These activities foster dignity of labour.

(xi) These directly and indirectly impart moral education.

In short, these activities develop virtues of give and take, cooperation, participation in social life, sharing responsibilities, cooperative endeavour, mutual adjustment, internal and self-discipline, friendly disposition, ideals of service, proper attitudes, etc.

22

Beyond Curriculum

The Significance

The Education Commission (1964-66) stressed their importance as, "We conceive of the school curriculum as the totality of learning experience that the school provides for the pupils through all the manifold activities, in the school or outside, that are carried on under its supervision. From this point of view, the distinction between curricular and extra-curricular work ceases to exist, and a school camp and games and sports are curricular or rather co-curricular activities."

Progressive education stresses that the school becomes a centre of vigorous life and provides different types of activities for children. The children do not learn from the lectures of the teachers. Observation takes the place of books. Experience becomes the prime educator. The motto of the educator is "Tell the pupil as little as possible and lead him to tell as much as possible from his own observation and education." The productive and creative activities become the centre of learning: Curriculum is not seen in terms of the tasks to be performed and goals to be reached rather than in terms of lessons to be learnt and taught. 'Learning by Doing' and 'Learning by Living' are the two slogans of the new education.

Productive and creative activities help in the development of 4 H's—Head, Heart, Hand and Health. A child receives valuable training in the 'art of living together' through productive and creative activities. A child is saved from cut and dried facts. 'Learning without tears' is another characteristic of new education.

The creative and constructive activities provide for the expression of the children's individual talents. They get preliminary training for their future vocation. To quote T.S. Avinashilingam, "Providing for various types of activities will give them opportunities for observation and in the use of their hands" and this will "offer them the fulfilment and satisfaction which nothing else confers."

Aims and Objectives

All-roundness is the theme of new education. The new education recognises that when the child comes to the school, he comes in mentally, physically spiritually, socially and vocationally and as such he must be educated in all of them. It is extremely difficult to emphasize sufficiently the tremendous importance of the co-curricular activities for the development of the whole man. To quote the Secondary Education Commission, "They are as integral a part of the activities of a school as its curricular work and their proper organisation needs just as much care and forethought."

The Background

These activities are as old as education itself though their sphere was not so vast as it is today. Monitor system was one of the important institutions of the ancient Indian system of education. The Gurukulas of old were residential institutions providing opportunities of social contacts on a large scale. In Athens and Sparta activities like athletics, music, students' participation in government were very common.

Essential Part

In the past, these activities were mainly organised after school hours and so were "extra-curricular". But now "they are as integral a part of the activities of the school as its curricular work and their proper organisation needs just as much care and fore-thought." At another place the Secondary Education Commission remarks, "Given a clean, pleasant and well maintained school building, we would like the school to see if it can provide a richly varied pattern of activities to cater to the development of their children's entire personality. It has to formulate a scheme of hobbies, occupations and projects that will appeal to, and draw out the powers of children of varying temperaments and aptitudes."

The crying need of the hour is the 'education for democracy'. Hence education must aim at producing those individuals who can intelligently and amicably participate in the various activities of life. Traditional curriculum failed to meet the demands of the changing conception of education. The co-curricular programme is a convenient tool by which an inadequate curriculum may be supplemented.

Psychologically these activities provide outlets for the flow of the energies of the students.

Different Forms

Broadly speaking Co-curricular activities may be categorised under thirteen heads :

Academic Development Activities

Subject Clubs : History Club, Geography Club, Mathematics Club, etc.

Aesthetic Development Activities

1. Drawing and Painting 2. Dramatics. 3. Fancy Dress. 4. Folk Dance. 5. Folk Song. 6. Flower Festival. 7. Music. 8. Organizing Exhibitions. 9. School Band. 10. Sculpture. 11. School Decoration. 12. Preparation of Charts and Models. 13. Variety Show.

Citizenship Training Activities

1. Mock Parliament or Youth Parliament.
2. Organizing Co-operative Bank in the School.

3. Organizing Co-operative Store in the School.
4. Visits to Institutions like the Gram Panchayat, Zila Parishad, Municipality, Legislative Assembly, High Court, Parliament etc.

Cultural Development Activities

1. Celebration of Festivals.
2. Visits to Places of Cultural Importance.

Emotional and National Integration Activities

1. Celebration of National Days.
2. Community Dining.
3. Educational Tours to Various States.
4. Organization of Camps.

Leisure Utilization Activities

1. Stamp Collecting.
2. Collection of Coins.
3. Collection of Pictures, Stones etc.
4. Album Making.
5. Photography.

Literary Activities

1. Book Reading. 2. Debates and Discussions. 3. Declamation Contest. 4. Essay Writing. 5. Extension Lectures. 6. Magazines. 7. Recitation. 8. Story Writing. 9. Symposium.

Moral Development Activities

1. Mass Assembly and Morning Prayer.
2. Social Service Activities.

Multi-purpose Activities

1. Community Survey.

2. Scouting or Girl Guiding.

3. Prize Distribution.

4. Undertaking Various Projects.

Productive Activities

1. Basket Making. 2. Book Making. 3. Card-board Work. 4. Clay Modelling.

5. Dyeing. 6. Embroidery. 7. Flower Gardening. 8. Kitchen Gardening. 9. Knitting. 10. Leather Work. 11. Spinning. 12. Smithy. 13. Soap Making.

14. Tailoring. 15. Toy Making. 16. Weaving.

Physical Development

1. Athletics. 2. Cycling. 3. Boating. 4. Indoor Games. 5. Mass Drill. 6. Mass P.T. 7. N.C.C. 8. Outdoor Games. 9. Swimming. 10. Wrestling. 11. Yogic Asanas.

Scientific Development Activities

1. Science Clubs
2. Science Fairs
3. Visits to Scientific Establishments.

Social Welfare Activities

1. Red Cross Activities.

2. Service on Special Occasions like Fairs.

3. Social Service in the Neighbourhood.

4. School Cleanliness.

Sublimation of Instincts. Gregarious instinct in the adolescent is very predominant. This tendency expresses the desire of the growing boys to behave socially. If no opportunities are provided to them, they will form their own groups. This grouping may be harmful to them and the society also and may take the shape of gangs etc. Their energies will be misdirected and they will indulge in anti-social acts. Without proper guidance, they are likely to develop wrong scales of social values and they may direct their energy and enthusiasm towards the end that will be harmful and even disastrous to them and to society at large. Various co-curricular activities, e.g. self-government, social service leagues, scouting, etc., will be very conducive to sublimate this instinct by providing them a field for doing something socially worthwhile through group activities. Similarly, their other instincts of self-assertion, sex and self-abasement will be sublimated.

Social Training. These activities are very useful in giving training in 'Art of Living.' According to the Secondary Education Commission, the 'Art of Living' is a much more comprehensive concept than the acquisition of knowledge, however, intelligently planned. It includes training in the habits and graces of social life and the capacity for cooperative group work; it calls for patience, good temper, sincerity, fellow feeling and discipline. These can only be cultivated in the context of the social life and the many curricular and co-curricular activities that must find a recognised place in every good school. By participating in co-curricular activities pupils learn valuable lessons in practical cooperation and the habits of team work; they realise the relation of the society to the individual and of the individual to the society.

Mohi-ud-din states that these activities have a social appeal. "By reason of the social appeal of extra-curricular activities, their co-operative method, their spontaneity, and their intrinsic interest, they are a significant social medium for the civic training of the young."

To be a good member one must sacrifice one's immediate interests if need be, for the welfare of the group. It is well known that boys and girls in the process of maturity, move from sheer individualism to social awareness. In the beginning every player wishes to carry the ball himself and does not realize that he must depend upon others to realize the goal. But with the passage of time, an individual discovers that one must play in a team if one is to win anything worthwhile. Thus a team spirit develops in him. Spirit of 'give-and-take' takes the place of selfishness.

Civic Training. The school should be a training ground for democracy. It should be organised and administered on democratic lines. Students in this manner will have opportunities and responsibilities somewhat similar in a small way to those they will have later as grown up citizens. The introduction of self-government provides experience of the life of a democratic society. In this, pupils determine the policies and the programmes. They plan and present assembly programmes. The individual pupil learns how to conduct a meeting in an approved parliamentary style. It gives him an opportunity to exercise his vote. While working together, the students will know that rights involve responsibilities.

They will get valuable lessons in cooperation which can be learnt by practice. In order to retain his position as a member in a Student Council, Athletic team, etc., a student has to exercise cooperation.

Moral Training. Students get opportunities of social contact. They also get opportunities of doing social service. This teaches them the lesson of morality. They acquire the virtues of honesty, sympathy and good etiquettes.

Supplementation or Academic Work. The teaching of civics, composition, history, geography, etc., will be greatly supplemented. Election to the students council will give them a picture of Central and State elections. Excursions to historical, geographical and industrial places will enrich the experience of the students. Writing for the school magazine will supplement the teaching of languages. Similarly, there are many practical activities which afford opportunities to supplement classroom work.

Provide Worthy Recreational Interests. Education for leisure is as important as education for work. If recreational interests are developed during schools life, they prove to be very beneficial in the leisure hours of adult life and make life fuller and richer.

Mohi-ud-din writes about the recreational value of these activities, "Provision in the school of a programme of free and creative activities, by way of crafts and hobbies, gives direction to youthful enthusiasm and training for healthy occupation.... The last, but certainly not the least important function of extra-curricular activities is thus to convert the leisure after-school life from a curse into blessing, from a burden into an opportunity for a fuller, richer and nobler life."

A good deal of educational work can be accomplished through recreation. In the opinion of G.D. Sondhi, "So wide is the field of recreation that there is no school, no teacher, no student that cannot find something of interest in it. If there are no playgrounds, yet there are school courtyards and school-rooms where some form of recreation can be introduced – be it group dancing, play-acting, clay-modelling, paper cutting, painting, group-singing, carpentry work, spinning, weaving and the like. Opportunities for joy-giving will be provided and boredom eliminated and invention, initiative and emotional control developed.

"Then there are outdoor activities like camping and hiking, gardening and even cycling and mountaineering which build up some of the basic requirements for success in life - the spirit of service, observation, grit, determination and courage." Further he observes, "pleasure and interest combined with some instruction and guiding sugar-coat the pill of learning and of discipline."

The fundamental point that these activities are means and not ends, should not be lost sight of.

Knowledge and learning are acquired as a by-product of interesting activity.

Development of the Sentiment of Loyalty. The more the students run the school administration, the more they feel that the school belongs to them and they belong to the school. The labour week, i.e. cleanliness of the school by the students themselves develops the idea: 'This is my school because I have made it with the sweat of my brow.' Tournaments and activities like school function also foster this sentiment.

Development of Discipline. Discipline becomes self-discipline. The students remain busy with different kinds of activities and develop their talents in different directions. They make laws for the various societies and come to realize the need for showing respect to other school laws.

Development of the Qualities of Leadership. Many programmes have to be organised. Many situations have to be faced in the running of various societies. All these inculcate in the students the virtues of initiative, clear thinking, originality, resourcefulness, good judging power, tolerance, patience, enthusiasm, self-confidence and reliance which are very essential in a leader.

Physical Development. Games, N.C.C., A.C.C., Physical Drill etc., contribute to the physical development of the students.

Scope for Self-expression. Someone has a talent for writing, another for speaking, a third for music and so on. These activities bring out these qualities and develop them. This self-discovery and self-knowledge will tell them in what direction they should turn their ability and talent to advantage and help them to make wise vocational choice.

Assistance in Guidance and Counselling. Students get opportunities to know their assets and liabilities. The teachers and especially the school counsellor comes to know them better and accordingly suggests programmes for their development.

Learning and Earning. Many activities provide students some opportunities to earn also.

Preparation for a Vocation. Some students develop such interests which prepare them for a vocation.

Cordial Relations between the Community and the School. Social service activities at fairs and the neighbourhood bring appreciation from the community.

Instruction Becomes Pleasurable. Principal G.D. Sondhi felt, "Pleasure and interest, combined with some instruction and guidance, sugarcane the pill of learning and discipline."

We may sum up the role of the co-curricular activities in the words of the Secondary Education Commission Report : "Thus by planning a coherent programme of these different activities, rich in stimulation, the school will not be frittering away either the time or the energy, of the pupils, but will be heightening their intellectual powers also side by side while training them in fine qualities."

Programme Requirements

Variety of Activities. A wide variety of activities should be planned in order to meet the different needs of a large number of students.

Activities during School Hours. As far as possible activities should be organised in school time.

Guidance of Teachers. The co-curricular programme should be strictly under the guidance of teachers.

Teacher as an Adviser. The teacher should not play the role of a dominator rather than that of an adviser.

Facilities to Teachers. Some credit either in the form of less teaching periods or in the form of extra-payment to teachers should be given.

Participation of a Large Number of Teachers. As far as possible each member may remain in charge of a particular activity of his interest.

Equal Opportunity to Students. All the students should have equal opportunity to be a member of school organisation.

Gradual Growth of the Programme. Activities should be started in a small way and developed gradually.

Careful Consideration. Every careful consideration should be given when a new society is to be started. Normally, when once an activity is organised and scheduled, it should not be allowed to die.

Maintaining Records. Record of the various activities must be kept by every organisation.

Reasonable Expenditure. Activity should be less expensive as far as possible.

Provision for Funds. Sufficient funds to meet the expenditure involved on various activities should be raised by the society concerned.

Balanced Stress. Funds should not be spent on a few elected stars (a few players or debaters etc.).

Regular Work. Regular time should be devoted to these activities.

Evaluation. Provision should be made for periodic appraisal of the services and values of these activities.

Publicity. Publicity should be given to the activities of these societies and the community should be well-informed.

Activity Time Table. An activity time-table and a calendar for activities may be prepared.

No Show Work. These activities may not be started merely for 'show work.'

Means not Ends. Co-curricular programme must be organised and considered as a means to the educative process.

The Counselling

To make the activity programme effective, a principal would do well to appoint a teacher as an activity director or coordinator. His teaching load must be lessened so that he may give sufficient time to the planning and execution of various activities in the school. His duties would be :

(i) To plan the schedule of the year's activities to set dates of special activities, such as concerts, parents' days, school dances etc.

(ii) To secure a list of clubs that the teachers desire to offer.

(iii) To take care of special disciplinary cases during club periods.

(iv) To coordinate with transport service to take students to various places.

(v) To issue bulletins of club activities.

(vi) To conduct research on the educative value of the co-curricular activities.

(vii) To select those activities which relate to the school curriculum.

(viii) To think of ways and means to make the activities less costly.

(ix) To provide opportunities to the students to participate in one or the other activity from which they derive immense benefit.

The Disadvantages

Disregard of Local Condition. Many schools undertake many activities simply because other schools have started these. They do not take into consideration their assets and limitations.

Lack of Accommodation. Some schools do not have playgrounds, no space for indoor games, no space for mass drill.

Lack of Funds. Some schools lack finances for purchasing equipment for sports, craft work, hobbies, workshop material, etc.

Lack of Variety. Some schools organize a few activities only with the result that students with diverse interests do not get opportunity to participate.

Lack of Adequate Staff. The number of teachers who can provide effective guidance to student in this field is limited.

Conservative Attitude of Authorities. Many Principals and teachers do not find any good coming out of a co-curricular programme and they are rather indifferent to it.

Over-emphasis on Academic Work. Generally speaking no regular time is allotted to the organization of these activities. Undue stress is laid on academic achievements.

Over-emphasis on Co-curricular Activities. Some schools follow the extreme course. They over-stress this programme.

Heavy Load on Teachers. These activities put a heavy load on the teachers and they feel over-burdened.

No Credit in the Annual Examination. Usually very little consideration is shown to students' performance in these activities while promoting them.

Causes of the Non-participation of the Students

1. Inadequate school provisions regarding these activities.
2. Lack of playgrounds in the crowded cities.
3. Inconvenient hours of meeting.
4. Interference with studies.
5. No credit in the examinations.
6. Insufficient number of trained scout masters and physical instructors.
7. More emphasis on intellectual development and less on other developments, e.g. physical, moral, aesthetic, social etc.
8. Poor economic conditions of the students compel them to work in their homes after school hours, leaving very little time at their disposal for participating in the activities which are organised after school hours.

Means of Motivating Students to Participate

1. Awarding certificates of merit to students.
2. Some credit to be given at the time of promotion.
3. Awarding prizes.

Causes of the Lack of Interest among Teachers

1. No extra pay is given to them for organising such activities.
2. Their teaching hours are not reduced.
3. Majority of the teachers do not possess proper training for organising such activities.
4. Some of the teachers do not see any good coming out of these activities as they do not fully realise that they should

aim at the all-round development of the personality of the student.

5. Due to the rigid outlook of the teachers and the Headmasters, the idea of the self-government is not allowed to creep into the minds of the students of the school. They feel that the students are not sufficiently mature and may misuse power invested in them.
6. The vain idea of superiority among the teachers checks them from allowing the students to share responsibility with them.

23

Maintaining Records

Records in Schools

Legal Requirements. School records and reports are used to satisfy the legal requirements of the State, to appraise the effectiveness of the instructional programme, to help in the administration of the school to furnish research data for statistical analysis and interpretation of policies and programmes and to develop cooperative and constructive relations with the parents of pupils in school.

Essential for Successful Working of an Institution. School is a social institution answerable to the parents, the managing committee, the department and the public in general and the records kept by the school serve as a useful means to judge its efficiency. Carefully and efficiently kept school records are indispensable for the successful working of the school.

Records Essential for the All-round Growth of the Child. School is entrusted with the task of the all-round development of the personality of each child and to discharge this function it is absolutely essential to keep a record of his day-to-day growth and development.

Records and Grant-in-aid. Sometimes certain conditions are laid down by the department for the payment of grants-in-aid to schools. For example, on the basis of average daily attendance of the school, block grants are sometimes sanctioned. This requires the supply of certain facts and statistics.

Educational Reforms. Educational reforms can be undertaken only when the school records provide a useful help in supplying comprehensive data to those who are asked to shoulder the responsibility of educational reforms.

Assessment of an Institution. School records assist us to assess the progress and needs of a particular locality.

Cooperation of Parents. To make the parents interested in school work and in their wards, schools send progress reports from time to time. This helps in establishing closer contacts between the home and the school.

L.M. Chamberlain and L.W. Kindred give the following advantages of the school records .

Records Help the School

1. To locate each pupil quickly.
2. To have available the significant facts about each pupil.
3. To explain and remove undesirable conditions.
4. To find if all legal requirements are met.
5. To determine if any administrative or other changes are desirable.
6. To make important investigations and case studies possible.
7. To find if school funds are adequate and wisely expended.
8. To reduce retardation and failure to a minimum.

Records Help the Classroom Teachers

1. To know pupils when the school year begins.
2. To determine what work a pupil is capable of doing.

3. To provide learning activities suitable to each pupil.
4. To formulate a basis for the intelligent guidance of pupils.
5. To explain the behaviour characteristics or unhappy conditions of any pupil.
6. To make possible the development of unusual capacities or exceptional talents.
7. To identify and make proper provisions for the mentally slow.
8. To make assignments to committee work and monitorial positions.
9. To make periodic reports correctly and in time.
10. To be properly informed when conferring with parents and others about a pupil.

Permanent Records Help the Pupil

1. To receive fair consideration in his classification.
2. To do his best in making a good record.
3. To make progress in accordance with his ability.
4. To secure development of his natural capabilities.
5. To secure transfer of correct information to other schools when desired.
6. To receive proper adjustment and guidance.

Record Keeping

Dr. Jaswant Singh remarks that office is really the king-pin in the enterprise, and its value cannot be minimised without undermining the efficiency of the school. It is the ultimate responsibility of the school Headmaster to maintain and preserve the school records properly and as such he should be well conversant with this aspect of school administration. The Headmaster, in no case, can transfer to his clerks or assistants blame for faulty discharge of what are his own primary responsibilities.

School Office. As a general rule every high and higher secondary school must have one separate room for office. The office-in-charge must be a person trained for the type of work to be done in schools. The head must be relieved of the mechanical details of the office routine if he is to make the best use of his abilities and to discharge his functions of guidance and counselling and supervising. The school office should be spacious and well ventilated.

Basic Requirements

Accuracy. All information contained in the school records should be accurate, well-organised, pertinent and justified solely on grounds of the contribution it can make either directly or indirectly to the welfare of the students.

Completeness. Data about a child should be gathered continuously, should be kept upto date and include information that reveals his true condition at any given time. In the case of his transfer from one school to another, his records should follow him.

Utility. Record system should provide for collecting and recording information that is relevant and useful in working with children.

Comprehensiveness. In view of the emphasis on the harmonious development of the child, different kinds of records will have to be kept. All members of the staff have a responsibility for keeping records peculiar to their field of activity.

Easy Maintenance. The records and reports should be easily maintained and should require a minimum of time and energy for making entries.

Systematic Maintenance. School records should be maintained and located where they will be used to the greatest advantage by staff personnel. The files should not be cluttered with unusable records and reports that teachers lose interest and become discouraged when they seek information related to the work they are doing. Separate files or note-books should be kept for each separate record or report.

Availability. School records should always be available in the school premises and should not be removed from the school premises for the purpose of scrutiny.

A record system then should be designed carefully, kept efficiently, located strategically and should contain all information that is essential to the achievement of the aim for which it was established.

The Functioning

1. Prepare a stock list of registers maintained in the school.
2. Write distinctly the following particulars on the outer cover of each register :
   (a) The name of the school.
   (b) The serial number of the register.
   (c) The name of the register.
   (d) The number of volume.
   (e) The number of pages of the volume.
   (f) The opening and closing dates.
3. Number the pages consecutively either in the red ink or with a number machine when a register is opened.
4. Keep the registers tidy. Avoid overwriting.
5. Make all the entries in ink.
6. Get each cutting attested by the head.
7. Do not open a new volume of a register every year, if the previous volume contains some blank pages.
8. Fill up every column provided in a prescribed register and do not leave any blank space between entries.

Kinds of Records to be Maintained. School records and registers can be broadly classified under the following heads :

General Records : (1) School Calendar. (2) Log Book. (3) Visitors' Book. (4) Service Registers. (5) Admission and Withdrawal Register. (6) Transfer Certificate Book. (7) General Order Book.

Financial : (1) Contingency Register. (2) Acquittance Roll. (3) Contingent Order Book. (4) Fee Collection Register. (5) Abstract Register of Fees. (6) Bill Register. (7) Register of Donations. (8) Register of Scholarships. (9) Boys' Fund Registers.

Educational: (1) Pupils' Attendance Register. (2) Teachers' Attendance Register. (3) Time Tables' Record. (4) Examinations' Results Record. (5) Monthly Progress Register. (6) Private Tuition Register. (7) Public Examination Register. (8) Register of Corporal Punishment. (9) Teachers' Diaries. (10) Cumulative Records.

Equipment : (1) Stock Book of Furniture and School Appliances. (2) Library Catalogue. (3) Accession Register. (4) Issue Books, Register of Newspapers and Magazines received. (5) Stock and Issue Register of Sports Material.

Correspondence : (1) 'From' and 'To' Registers. (2) Peon Book. (3) Memo Book. (4) File of Departmental Orders and Circulars. (5) Register of Casual Leave Granted.

Account Books : (1) Cash Book for Daily Receipts and Expenditure. (2) General Ledger or Classified Abstract of the Monthly Totals. (3) Remittance Book. (4) Register of Pay Bills.

Special Registers Maintained by the Basic Schools and Schools Providing Work Experience etc. (1) Craft Work Record. (2) Production Register. (3) Producers' Register. (4) Art Work Record.

The list is no way a comprehensive and complete one. It includes only those registers which are commonly used. Additions will have to be made to suit the needs and requirements of individual schools. A few of the important school records, relating mainly to the educational side of school administration, are described below :

Admission and Withdrawal Register. This is one of the most important school registers. The head of the institution is personally responsible for its sanctity. According to departmental rules, it is to be kept permanently and therefore it should be specially got bound and arrangements made for its safe custody. Entries should be made as soon as a pupil is admitted or at any rate before the close of the day. Every admission or re-admission made in any part of the year should be entered in it. Successive numbers should be given to the pupils on admission. Each child should retain this number as long as he remains in the school. A new entry should be made if a pupil leaves a school and rejoins it with a leaving certificate issued by another school. This register contains the following information : (a) The number of the child in the register. (b) Date of admission or re-admission. (c) Name of the child in full. (d) The exact date of birth of the child. (e) Name and address of the parent or guardian. (f) The class to which admitted. (g) The date of leaving and the class in which the child was at that time.

Special care is to be taken in recording the date of birth of every child. Many heads have invited trouble due to lack of proper care in recording date of birth. The entry once made should not be altered unless authorised by competent authority and that too in writing. The entries are to be made both in words as well as in figures. The exact day, month and the year of the birth should be recorded. This entry regarding date of birth is very important as it is often required as evidence in important matters.

Pupils' Attendance Register. Each class has its own register showing the names of the pupils on the rolls of a class during a month. As far as possible only one attendance register should be kept by any one teacher. Attendance should be marked both for the beginning of the school day in the morning and its end towards the evening. Ink should be used for marking attendance. No blanks should be left. It is also not a good practice to put dots. The students are to be marked as 'leave' or 'sick' only when their leave applications are sanctioned by the competent authority. Holidays should be indicated in red ink. The name of the student who has been absent without leave for 12 consecutive attendances should be struck off the rolls. Names of girls shall be struck off the rolls for absence without leave after ten consecutive days. The reason for this action should be given in the remarks column against the name of the boy or girl and the necessary information should be given to the school clerk. The entries thus made should be got signed by the Headmaster simultaneously both in the attendance register and withdrawal register. On the last working day of each month, the summary at the end of each page in the register should be carefully prepared and the register got checked by the teacher deputed for this purpose and then got countersigned by the Headmaster. All amounts received by way of fees and funds must be entered in the register immediately on their receipt.

Truants should be noted particularly and their cases reported to the Headmaster and the parents concerned.

Leave application for long sick periods should be supported by medical certificates.

School Calendar. It is drawn up at the beginning of each school session. If possible all schools in the same area should have a uniform school year so that the migrating children are not handicapped and put to inconvenience. It should contain the following items of information :

(i) General, partial and local holidays.

(ii) Dates for the submission of monthly, quarterly, half-yearly and annual reports and returns.

(iii) Dates of public and school examinations.

(iv) Dates of meeting of School Committees, Teachers' Associations, Local Excursions, School Tournaments, etc.

(v) Dates of the monthly tests and the subjects in which they will be held.

The school calendar is very conducive to the better and more systematic organisation of school activities.

Cash Book. It contains a record of all money transactions that are being carried through from day to day in the school. The credit side of the cash book shows all the money received by the school from different sources, e.g. donations, grants-in-aid, fees, boys' funds etc., and its debit side indicates all the payments made, e.g. salaries paid, deposits made in the post office or bank, contingent expenditure incurred, etc.

Cash Book should be well-bound and the pages should be carefully numbered in print.

Cash Book should be written up from day to day. The entry relating to each item of receipt and expenditure should be made at the time of transaction.

As far as possible the cash balance should be immediately deposited in the post office or bank. Daily balancing of the cash book avoids chances of errors.

Ledger. It is a necessary complement of the cash book. All entries made in the cash book are carried to the ledger in their respective accounts. It facilitates the preparation of monthly and annual accounts. It is also helpful in controlling future financial commitments.

Contingency Register. Every Headmaster is generally provided with a contingency advance which is to be spent for day-to-day expenses on petty items such as purchase of office stationery, postage, repairs to building and furniture etc. All such expenditure is entered in the contingency register. All entries in this register are supported by proper receipts which are placed in a separate file.

Boys' Fund Register. The head of an institution is the sole incharge of the boys' funds. The school management is not concerned with boys' funds. The Headmaster is responsible for keeping a regular account of the same and rendering it to the departmental auditors and the inspecting staff.

All income and expenditure pertaining to boys' fund should be entered regularly in the Boys' Fund Register.

It will not be out of place to mention that most of the troubles in our educational institutions owe their origin to the use of these funds. Undue funds charged from the students lead to indiscipline. Wrong use of funds leads them to suspect the integrity of the authorities. Unfortunately the present trend is to use funds for all and sundry purposes. A wise head will make a very judicious use of these funds. He will take his students into confidence and spend this fund through their committees working under the guidance of teachers.

Property Register. All items of a more or less permanent nature bought and placed in the school are entered in the property register. It contains the name of the article, its price and the ordering authority for its purchase.

The Headmaster should get the stock of equipment checked once a year. Room-wise property list facilitates the work of checking. Proper checking of the equipment has a very good advantage. It helps the Headmaster to know which article of equipment or furniture stands in need of repairs or is missing.

Nothing should be struck off the register without the permission of the head who is generally competent to do so.

Service Register. This register contains the record of the official life of every officer working in the institution. On the basis of this record, matters concerning promotions, leave, superannuation, etc., are determined. It is, therefore, very important to make correct and complete entries in it. The entries in the service register should tally with other records. The date and the number of the appointment order should be noted in the case of the first appointment and in the case of transfers. No change in the date of birth is permissible except with the permission of the competent authority. All cases of fine, suspension, degradation or other punishment should be noted along with the reasons and the authority for the punishment. All questions relating to previous service should be settled immediately. Service registers should not be handed over to the persons concerned on their transfer from one school to another but should be sent to the officer responsible for the custody of the registers. Every Headmaster should make it a point to ensure that the registers are free from faults of omission and erroneous insertion.

Teachers' Attendance Register. This register shows the daily attendance of the teachers in a school, their time of arrival and departure, leave taken by them, holidays, and their nature. It is generally placed in the Headmaster's office. Every teacher must sign this register everyday when he comes to the school in the morning and leaves at the termination of the school day.

24

Library as Institution

Books are, apart from the work and influence of the teacher, the chief instrument of education. Children need an environment of attractive books from the beginning; and it is one of the first duties of the school to see that this environment is provided. If a child's early experiences with books are pleasurable, a sound foundation is laid for their use in his future development. The value of a school library lies on the beautiful books on which he may at all times draw inspiration Suitable to his age and development, in which he may follow up and enlarge his own interests and enrich and illumine his growing consciousness of the world around him, and as he grows, so will the range on which he will draw widen.

Centre of Intellectual Life. "The library should be the centre of the intellectual life of the school, available at all times for reference, for study and for private reading. It should be a quiet space, an environment which encourages study and reading, furnished and equipped for comfortable use, it should be very much more than a store room and distributing centre for books."

- (Building Bulletin).

It is the school librarian's function to see that the individual reading is progressive in quality. He must use methods persuasive rather than imperative, indirect rather than direct.

- *(School Library Association Report).*

Live Workshop. "In a school that educates pupils for a changing world the school library should be a live workshop," writes S.R. Ranganathan.

K.G. Saiyidain has observed, "No school or university without a library, adequate for its needs and size, should be recognized as a worthy centre of education."

Hub and Centre. In the opinion of the Secondary Education Commission, "The library will be the hub and the centre of the intellectual and literary life of the recognised school and play the same part vis-a-vis all the other subjects as the laboratory plays for science subjects or the workshop for technical subjects." The dynamic role and the educational possibilities of the school library have long been realised in all progressive countries. In countries like the United States and Great Britain, the school libraries are usually well-equipped and are used fully in the education of children.

The modern philosophy of education stresses more on the child's learning through experience than on anything else. "Individual work, the pursuit of group projects, many academic hobbies and Co-Curricular activities postulate the existence of a good, efficiently managed library," wrote the Secondary Education Commission. So library - a good library - is one of the essentials of a school. Oliver Lodge writes, "Part of education should consist in familiarity and practice, with the looking up of details, with the use of books in general, not only of books of reference."

In the words of Bacon, "Libraries are the shelves where all the relics of saints full of virtue and that without delusion and importance are reposed."

The Purposes

Properly conceived, it is the correlating centre of the school activities. It serves the following purposes :

Introduction of Progressive Methods. The library proves to be instrumental in putting progressive methods into practice.

Opportunity for Self-study. It provides self-study and self-education. It supplements class work by increasing students' vocabulary. There is no doubt that it is not possible for a single student to afford to purchase all the books that he needs. The school library comes to his assistance and helps him to read any number of books, he feels interested in.

Scope for Broadening Interest. It broadens the outlook of the students by placing before them a vast store of useful information that has accumulated through the ages. The students develop wider interest and are encouraged to write their own books when they grow up.

Participation in Co-curricular Programme. It assists the students to prepare themselves for taking part in the various co-curricular activities of the school. They get valuable information which is of great help to them in taking part in debates, declamation contests, giving lectures and writing for the school magazine.

Leisure Time Hobby. Library reading is a good leisure time hobby and it provides an opportunity for the right use of one's leisure time and thus conserves the time and energy otherwise to be used in card games, other indulgence and cinemas.

Increase in Information. It tends to develop habits of the students to derive pleasure and information from recreational and informative books.

Source of Inspirational Books. A good library service helps the students to turn to inspirational books which may ennoble their lives. It provides suitable books to students to satisfy their hunger of reading books and saves them from the harmful effects of reading unsuitable and injurious literature.

Training in the Proper Use of Books. The library imparts training to the students in the proper use of books. The library rules demand that the books should be well-kept and thus the students develop in them the habit of keeping books neat and tidy. H.C. Dent observes, "With a good school library widely used, it is possible to teach children how to use books efficiently—a lesson all of us must learn if we are to get the most out of them. It is a lesson not too easily learnt, and far too rarely taught."

Moral Training. The library imparts training in punctuality by impressing upon them the necessity of borrowing and returning books in time.

Development of Study Habits. The library develops the habit of silent reading. Reading, borrowing and returning are the watch-words of a library room.

Constructive Discipline. It lessens the chance of indiscipline in the school by providing an opportunity to the students to make the best use of leisure time.

In the words of Edmonson, "The modern school library is conceived as a genuine service unit. It supplies materials for developing and expanding interests. Through its reference tools, indexes, bibliographies and catalogues, the realm of knowledge may be explored. The library cooperates with other agencies of instruction in helping students learn to use books and libraries, to find information, and to study. By its bulletin exhibits, posters and atmosphere, the library teaches informally. By its introduction to books, it suggests the life-time use of reading to further any interest."

The functions of the school library may be summed up in the words of the Joint Committee of the School Library Association in Britain, "We seek in the library to make children familiar with the sight and use of a collection of books and to help them to grow to love and care for them, to provide material for child's own recreational reading and explorations, to supply additional reading material illustrating the subjects taught in class, to give opportunities for elementary instruction in the use of books and for carrying out group and individual projects, to give scope for the exercising of simple responsibilities and finally to prepare the way for the use of larger libraries including public library, in adult life.

Current Situation

Our schools do not seem to have been much influenced by the new trends in education especially in the school library organisation. The Secondary Education Commission has expressed that our present libraries are not worth the name and, therefore, do not inspire students to read and cultivate in them a sincere love of books. Some of the main defects of the existing school libraries are:

First the books are usually old, out-dated, unsuitable, selected without reference to the students' tastes and interests.

Secondly, there is a lack of suitable books for children.

Thirdly, books are stocked in a few book-shelves.

Fourthly, generally speaking there are no trained librarians in schools and library work is entrusted to teachers who are very busy in their teaching work and show little interest in library work.

Fifthly, school library is generally housed in an inadequate and unattractive room.

Sixthly, the general tendency of the school authorities is rot to encourage students to read extra books.

Seventhly, the books are beyond the comprehension of students.

Eighthly, the books do not meet the needs of the students. Teachers stuff the library with those books which they need for some examination or some other purpose.

Factors Responsible for the Poor Conditions of the School Library. These factors relate primarily to our:

(a) School curriculum.

(b) Present system of examinations.

(c) Text-books.

School Curriculum. It is generally recognised that our secondary school curriculum is very heavy and it imposes a terrible strain both on students and teachers with the result that they can hardly think of anything else than curriculum itself. The teachers and the students have to work within the prescribed syllabus. It is, therefore, obvious that under these rigid conditions, no dynamic teaching is possible and the school library which forms an integral part of any programme of dynamic teaching remains neglected.

Present System of Examination. Our examinations stress the importance of facts and the students run after those books and notes which provide 'shortcuts' to examinations. The teachers on their part are also forced to spoon feed their pupils rather than encourage habits of independent study.

Text-Books. The present practice of prescribing text-books on all subjects is to be depreciated. The dependence on the prescribed text-books leads to the neglect of original books written by master-minds. Most of the prescribed books are not of a good quality - the paper is not good, the printing is poor and illustrations are inadequate and unsatisfactory. Such books fail to inspire students to acquire any love of books.

Significance of Library

Tagore has given a very good description of a good library, "My idea of a small library is one that keeps books on every subject, but only selected books, not one of which is there merely as an offering of worship to number, but each of which stands on its own merits; where the librarian is a true devotee, devoid of ulterior seeking, free from pride in the mere loading of shelves, capable of discriminate rejection. A library, in short, which makes just enough provision that can be placed before its guests for their delectation, with a librarian who has the qualities of a host, not a store-keeper."

Organisation of a Good Library. The efficient running of the school library depends on a large number of factors which are discussed as under :

1. Role of the Librarian.
2. Library Room and Equipment.
3. Books.
4. Cataloguing.

5. Publicity.

6. Library Rules.

7. Role of the Teachers.

Role of the Librarian. Arnold Bennett states that if libraries spend less on books and more on educated staff, far better results would be obtained. A trained librarian should be appointed in every school. He should have knowledge of contents of every book. He should know the aptitudes, tastes and interests of every student and should help students for extra reading by suggesting them good books. He is expected to play the role of a sympathetic friend and guide to students. His function is also to maintain a study atmosphere and discipline in the library room besides regulating library hours. He should help the school authorities to buy good books. In short, the librarian should possess the following qualifications

(i) General educational.

(ii) Professional, i.e. indexing and cataloguing.

(iii) Pedagogical,, i.e. adept in child psychology, familiarity with the present trends in the educational field, sympathetic nature, etc.

The Secondary Education Commission has observed that if the library is to be the hub of the academic and the intellectual life of the school, if it is not only to meet but guide the reading interests of the students, if it is to work as a centre of free and supervised study as well as group of work on projects undertaken by them - if it is to do all these things, the librarian will surely have all his work cut out. He will also give due publicity to good books, old and new available in the library. He will prepare and circulate book lists suitable for different grades. He will display 'blurbs' and cuttings of book reviews on the notice board. He will also arrange book exhibitions and conduct a few reading projects.

Librarian at Work

1. Preparation and display of library rules and regulations.
2. Preparing catalogues—subject-wise and language-wise.

3. Classification of books.
4. Numbering of books.
5. Stocking books in the proper manner.
6. Training students in the art of looking up reference material, in using catalogues in selecting books.
7. Instructing students in keeping books neat and tidy.
8. Taking annual stock of books.
9. Making plans for the purchase of books.
10. Attaining skills in the use of audio-visual aids like film-projector, tape-recorder etc,
11. Maintaining an atmosphere or perfect silence in the library room.
12. Displaying cuttings and folders on the notice board.

The Secondary Education Commission observes, "He will also be responsible for giving due publicity to good books, old and new, available in the library – preparing and circulating book lists suitable for different grades, displaying 'blurbs' and cuttings of book reviews on the notice board, arranging book exhibitions, perhaps conducting a group reading project when a few students of similar interests may come together to read aloud poems, stories or dramas."

V.B. Pathak observes, "In addition to the routine work, the librarian is required to see that the library is situated in a central place in the school; that it is adequately equipped; that every student has an easy approach to the library material; that adequate arrangements for seating according to the age-groups are available; that books are arranged in the shelves in such a way that students do not find much difficulty in tracing out the required information; that the tools for finding out the information are adequate; that the library meets the demands of the gifted as well as the backward children; that the library helps in forming a good reading habit in the students; that there is coordination with the teaching staff, that the students and the staff get the right type of books; that the funds of the library are not misused; that the library is made a place of attraction; that there is a temperamental adjustment with the staff, and last but not the least that the important factor of economy in time, labour and money receives special attention in such a way that it does not serve as an obstruction in achieving the ultimate goal of education."

Role of the Teachers. The importance of the close connection and cooperation of all members of the staff with the librarian must be stressed. The teachers should acquaint themselves with the contents, important topics and the stories within the books and should suggest suitable books to the students. They should advise students as to what type of books they should read and what sorts of books they should avoid. They should quote references in the teaching of various class lessons in order to stimulate to read extra books. They should stimulate, guide and direct the independent study on the part of children. They should keep records of the books read by the students.

It has been stated by Don W. James, "Teachers and librarians together must plan for maximum utilization of a school library They must break down old barriers that separate library and classroom and discover the unity that can support the learning process."

Location of the Library Room. It should have an exposure admitting plenty of light and sunshine. It should be separate from the study hall, but should be as near as possible to it. The floor should be covered with carpet to deaden sound. All possible surface downward from a point 7 feet above the floor should be utilized for shelving. White ceiling and light buff walls give the best lighting effects.

Regarding library room and equipment, S.R. Ranganathan observes : "It should be equipped with plenty of attractive well-built, well-printed, well-illustrated books; with comfortable furniture, open shelves, charming pictures, flowers, hangings and bright and cheerful outlook, with a librarian who loves children as well as books." Reading, lending, borrowing and returning, should be the watch-words of a library room. Spitting, smoking, noising, sleeping and quarrelling should be prohibited.

Selection of Books. According to the Secondary Education Commission, the guiding principles in the selection of books should be not the teacher's own ideas of what books the students must read but their natural and psychological interests. The contents of a library as regards books may be classified as:

Books for Younger Children. This will include well-illustrated and attractive books giving information on fairy tales and fables etc. They should be moderate in length and should be handsomely bound.

Books for Older Children. These include (i) books depicting stories of travels, explorations, adventures, discoveries and inventions; (ii) biographies of great men and women; (iii) suitable works of fiction, fun and hobbies ; (iv) parallel text-books; (v) books on different subjects; (vi) source books; and (vii) dictionaries.

Books for Teachers. The librarian should remain in intimate touch with the work of the different departments, and the specific projects of the classroom, and should make available all that the library contains in connection with classroom work. A faculty committee including a representative of each department should be appointed, with the librarian as Chairman. The committee should determine policies for the development of the library, draw up rules governing its use and use funds in such a way as each phase of the school work may be provided for equit. Lists of usable books and periodicals indicating those that are most immediately desirable, should be prepared by each departmental representative in excess of the number that can be secured in any given year. Such a step will increase the service of the library and will make it the real unifying centre of the school.

Books for Adults. The school library should contain books for the adult population also in order to serve it a centre of community service.

In general, the following types of books should be selected for the school library :

1. They should be selected with reference to the general aims which the school sets up.

2. They should be selected, with reference to the vocational needs of the students.
3. Recreational interests of the students should be given due consideration in the selection of books.
4. There should be included carefully selected works for general reference such as dictionaries and encyclopaedias.
5. Duplicators of books much in use should be secured. In order to provide common intellectual link for the budding scholars it is advisable to have many copies of a few useful books than to have one copy each of many different ones.
6. There should be some well-illustrated editions of standard books and of works on art and travel.
7. There should be as liberal a supply as possible of current periodicals and newspapers, selected on the basis of their natural interests to young people and their relation to classroom work and to co-curricular activities of the student.
8. Books which inspire students for noble ideas, higher thinking; good morals and social virtues should be placed in large numbers in the school library.

In fact a library should be made as attractive as possible. The students are to be drawn and driven to the library.

The Cataloguing. Views of Rabindra Nath Tagore are worth noting when he writes, "The usual thing is for a library to say, 'Here is my catalogue, come and select for yourself.' But in the usual catalogue there is no introduction, no invitation, no spirit of welcome. That library alone can be called hospitable which shows an eagerness to invite readers to the feast at its disposal. It is such hospitality that makes a library big, not its size. That the readers make the library is not the whole truth the library likewise makes the readers."

Encouraging Students to Read Library Books. In the words of Tagore, "In order to bring a library into the fullest use, it is necessary that its contents should be clearly and specifically brought to notice, otherwise it is difficult for the ordinary man to find his way about them, and the library is left as a city of vast accommodation that lacks sufficient means of communication. Those who frequent libraries on some special quest of their own may manage to make a track for themselves by dint of the urgency of their particular pursuit. But the library itself should recognise its share of responsibility in the matter. Because it has the books, it is incumbent on the library to get them read, for that alone it is justified; it is not enough that it passively permits visitors, its invitation should be active. For, as the Sanskrit proverb tells us: 'tannashtam yannadiyata', that which is not given is wasted."

The following steps are likely to encourage pupils to read library-books:

1. Thorough and systematic instruction in the use of the library should be given to all pupils. The instruction should aim at teaching pupils not only how to find out the books and other materials in the library but also how to make the best use of the material which the library contains. The librarian should give this instruction to regularly scheduled classes. The teacher should give occasional talks to pupils on the importance of extra reading.
2. As far as possible, the open-shelf system should be introduced so that the students may have free access to books, may learn to handle them and browse on them at their leisure.
3. The Secondary Education Commission recommends that it is necessary for the Headmasters and the teachers to keep their finger, as it were on the pulse of their students' general reading. "Where ordinary issue registers—rather issue cards - are maintained, each student must be allotted a few pages of the register in which all books studied by him are entered date-wise so that the class teachers and Headmasters may see at

a glance that each individual has been reading and give him necessary advice and encouragement."

4. Each student may be asked to maintain a diary in which he may enter date-wise, the names of all the books (along with the names of the authors) which he has read. He may also be instructed to write brief quotations or extracts that may appeal to him. If possible, he may write short reviews or appreciations of those books. Such a diary, maintained throughout the school years, will provide a fascinating map of his intellectual development and literary growth which will not only be of value to him here and now but may be of interest even in later life.
5. As far as possible, the open-shelf system should be introduced so that the students may have free access to books.
6. Bulletin Boards may be used in schools and beautiful pictures, cuttings from newspapers and illustrations from current events and topics should be displayed on them.
7. To encourage the students to read books, marks may be allotted. There is a practice in some schools to make a mention of the number of books read by each student during the month in the monthly progress reports which they send to the parents.
8. Library periods should be provided for each class in the time-table. The teachers may be deputed to supervise.
9. A Book Lovers' Club may be formed and the students asked to give a short review of the interesting stories or other comments of the books read by them.
10. Book competitions should be arranged from time to time and questions on titles, authors and the subject matter should be set. This will prove helpful in stimulating children to read.

11. Books suiting different tastes and interests should be provided in large numbers.
12. It should be made possible to keep the school library open during the vacation and long holidays for the benefit of the students as well as the local community.
13. During the vacation books of interest to suit different grades of students should be collected from various school libraries and placed in a central locality. This will encourage the students to visit such improvised libraries and to study whatever books they may be interested in.
14. A whole-time and a very competent librarian should be appointed in the school.
15. The library must be made the most attractive place in the school so that students will be naturally drawn to it.
16. In decorating the library, full cooperation of the students should be obtained in order to give them the feeling that it is their own library.

The Guidelines

(1) The students should be asked not to spoil or disfigure books.
(2) They should be asked to keep a diary in which they should write their comments regarding books which they have read.
(3) They should be told the implications of the library rules.
(4) They should be instructed to maintain a study atmosphere in the library.
(5) They should contemplate upon whatever they read.
(6) They should discuss their doubts with the teachers.
(7) They should quote the material read (whatever necessary) in their own compositions.

Classroom Library. By classroom library we mean library in the room of each class and managed by the class teachers. Every school is expected to organise class libraries. It is wrong to imagine that class library is competitive to central library. It is to supplement the work of the central library. "The class library is an important and essential adjunct to the central school library," writes the Secondary Education Commission. It is full of educational potentialities.

The class teachers spend much of their time with students and therefore they are in a better position to suggest suitable books to them according to their taste and aptitudes.

The teachers get opportunities to see how much reading each pupil is doing and can thus encourage the keen students and stimulate the slow goers. They can also assess whether the students are reading carefully and intelligently. It is also easy for them to organise book competitions.

The administration of class library is very simple. It does not require any elaborate method of recording.

The organisation of the classroom library can very easily be entrusted to the students thus affording them an opportunity to manage their own affairs.

Teacher's Attitude to the Class Library. The class library service is never up to the mark unless class teachers are full of enthusiasm and are ready to put in some extra work. They must see that the collections are frequently changed and replenished so that even within the walls of classrooms the children have a wide variety of intellectual flair spread out before them. They will also continually, in all their lessons talk about books, refer to characters and scenes in them, quote from them and put them in their pupils' minds.

Subject Libraries. It has been recommended by the Secondary Education Commission that besides the class library in every high school, there should be subject libraries under charge of subject teachers. In addition to text-books, there should be advanced works, reference books on related subjects and books on allied fields. Such collections are expected to help the teachers in enriching their teaching. The students are also likely to get a wide view of the subject in all its bearings.

Reading Room. The reading-room should be provided with facilities to accommodate at one full period readers numbering from 5 to 10 per cent of the total daily attendance of the school. In high schools enrolling 500 pupils the reading rooms should have a seating capacity of 40 to 50, those enrolling 1000 should have a seating capacity of 75 to 100. The minimum capacity in the small high school should be that of an average classroom. The reading-room should contain tables, comfortable chairs, a charging desk for the librarian and a card catalogue case.

The room should be well-illustrated with informational illustrations. A large number of daily newspapers, periodicals, journals and well-illustrated magazines dealing with current affairs in every walk of life should be placed in the reading-room. Of course, care should be taken to select magazines, etc., which are of great interest to children. Latest copies of the reading material should be kept and the old should be removed and kept up for reference purposes.

25

Building of the School

Jacobson, Reavis and others observe : "The school plant is a comprehensive term which includes building, grounds, school furniture, other equipment and apparatus. The head of the school must look upon the plant as an integral part of a learning environment."

Exemplary Building

Shri K. G. Saiyidain observes, "Ideally a school building should be planned spaciously, functionally and with pleasing architectural features. It should stand out in the village or the city as something of which the local community can be proud. In fact in some educationally advanced and wealthy countries, schools are housed in beautiful buildings which are not only stimulating centres of education for children but also vital centres of community life."

Ideal Environment

The importance of a healthy, beautiful and refreshing environment which soothes the eye and refreshes the soul and where the intellectual forces of teachers and pupils function at their best, is apparent when we realize that the students spend a good deal of their time in the school premises. A school cannot be put everywhere and anywhere. Some very definite considerations have to be taken into account in the selection of the site which is the first requisite of a good environment.

William Yeager thinks : "Nothing in the whole educational programme is more conducive to cooperative attitude among the pupils and a love of school than an attractive and wholesome environment."

Common Principles

Principles of Adequacy. The school plan must provide for all the necessary facilities for curricular and co-curricular activities.

Principle of Safety. The building must be planned in strict conformity with hygeine laws. Full attention must be given to site, soil, ventilation, light and other allied problems. The school plant must be able to protect the health of the students and teachers.

Principle of Durability. As far as possible, the building must be 'pucca' rather then 'kacha.'

Principle of Economy. The school plant should be economical in original cost, upkeep and operation. Economy can be affected by the adoption of a standard classroom unit.

Principle of Accessibility. The school should be built at a place which is easily accessible to the students and free from road dangers.

Principle of Mobility. The question of easy movement, particularly in large schools on more than one storey is important.

Principle of Flexibility. There should be no rigidity in the design and use of the plant. Scope must be left for modifications in accordance with the needs.

Principle of Coordination. There must be full coordination among the various parts and their location at a particular place must have a purpose. For instance a workshop will be away from the classroom and the staff room very near to principal's room.

Principle of Simplicity. The design of the building should be simple but artistic.

Principle of Comprehensiveness. A comprehensive vision is necessary in which function, form and space are so harmonized that the soil from which the synthesis grows, will be enriched by such a pattern.

Principle of Utility. It must give the maximum utility to the students as regards accommodation, protection from weather, maximum light and ventilation, free movement and comfortable stay in rooms for longer hours.

Need for a Plant

Site

1. The school is located in congenial and healthy surroundings.
2. It is free from noise and disturbance.
3. It is easily accessible.
4. It has the following:
   (a) Playgrounds. (b) Gardens. (c) Cycle stand. (d) Lawns. (e) Agricultural Land.
5. The site has scope for expansion and extension of school building.

Building

1. The school is well protected by a boundary wall/fence.
2. The school building is structurally stable.
3. The school building is planned in a way wherein the free movement of the inmates is possible.
4. The accommodation for various special rooms is adequate.
5. The accommodation for various purposes is adequate.

6. The school building meets the requirements of the school and provides for the following rooms :
   - (i) Principal's Office.
   - (ii) School Office.
   - (iii) Staff Room.
   - (iv) Library.
   - (v) Reading Room.
   - (vi) Girls Room (in co-educational institutions).
   - (vii) Assembly hall.
   - (viii) Auditorium.
   - (ix) Museum.
   - (x) Workshop.
   - (xi) Audio-Visual Room.
   - (xii) N.C.C. Room.
   - (xiii) Guidance Room.
   - (xiv) Subject Room.
   - (xv) Store Room.
   - (xvi) Laboratories.
   - (xvii) Class Rooms.
   - (xviii) Cycle Stand.
   - (xix) Drinking Water Room.
   - (xx) Doctor's Room.
   - (xxi) Sports Room.
   - (xxii) Urinals and Lavatories.

Building Services

1. Proper ventilation is provided in the school building.
2. There is proper provision for lighting arrangements in the school.
3. There is sufficient provision for fans.

4. The drinking water facilities are sufficient.
5. The drinking water facilities are in hygienic order.
6. There are proper sanitary arrangements in the school.
7. Adequate number of urinals and lavatories are available in the school.

Equipments

1. The rooms and subject room furniture and equipment are adequate to meet the requirements of the pupils.
2. The furniture is convenient for work and suitable for the correct postures of the pupils.
3. The furniture and equipment are properly arranged to facilitate efficient working in the school.
4. The library is well-furnished and properly equipped according to needs.
5. The reading room is well-furnished and equipped.
6. The principal's room is well-furnished and equipped.
7. The staff room is well-furnished.
8. The office is well-furnished and properly equipped.
9. The unserviceable furniture and other equipment are written off and disposed of regularly.

Maintenance and Repairs

1. The school campus is kept neat and tidy.
2. The furniture and equipment are in serviceable conditions and properly maintained.
3. Repairs of the building-furniture equipment and building services. i.e. taps, walls, electric fittings are done regularly.
4. Proper steps are taken to make the campus look attractive and beautiful by means of gardens, flower beds.

Site Selection

The following points should be kept in view:

Surroundings. The site should be located in healthy surroundings. It should be near a road so as to be accessible by bus or other means of transport, yet back from the road. It should be located in a quiet and pleasant environment.

Level. The level of the area should be raised a little so that water-logging does not take place. There should be no danger of floods or beach of any canal.

Direction. The site selected should permit the construction of the rooms in such a way that no corner remains bereft of sunlight.

Shape. The shape of the site preferably should be rectangular.

Public Service. Various public services like drainage water-pipe arrangement and lighting arrangement should be easily accessible.

Scope for Future Expansion. The site for a school should be so selected as to allow normal expansion towards one direction at least.

Situations to be Avoided

1. Noisy and busy roads.
2. Public places like bus stand, railway stations, grain market, etc.
3. Places like cremation ground and burial ground.
4. Marshy lands.
5. Uneven and undeveloped lands.
6. Stagnant pools, cattle ponds and other unhealthy surroundings.
7. Places of public entertainment like the cinema houses.

Area Requirements

Area is another determining factor in the selection of a site. It is possible to prescribe any definite limit. The area required for a school site depends upon many factors.

The Strength of the School. As every child is to be provided with 15 square feet of floor space, the area of the site will depend upon the number of students in a particular school.

Type of School. For residential schools, a big area is required. They will require provision for hostel and staff quarters also.

Subjects Taught. Schools which provide for the teaching of agriculture must have agricultural farm. Naturally, such schools will stand in need of a far greater area than an ordinary school. Multipurpose schools will also require larger areas.

Co-curricular Activities. Generally speaking greater area is required for the public schools as they organise a large number of co-curricular activities than the ordinary schools. They provide activities like swimming etc.

Recommendations of the School Building Committee of the Central Advisory Board of Education regarding the Minimum Area for a Higher Secondary School.

No. of Children	*Area of the Building*	*Area for Playgrounds*
160	2/3 Acre	2–3 Acres
320	1 Acre	4–5 Acres
480	1½ Acre	6–7 Acres

Various Designs

No single type can be recommended. The common types are:

(i) The simple I type, a row of classrooms.

(ii) L type i.e., I type with an extension of one side.

(iii) T type i.e., I type with extension on one side both ways.

(iv) U type i.e., two I's joined on one side.

(v) E type.

(vi) H type.

Current Conditions

Open Air Schools. The task of providing 'Schools for All' is a stupendous one. Our resources are limited and it is, therefore, imperative for us to see that each rupee that we spend is fully utilised to the last paisa. It has been observed in a pamphlet "Schools for All ." "If we put up school buildings, as in the past, it will not leave us with enough resources to undertake improvement in the quality of education or in the status of teachers, or provision of equipment and other necessary material needs of the school." Our first Prime Minister who was deeply concerned about this problem, wrote as follows : "Let us take primary education which must necessarily be the base. We hold it up because of lack of money and lack of teachers especially for Basic education. Probably we still spend much more on buildings than on equipment or teachers. Can we not stop putting up any buildings in rural areas and devote the money thus saved to a better class of teachers as well as to some equipment ? The equipment would have to be kept somewhere and there should be a small room or hall for this purpose. But all the teaching might well be done in the open under trees or under very simple sheds. It must be remembered that our climate helps and normally it is healthier to sit outside under a tree or in a grove, except during the rainy season. Also our old traditions fit in with this open air teaching."

"It seems to me more important to have a proper house for the teacher than to put up a building for the school. The school revolves round the teacher and not round the building."

"I should like the village to give a small plot of land for the school and the teacher. A vegetable garden could be laid down there. The status of the teacher would go up, even though his salary may not be as much as we would like it to be, though it would be substantially higher."

K.G. Saiyidain, a formerly Educational Adviser to the Government of India, observes, "In the matter of buildings, there have been two schools of thought - those who ask for impressive buildings for schools and those who favour the 'one-tree-one-school' approach. I am putting the two points of view in their extreme form. It is obvious that there are some considerations which weigh in favour of each. Ideally, a school building should be planned spaciously, functionally and with pleasing architectural features. It should stand out in the village or the city as something of which the local community can be proud. In fact, in some educationally advanced and wealthy countries, schools are housed in beautiful buildings, which are not only stimulating centres of education for children but also vital centres of community life. Personally, I am of the view that, given the resources, nothing, in reason, can be too good for our children. On the other hand, in our existing conditions, there is much to be said - not only on financial, but also on educational grounds for keeping education close to Nature, for teaching children not within the confines of small, cramped and dingy school rooms but in the open air, so far as possible, so that contact with the earth and sky and trees and flowers and birds and animals becomes part of their environment. This approach, however, has certain limitations. In many regions of the country there are rigours of climate which make open air schooling difficult in certain parts of the year. Moreover, some covered space is needed not only for sheltering school apparatus books and furniture but also for organised craft work. It becomes necessary, therefore, to strike a balance between these various considerations and, in view of our resources position. We must perforce strike the balance in favour of economy. We have to think of ways to provide the minimum necessary accommodation as economically and quickly as possible and leave it to local effort and initiative and civic sense to complete the school building in due course. In the case of rural schools, it is necessary to utilise local materials and not impose on the village a style of construction which is out of tune with its general set-up. This does not, however, mean that school houses need be drab or unattractive like most of the existing village houses. Far from it, with cheap local material, it is possible to build schools which will be functionally useful and artistically attractive."

In the opinion of the Secondary Education Commission, under certain conditions some of the activities of the school may be carried on in the open air during part of the year. The Commission further notes :

(1) The open air system lends itself to small groups of students being taught there, and it also requires good shade and a large area for carrying on instruction satisfactorily.

(2) While much theoretical instruction in certain subjects may be given in open air classes, it is impossible in certain other subjects unless suitable accommodation is provided for them. Thus the laboratories, libraries and workshops should be located in buildings suitably constructed. In any case the school requires considerable grounds for the physical education programme to be carried out for group games and many of the extra-curricular activities of the school. There is also the need for agricultural farms in schools where agriculture is taught as a practical subject.

A "Nucleus First" Type Schools. The brochure "Schools for All" gives a scheme for the construction of school buildings. The scheme may be described thus : Instead of building a complete school right from the start, we should try to build it by stages, starting the institution with a nucleus. There should be a provision for storage, display and black-board space in the nucleus. The actual teaching may be carried out in the open. A 'pucca' room of suitable size may be built and partitioned into four equal isosceles triangles. There will be two openings of each triangular room so formed. A chalk board will be fitted between them to the wall. There will be storage space for equipment, craft tools and materials and various other teaching aids in the triangular rooms. The doors will carry bullet in boards for display of pictures, newspaper clippings, wall magazines and a variety of other materials.

The classes will be seated in the open and make use of the chalk boards and the improvised bulletin boards. Given a suitable point, chalk boards can be used as screens for arranging film shows for children in the evening. A portion of the outdoor space can also be used for construction activities, for rhythms, dances and class dramatics.

Spaces X1, X2, X3, X4 between the classes (as shown in the diagram) are to be used by the classes for activities like gardening, planting and other craft work. The nucleus will thus provide excellent facilities for four grades in an Elementary School.

A. NUCLEUS (storage, workbench, display space on back of door, black-board).

B. SHELTER (floor, roof, wind break) to be provided with local effort trees or canvas or bamboo at first, permanent construction later.

C. PLANTING AREA - Adjacent planting area to be developed entirely by pupils and teachers.

Advantages. Advantages as envisaged in the brochure are :

1. It will enable us to get a well equipped school functioning quickly and with a minimum of expenditure.
2. It would provide a flexible long range plan within the means of every community.
3. It would provide the teacher with better tools than are available in present school buildings.
4. It would induce and inspire local effort.
5. It would give local effort a simple plan of action.
6. It would provide an environment that will almost automatically lead to adoption of some form of Basic education. The nucleus will free the children from drab, limited and walled-in classrooms with nothing but bookish instruction and on the other hand will bring them into close partnership with life and nature.
7. The nucleus will be provided by the State and the local community encouraged to proceed with the rest. Thus it would shift financial responsibility from the State to the local effort.
8. It will bring about better team work between pupils, parents and the State. More local effort will bring about more local interest. More local interest will result in better schools. The pupils and the teachers would also have a definite part in the building of this new school as has been suggested.

RECOMMENDATIONS OF THE REPORT ON HIGHER SECONDARY SCHOOL BUILDING (1960) PUBLISHED BY NATIONAL BUILDINGS ORGANIZATION

School : Big and Small

On purely economic considerations, a school with high enrolment is justified. But to obtain the desired student-teacher relationship, it is necessary to limit the size of school. Considering both economy and educational requirements it is recommended that ordinarily schools should be planned for an enrolment of 960 students. The limit may, however, be increased in exceptional cases where the Director of Education is satisfied that the increase in enrolment will not adversely affect the standard of education.

Number of Students in a Class. Almost all educational authorities agree that 30 is the ideal number of students in a class but on economic grounds it is not possible to achieve this ideal. Even in public schools, 35 is the average class strength. Analysis of data showed that 66.7% of schools have 40 to 49 students per class with an average of 45 students.

Area per Student in a Class

(a) The educational authorities insist on 8 to 12 sq. ft. per student in class.

(b) Foreign standards and changing educational needs require 16 sq. ft. per student. Twelve sq. ft. per student, however, would not permit flexibility of space and provision of a small work bench in the class as required by the modern methods of teaching. But in view of the present financial stringency, the minimum functional requirement of 12 sq. ft. per student is recommended.

Various Facilities

The area of laboratories will depend on the average number of students taking science group. The number and area of laboratories should, therefore, be worked out in each case on the basis of actual requirements. Laboratories should always be planned for even number of students subject to a minimum of 210. Taking both educational and economic factors into consideration, an area of 20 sq. ft. per student in laboratories was considered essential. In addition a store of 80 to 120 sq. ft. may also be provided.

A separate room for library centrally located to all the teaching spaces should be must in every school. But the standard for library accommodation should be rational and consistent with its utility. Considering the economy, utility and function, it is recommended that a library of 600 sq. ft. would be adequate to meet the present educational needs. The area in certain cases may be increased to 960 sq. ft. where instructions in library science are to be given or if library is to be used both by teachers and students.

Ordinarily the hall should be planned in all school designs for future construction only, the hall should be planned and located in such a way that it could be divided into 2 or 3 smaller halls for use of teaching purposes also. Size of hall will depend on the number of students. It is recommended that 7 sq. ft. per student may be taken as the basis to calculate the floor area of the hall. This figure is inclusive of the passages, gang ways, etc. in the hall but does not include the area occupied by stage. Ordinarily, a hall should be provided for 50% of the total enrolment. It was desired that the hall should be so designed that verandah or entrance hall or any other room close to it could be used to accommodate the over-flow from the hall. It is also suggested that one side of the hall should not be more than 11/2 times the other for best hearing and seeing conditions.

Administrative Offices

The area required for the school office will depend on the size of the school and number of staff members. It should, therefore, be worked out on the basis of exact requirement. Whereas it is necessary to reduce the non-teaching areas to absolute minimum, it was felt that for efficient functioning of school, suitable accommodation for staff and the office was necessary. Suggestions made by the Principals of schools on this point were carefully examined. Taking all the factors into consideration the following scale of accommodation is recommended

Principal's office	200 sq. ft.
Staff common room	for 75% members of the total teaching staff at the rate of 20 sq. ft. per staff member subject to a minimum of 200 sq. ft.
Guidance room (which may also be used as visitor's room)	200 sq. ft.
First-aid or doctor's room with attached lavatory.	150 sq. ft.

Storage. One of the most common complaints registered by the Principals of schools was the absence or inadequacy of storage space. Only 35.3% of the schools had a general store. Wherever provided the accommodation for storage was generally considered insufficient.

In all kinds of instructional areas, storage space is needed so that materials can be conserved or laid temporarily for subsequent use. The general practice is to plan the educational spaces and then designate spaces lacking natural light or ventilation as storage. Sometimes this provision is omitted or very small store is provided resulting in the use of spaces for storage designated for quite a different use.

Storage space is required in classroom and other teaching areas. In addition separate rooms for storage of general teaching equipment, sports goods, furniture and dramatic and other equipment are needed.

It is recommended that adequate built-in storage space in the shape of cupboards, open shelves, etc., should be provided in classrooms, etc. The space under the window sills should be utilised for storage as it would not take any floor area. Cupboards at the teacher's wall are necessary for keeping teaching equipment such as duster, chalks, students' note-books, etc. These should, however, be so provided that they do not take additional floor area or increase the wall thickness, etc.

Well planned separate storage space is needed for housing other equipment stated above. Whereas it is necessary to provide adequate storage space the exact requirements could best be worked out by the architects and the educationists. Normally, the storage space should be in the neighbourhood of 5% of the teaching area.

Personal Facilities. The requirements of cafeteria and students' common rooms, etc., were considered and it was felt that these were not essential requirements. Even the analysis of data shows that only 12.7% of schools have a room for cafeteria. It is recommended that cafeteria, etc., need not be provided unless it is absolutely necessary due to the distance between student's house and school or because of eating habit or some other reasons.

Sanitary Facilities. It is universally agreed that the provision of proper and adequate sanitary is essential. But it is here only that there is wide gap between the standard recommended by different authorities and the actual conditions. It was surprising to note that out of 103 schools, 20 schools did not have a single latrine, 26 were without urinals, and 74 had no wash-basins. The provision varies from I latrine for 1,344 students to about 40 students. In case of urinals, the variation is of the same order except that the minimum goes up to 60. Provision of wash-basins is most inadequate and one wash-basin is used by 200 to 800 students. On the basis of observations in the use of urinals, etc. in schools, the following scale of sanitary fittings is recommended. However, a systematic study and further investigation would be required to ascertain the actual use and exact need of sanitary fittings.

Latrines or W.C.	1 for every 100 students or part thereof
Urinals	1 for every 25 students or part thereof
Water taps with troughs	1 for every 50 students or part thereof In addition, facilities for drinking water should be provided at each floor.

(In case of girls schools urinals shall be provided in separate enclosures with foot squatting.)

Circulation. Analysis of some of the recently constructed schools show that circulation space varies between 20% to 30% of the total floor area. In foreign countries 20% of the floor area is a standard. It is recommended that area under circulation should not exceed:

(a) 20% of the total area in the case of single storey structures or double storey structures with doubly loaded corridors.

(b) 33% of total building area in the case of double storey structures.

Ventilation. Till such time the present method of fixing the light area in terms of floor area may be followed, the standards prescribed by most of the authorities i.e., 15% to 29% of the floor area is recommended. The height of window sill should be such that adequate light falls on the student's desk. It should not normally exceed 3 ft. unless it is so required due to some special reasons. Where the students' chairs and desks are not provided but instead squatting arrangement is provided the height of window sill should be reduced suitably.

Accommodation for Staff

Place for living in close proximity of place of work is advantageous both for the work and the worker. In educational circle there is growing demand for staff residences in the school compound.

Dwelling units for the principal, one senior teacher and a member of the office staff in the school compound are recommended by majority of the principals. The main reason for their recommendation appears to be difficulties that teaching staff might be experiencing due to shortage of housing. It is true that sometimes the distance between the residence of the Principal and the school would seriously interfere with his educational responsibilities.

It is, therefore, recommended that residential accommodation for Principal, a member of the staff, chowkidar and a sweeper or a peon only be provided in the school compound in case of urban areas. For rural areas, however, it may be necessary to provide residential accommodation for the principal and 50% of the staff to attract talent to rural schools.

It is further recommended that the local authorities should requisite suitable houses in the locality to ameliorate the difficulties of the teaching staff. Such an action will indirectly help the cause of education.

Land Requirements. Analysis of data shows that out of 83 schools, 36 are housed on plots with area between I to 5 acres; 18 schools have plot areas of 5 to 10 acres. 3 to 6 acre size seems to be quite common.

As in the past, the area of a school site would, to a great extent, depend on the availability and cost of land at the places suitable for building a school. Recommendations of land requirements would, therefore, serve only as a guide in the selection of site otherwise suitable for school purposes. The area of a school site will depend on :

(i) The area required for school building with necessary open spaces for outdoor teaching and physical exercises.

(ii) The areas required for playing fields.

(iii) The area required for staff quarters, etc.

Depending on the availability of funds and the land, larger sites should be acquired. Any economy on this account is likely to create serious difficulties later on due to growth of town or change in educational needs. Expansion or improvement scheme of most of the schools are handicapped due to site limitation.

The area of site to a great extent depends on the number of playing fields required. If there are community open space or parks, which could be used by the school as playing fields, the area required for games could be substantially reduced.

Volleyball, football and hockey are the most popular games in schools. In the schools examined, it was found that volleyball is played in 82.8% of the schools; football in 77.8%, badminton in 75.8% and hockey in 59.6% of the schools. Badminton and volleyball are very popular because these games require much smaller area of land.

The area required for hockey and football fields are 11/2 acres and 2 acres respectively. The area required for most of the games and athletics meets is 3/2 acres.

It is recommended that at least an area of 3 acres should be aimed if community parks or open spaces are available in close proximity to schools and could be used by the school as playing fields. In case where these facilities are available but the land is cheap and easily available it could be advisable to earmark 11/2 acres of land for future needs of education or game. In case suitable site for school is not available near community park or open spaces or where such open spaces cannot be made use of by the school as play fields, etc., it is recommended that minimum area of 5 acres should be aimed at.

Temporary Structure

The Report of the Temporary School Buildings in Delhi (1961) deals with the problem of requirements and describes the type of structure recommended and adopted with success. The plan effects economy in space by : (a) omission of the provision for a separate hall, (b) reduction in the area of laboratories commensurate with the number of students using it at a time and the type of work to be done and (c) reduction in the administrative area of schools such as the Principal's room, staff room, office room, record room, etc. The reduced space requirements for a temporary higher secondary school of 15 sections and having a strength of 600 students comes to 14,640 sq. ft. as against the original requirements of 21,020 sq. ft. effecting a saving of 30.4 per cent in carpet area.

The design envisages the use of precast concrete columns and panels, prestressed concrete purlins and A.C. roofing. The shape and size of the columns and those of the panels are so adjusted that they could be erected without any difficulty, providing at the same time, an architecturally pleasing exterior and an interior reasonably protected from the effects of weather. The flooring can be either of cement concrete or dry brick on edge laid over well-rammed earth. The latter is much cheaper but not so durable and clean.

There are no corridors or verandahs, therefore, bajri or brick paved paths are necessary. A block of WCs and urinals would be provided away from the main building.

On the structural side, several minor details have been looked into with great care resulting in the omission of frames for doors and windows and lintels over openings. The columns themselves are so shaped as to facilitate the attachment of doors and window shutters while some of the wall panels are so made as to act as lintels over openings and as window sills.

Unpleasant State

In the words of the Education Commission 1964-66, "The provision of school buildings is extremely unsatisfactory at present. At the present stage, only about 30 percent of the schools are stated to have been housed in satisfactory buildings."

The Difficulties

1. Heavy costs.
2. Delay in the construction of Government school buildings.
3. Availability of site.

RECOMMENDATIONS OF THE EDUCATION COMMISSION 1964-66 ON SCHOOL BUILDINGS

Funds for School Buildings. The Education Commission recommends that the allocations for construction of school buildings in the Central and State budgets should be increased. This is one area where the local community can make a significant contribution. Schemes of grant-in-aid should, therefore, be devised under which assistance from the State will be available to local communities, on a basis of equalisation, for the construction of school buildings. Wherever possible, loan programmes for the construction of buildings should be encouraged. Grants-in-aid and loans should also be available to private schools, on a fairly liberal basis, for building constructions.

Less Costly Buildings. The Education Commission feels that the prejudice against the use of 'temporary' buildings or thatched huts for school purposes is totally unjustified. Designed and constructed with a raised floor and high doors and windows with plenty of ventilation, these structures serve more than adequately as school building. This should not, however, be misunderstood to imply that kaccha buildings are always better. This is not so; and some kaccha buildings prove costlier in the long run because of heavier costs of maintenance. What we wish to emphasize is the need to accept well-planned kaccha structure as part of our system and to highlight simplicity and utility rather than ostentation in the construction of buildings.

Buildings in Rural Areas. The problem of school buildings has been discussed by the Commission separately for urban and rural areas.

In the former case, land values are high; and very often enough land is not available at all. Sophisticated structures are, therefore, necessary, even in order to keep in tune with the immediate environment. In the rural areas, on the other hand, land is cheap and readily available; and sophisticated structures often look grotesque in a village atmosphere.

The Education Commission recommends that everything should be done to encourage local initiative and local contribution (in cash, kind or labour) for the erection of schools. A special device that can be of great use is that Government should supply only the framework, which can be prefabricated, and the local people should be expected to raise the plinth and fill up the walls. The 'nucleus' approach recommended by the Ministry of Education will be of great help and deserves to be generally adopted.

Judicious Selection or Specifications and Local Materials. The existing practice of playing safe by adopting conventional specifications is not conducive to economical construction. The economy can be achieved through the selection of locally available materials, use of cheaper materials, omission altogether of certain finishes and acceptance of a lower standard of construction. In all these steps, the governing factors would be the availability of materials, climatic conditions, safety of buildings and recurring costs on maintenance.

Techniques of Construction. With careful planning and designing, even the so-called 'temporary' structures can be made to serve a better purpose than many of the rented buildings in which schools are often housed. Such structures should be built, wherever climatic and other conditions permit. If pucca buildings are absolutely necessary, an increasing reliance is needed on the improved techniques of construction such as the use of framed structures, cavity walls, pre-fabricated components, RCC frames for doors, and windows and components evolved by the Central Buildings Research Institute and other research organizations.

Expeditious Construction. In order to expedite the construction of school buildings, the following steps are recommended by the Education Commission:

(i) In rural areas, there are no local contractors available. Contractors from urban areas generally charge higher rates when they are required to work in villages. The departmental machinery is also not adequate to reach most of the outlying villages. For the construction of village school buildings, therefore, the Commission recommends that the agency of the local communities or village panchayats should be utilised to the fullest extent possible.

(ii) In urban areas, it has been recommended that the local agencies like Municipalities and Corporations should be utilised fully for construction of school buildings. They have the necessary technical staff and can also contribute towards the cost of such buildings. If the responsibility for providing buildings for local schools is placed on municipalities and if a suitable system of grant-in-aid is devised, the progress in this sector would be accelerated.

Formation of Development Groups. Each State should have an Educational Building Development Group within the Public Works Department but working in close association with the Educational Department and consisting of an architect, an educationist, all working on a full-time basis with power to co-opt representatives of special technical skills whose main function would be to improve the planning and construction of Government school buildings and whose advice should be available for private schools also. There should also be a Building Development Group working at the Centre, for effectively coordinating the working of State Level Groups.

Functions of the State Groups. 1. To study building requirements in the light of new teaching techniques.

2. To develop in cooperation with manufacturers new building techniques and specifications.
3. To evolve functional and economic type plans for various types of educational buildings.
4. To arrive at a correct assessment of costs of materials and labour required.
5. To conduct field trials.
6. To evaluate the plans, specifications and building techniques already in use.
7. To study methods of maximising the use of indigenous materials.

The State Government should ensure that the recommendations of these Development Groups are followed.

Publication of a Building Journal. The Group at the Centre could profitably bring out a journal highlighting the latest techniques of construction, researches at home and abroad on conventional buildings.

Separate School Unit or PWD. To avoid delays in the construction of government buildings a separate unit of PWD should be set up for execution of educational building programmes.

Educational Building Criteria. After the Educational Building Development Groups have standardised the plans and the techniques of construction, the possibility should be examined for establishing Education Building Consortia, (on the lines of similar associations, popularly known as CLASP, in the U.K.) to exploit fully the advantages of industrialized building.

Other Aspects

Lay-outs, dimensions, specifications and methods of construction for any particular region should be mentioned so that mass production of the different components on a factory scale can be undertaken resulting in economy as well as speed of construction. Considerable work in the field of standardization has been done by organizations like the Indian Standards Institution which could serve as a basis for further studies.

Buildings for Private Schools. The economy measures worked out by the Educational Building Development Group in each State for reducing the cost of educational buildings should be made known to the managements of private educational institutions in the State, and the grant-in-aid given to a private management for a building subject to upper cost limits worked out.

Legislation Acquiring Open Spaces. It has become a great problem to select suitable sites in big cities due to encroachment upon open spaces for building programmes. The Education Commission has recommended that the State and Central Governments should immediately take steps to see that a survey of open spaces, parks and playing fields in all cities, municipalities and in the bigger villages is made and that a complete record of this is maintained and necessary legislation passed to prevent encroachment for industrial and commercial purposes or for housing societies without proper sanction by the government. They have further stated that if the youth of the country are to be properly encouraged in physical education and their health improved, early legislation should be passed towards this end.

Lighting Arrangement. The increase of short-sightedness among school going age imposes heavy responsibility upon the school authorities for providing proper means of lighting. It is hardly necessary to add that every classroom should be well-lighted. Light should be weli-diffused and it should not fall directly on the eyes of the students. It should come from the left. Where left light is not possible, right light may be allowed. Direct front light is not allowable in any case. The desks, therefore, should be arranged in such a manner so as to take full advantage of light coming from the left otherwise the light will either shine in the teacher's face or dazzle the children. The colour of the walls should be such as it does not tax the eyes of the students.

Windows. Two purposes - admission of light and admission of air are served by windows. The window area should not be less than one-fifth of the floor area. The window sills should be placed at not more than four feet and not less than three and a half above the floor of rooms in which the students are seated.

Ventilation. There are two methods of ventilation, natural and artificial. Natural ventilation depends upon natural forces while artificial ventilation is brought about by the use of fans, etc.

Desks. We can hardly ignore the seriousness of poor postures. They affect health, physical efficiency, mental attitude and appearance of an individual. Most of our diseases are the outcome of poor posture. As a result of poor postures says Dr. Mosher, "Constipation, diarrhoea, flatulence, disturbance of the circulation, nervous irritability and most marked of all, fatigue out of proportion to the effort expended, lessen the efficiency of the individual and then make life a burden." As a child spends a good deal of his time at desk, it is but obvious that right postures can be maintained only when good seats are provided. A child who is comfortable is likely to pay more attention and concentrate on his work than one who is not. The seat and the desk should be made to fit the child - not the child to the seat and the desk. J. Mace Andress states, "If a child is properly seated he should be able to rest his feet comfortably on the floor without pressing upon the nerves and blood vessels under the knee; the seat should be so shaped as to encourage the sitter to sit with the pelvis well back in the chair; the distance of the chair from the desk, its height and slants should be such that bending forward will not be encouraged." Another writer Dressler states, "If the back of school benches or chairs be just a little lower than the shoulder blades of the pupil when sitting properly, the best results, other things being equal, may be obtained."

Following points should be borne in mind while providing furniture to the students :

(i) There should be, as far as possible, single desk with a slight slope towards the seat.

(ii) The seat should be supported by a back.

(iii) The maximum length of the desks should be twelve feet.

(iv) Inkpots should be fitted in the desks.

(v) The desks should not be arranged more than six rows deep.

(vi) 18" of space should be provided to each pupil.

(vii) There should be sufficient space between the rows of desks as well as between desks and walls so as to have free movements.

Black-board : The black-board plays a tremendous part in making the teaching more efficient and effective. It is a necessary equipment of a classroom and a handy apparatus at the hands of a teacher.

Black-board should be placed at a place from where the writing on the black-board could be seen very easily. It should never be placed between windows. Its back should not be towards the light as in this position its surface would be in the dark and it will tax the eyes of the students in trying to read what is written on the black-board. It should be either black or green in colour. It should not be glossy, otherwise it will adversely affect the eye-sight of the pupils. Its height from the floor should vary from 26 to 39 inches according to the height of the students. It should be four feet wide. Easel black-board is better as its both sides can be used and it can be raised or lowered. It is also easily removable. Damp duster should be used to clean it so as to avoid the inhalation of chalk dust which leads to consumption.

In order to develop aesthetic sense in the minds of the pupils and to provide a pleasing and joyful surroundings, a project for beautifying the school plant may be undertaken and the students guided and actively engaged in this educational activity. The following activities may be started

1. Growing hedges.
2. Decorating the lawns with green turf, flower beds, flower pots, creepers and trees.
3. Demarcating pathways with lime and bricks.
4. Flooring the pathways with either tar coal or bricks.
5. Decorating the walls of the rooms and the verandahs with beautiful charts, pictures, etc.
6. Decorating notice boards, bulletin boards, etc.
7. Decorating the school hall, library room and laboratories, etc.
8. Whitewashing the building if possible.

Hostel for Students

Importance of the School Hostel. There is no doubt that a good hostel plays a very important role in education by providing right conditions for the development of the many-sided personality of the child. Hostel life is very rich in its educational values. A well-supervised hostel life is very conducive to the training of ideals of citizenship. An ordinary school sets limits to the possibilities of social and corporate living. Hostel life provides conditions for securing all the values of social life. The institution serves as a boon to a large category of persons. It caters to the needs of the children of those parents who are transferred frequently, leading to the disruption of their studies. It comes to the rescue of those parents who do not find good schools for their children in the neighbourhood and who want to send them in good schools having hostel facilities. To some students it will be a welcome change from their unhappy and unhealthy home environment. Still others who have to travel long distances to go to school, find this institution of immense value.

School for Day and Night

A Boarding School is different from a Day School in several ways.

The students of a Day School generally come from homes that are within daily walking distance from the school. But most of the students of a Boarding School come from places that are far away.

A Boarding School brings together children of different sections of society. It provides the opportunity for these children to understand one another's different customs and ways of life.

At a Boarding School the Head of the institution has to make arrangement for feeding, sleeping and recreation.

As the pupils 'live' at school, there are long periods when they are not actually at lessons - on Saturdays and Sundays for instance. The Head has to think out how these out of school hours can best be occupied.

At a Day School, the work of the teachers may end at the conclusion of afternoon lessons but at a Boarding School they have duties of supervision during out of school hours. For three quarters of the year, they are in the homes of parents. So they have a big responsibility and their influence on the lives and character of their pupils will be great.

Hostel Building. The same principles which govern the selection of site for a school also apply to the selection of site for a hostel. As regards the shape and equipment of the hostel.

Cottage System and Dormitory System. Cottage system resembles a small village. In the cottage system, small houses are built more or less close together. Each house of cottage accommodates 8 to 12 students. A teacher's quarter is attached to each cottage. The teacher (his family if he is married) and the pupils live together as one family. A much closer contact between the teacher and the taught is established. Every cottage is a self-sufficient unit with its dining room and kitchen etc. The system, though an ideal one, cannot be adopted in our country due to its heavy demand on purse.

Dormitory system as adopted by the Punjab Education Department seems to be a suitable one. This system is economical as compared to the cottage system. The building should be such as can be enclosed easily and shut at night. A floor area of not less than 50 to 55 ft. should be provided for each student and the distance between beds should not be less than 3 ft.

26

Community in Action

"A 'people's school' must obviously be based on the people's needs and problems. Its curriculum should be an epitome of their life. Its methods of work must approximate to theirs. It should reflect all that is significant and characteristics in the life of the community in its natural setting," observed Prof. K.G. Saiyidain.

The importance of linking the school life with the life of the community has been stressed by he Secondary Education Commission in these words, "The starting point of educational reform must be the relinking of the school to life and restoring of the intimate relationship between them which has broken down with the development of the formal tradition of education." Dewey also in his book, School and Society emphasises this when he writes, "The great thing to keep in mind, then regarding the introduction into the school of various forms of active occupation, is that through them the entire spirit of the school is renewed, it has a chance to affiliate itself with life to become the child's habitat, where he learns through direct living, instead of being only a place to learn lessons having an abstract and remote reference of some possible living to be done in future. It gets a chance to be a miniature community, an embryonic society. This is the fundamental fact and from this arise continuous and orderly streams of instruction." According to Raymont, "The school should be a bit of life, or rather, perhaps, it should be, in some sort a miniature of the best elements in the great society outside."

K.G. Saiyidain describes the significance of school–community relations in these words, "If we continue the present practice of working in isolated compartments, the school not enriching the community, the community not supporting the school, not only will it defeat our real educational objectives, but whatever education we provide, will be stale and anaemic."

Ryburn describes the relationship between the school and the community in these words, "There must be a vital connection between the life of the pupils in school and the life of the community from which they come. There must be a vital connection between the school, which is the corporate life of pupils and teachers and the community. Otherwise, the school can never succeed in its aim of enabling its pupils to go out and to face society and make necessary adjustments nor can it, as a corporate body, even have the vital influence on the community which it ought to have."

School is a social institution set up by the society to serve its ends. It is charged by the society with the duty of training and bringing up the students so that they may be able to take part effectively, harmoniously and efficiently in the group to which they belong. They cannot inherit automatically their social heritage as they inherit their ancestral property. Constant efforts have got to be made to bring the activities of the school closely in touch with the life outside the school. School is a society in 'miniature'. It must be brought out of its isolation and connection with all the nobler, and the worthier aspects of the life of the community. Knowledge gained in the school must be linked with the life of the community. Failure to do so, will only produce shiftless, aimless, helpless and perhaps worthless individuals. All the possibilities of connecting the school life with the community life be explored and the child fully prepared to take his rightful place in the community. Curriculum, methods of teaching, school building, library and the experience of the teachers are the various tools to link the school with the community.

Community Centre

The present conception of education differs radically from the old conception of education and consequently the functions of the present school differ from the traditional school. The traditional conception of a school has been too academic. According to it the school was "a knowledge shop and the teachers information mongers." Teaching activities were carried on in it in an academic seclusion out of touch with the social and economic life surging around. It was preoccupied with one narrow but clear-cut problem - how to prepare its pupils to pass certain examinations which were prescribed by the educational authorities. Knowledge was the be-all and the end-all of education. The modern sociological view of education postulates that "the school should constantly draw upon social life and activities for its subject-matter, its methods of teaching and its methods of work. There must be a conscious and continuous intercourse, a free give and take, between the little world of the school and the bigger one outside."

Secondly, the school is not a place where merely the children are educated but the whole community. With tons of money invested in school buildings and equipment, it is a poor economics as well as bad educational philosophy to restrict its use to a few hours each day, five and a half days a week and for only a few months in the year. Its use must be made of by the whole community regardless of creed or religious or political affiliation. The Folk High Schools of Denmark, the Tushegee Institute for Negros in the United States and the Gary Schools of U.S.A. furnish notable instances of the community service which schools can render. The school building and equipment must be thrown open for public use after the regular school hours are over.

Thirdly, the tax-papers will feel that they are really getting a fair return for their money and will take all the more interest in the school if it is taken out of its isolation.

Fourthly, the school teachers will get chances to become the leaders of the social group and can improve their position and prestige.

Rural School and its Community Functions. What has been said above applies to all schools, rural and urban. But India being a village country, the rural schools have an important duty to the nation. Rural uplift is the only solution if we want to see India standing in the row of all advanced countries. The Community Projects and National Extension Service Schemes have in view the object of making our villages pulsate with life as in the old days and not continue to decay as at present. Gandhiji raised the slogan

"Back to villages". The village schools have to play an important role in the reconstruction of the villages. Mr. F.L. Brayne remarks that there is no better and cheaper agency possible for the remaking of village India than the village school. The village school must serve as a centre of light to the villagers and supply cohesion, initiative and knowledge required for the great task of rural reconstruction. To quote Mobel Carney, "The interpretation of the function of the country school as one of social leadership and community service implies that it must reach not only children but adults also. No argument is needed to establish desirability of this service. To educate properly is to cause a change of conduct and the hypothesis that the country school shall so govern its instruction as to cause a change in social attitudes and community conditions and relationships in no way clashes with its original purpose (to educate)."

Village schools are to be organised on a different pattern than that of an urban school. At present the position is that there is no particular difference between a rural school and an urban one. So far as the aims, curricula and methods of teaching are concerned, both are alike. The same curriculum and the same methods cannot be suitable to rural and urban children. So the present curriculum should be 'ruralised.'

Serving Methods

The school will employ the following three methods to influence the community:

I. Producing good individuals or imparting training for citizenship.

II. Organising community service programmes.

III. Throwing open the school building for social, cultural and recreational programmes.

Education for Citizenship.

Vocational Efficiency. The old system fails to prepare students for a vocation and simply produces persons who are fit for white collar jobs only. Such individuals fail to harness the resources of the community and are unable to serve the community to which they belong. In a Basic school adequate stress is laid on the development of sound working attitudes and habits and appreciation of the dignity of labour. The introduction of various crafts helps the students to develop vocational efficiency and thereby saves them from becoming misfits in life.

Appreciation of the Rights and Responsibilities. A Basic school provides many opportunities to the students to appreciate that rights and responsibilities go hand in hand. The introduction of student self-government in a limited form helps very much to teach this lesson to the students.

Physical and Health Development. It must be constantly impressed upon children that a healthy body contributes much to become happy and efficient citizen. A course in scientific knowledge of food and nutrition should form a part of the curriculum. The importance of good food and living in healthy surroundings should be told to them. School building, school hostel and school surroundings should be made model of cleanliness. The idea is to develop good health habits in the students so that they may spread these in the locality to which they belong.

Appreciation of the Inter-relatedness of Different Agencies. A man is never self-sufficient and is dependant upon others for the satisfaction of his needs. From the very beginning a child should be made to realize that cooperation is the basis of all the activities of man – social, economic, political and educational.

Organising Social Service Programmes

The field of social service activities is very vast and may be grouped under the following heads :

Physical Activities. The students may be asked to clean the lanes and homes of the locality, to construct open air theatre, to dry up marshy lands, etc. These activities have immense educational and social values.

Cultural Activities. India is a land of festivals. The school should organise seasonal, national and cultural festivals and invite parents to attend these. The elders or the experienced persons of the locality may be asked to address the audience.

Campaigns against Social Evils. Periodical campaigns by the school may be organised and the evils of drinking, gambling and borrowing pointed out.

Literacy Campaigns. Night classes for the adults may be started and conducted by the elder students of the school and the teachers also.

Miscellaneous Activities. Social service by the students may be rendered during fairs, floods, epidemics etc. Occasional trips to the various parts of the locality may be arranged by the school authorities, with the idea of making the students know of the problems confronting the community and creating an urge in them to remove defects which they notice. Local surveys may take the form of projects like the extent of literacy in the locality, cleanliness, living conditions in the homes and the like. The school may serve as a 'clearing house' as K.G. Saiyidain points it, where teachers and parents of the boys meet and discuss in a friendly way their problems, social, economic and educational, with which they are faced and in which both are interested.

Utilising School Building. It will be very desirable if the above mentioned programmes are organized in the school premises. Besides in places where there is no public library, the school should consider the possibility of throwing the school library open to the public after school hours. A special section catering to the needs of the adults may be opened.

Basic Principles

First, the work of planning and organisation of these programmes should be undertaken very carefully beforehand by the teachers and students in collaboration.

Secondly, programmes should be so varied that they give scope for many students to participate in them.

Thirdly, cooperative aspect of the work should constantly be emphasized.

Fourthly, these programmes should be linked up with the academic work also.

Fifthly, the quality of the work done by the students should improve gradually.

Lastly, the students must be made to feel that year after year they are not merely carrying out a routine activity, but they are doing something which is really useful to the community and that their abilities are utilised for noble causes.

Community and the School. "What we would like to see is a two way traffic," thus wrote the Secondary Education Commission. In this context they have suggested that interested members of the community, engaged in various useful vocations and professions should be invited to the school from time to time to talk about their particular work, to show its place and significance in the life of the community.

Projects for Improvement

1. Construction of school buildings; provision of additional accommodation.
2. Electrification of buildings.
3. Construction of quarters for teachers.
4. White-washing and repairs of buildings.
5. Construction of compound walls, provision of sheds for cooking free meals and provision of fence for garden.
6. Donations of lands for free meal scheme.
7. Donations of lands for agricultural and garden purposes.
8. Acquisition of land for playground.
9. Provision of classroom equipment like screens, painting of black-boards, supply of classroom furniture, supply of equipment and teaching aids and supply of portraits of great leaders.
10. Supply of slates and text-books to poor children.
11. Supply of free clothing.
12. Supply of personal hygiene materials (soap, towels, mirrors, etc.)
13. Supply of grain, firewood etc. for free meal scheme, supply of cooking vessels for free meal scheme and supply of plates and tumblers etc.
14. Provision of drinking water.
15. Provision for night study and supply of petromax and hurricane lights.
16. Supply of equipment for handicrafts like sewing machine, etc.

17. Supply of musical instruments and radio.
18. Supply of play and hobby materials.
19. Supply of garden tools.
20. Maintenance of existing wells and sinking of new ones.
21. Provision of sanitary conveniences.
22. Supply of books, newspapers and magazines.
23. Provision of first-aid materials.

Mutual Cooperation

In the words of S. Balakrishna Joshi, "Close cooperation between the parent who is the first teacher and the teacher, who is the second parent, is the very foundation on which rests the fruitfulness of the training imparted in our institutions." Mr. George Tomlinson has fully stressed the need of cooperation between home and school in these words : "Let us fashion our homes and organise our schools with the well-being of children always in mind. In particular, remember that any clash between parents and teachers must always be harmful to the child. Harmonious working together can alone bring us the results we want." Teachers are interested in the welfare of the children, they want their pupils develop mentally, physically, morally and socially. So is the case with the parents. Hence the need for united efforts on the part of parents and teachers who are the custodians of the welfare of children.

The Requirements

From the Point of View of Teachers

(i) To seek maximum information from the parents about the child to have fuller understanding of him.

(ii) For getting help from the parents in the regular attendance of the child.

(iii) For getting help in regular supervision of home work of the child.

(iv) For providing the child necessary equipment at proper time.

(v) For getting help in stressing upon the child the necessity of having respect for the school laws.

(vi) For securing funds and gifts for the school.

From Parents' Point of View

(i) They need information regarding the progress of their children.

(ii) They want necessary warning regarding expenditure on books etc.

(iii) They need information about problem situations before they become serious.

(iv) They want careful assignments.

(v) They need advice as to how they could supplement the efforts of the school in promoting the progress of their children.

Various Problems

From the Side of the Teachers

(i) Their unwillingness to face criticism.

(ii) Their conservative outlook and doubts about the success of this programme.

(iii) Lack of time to make sincere efforts in this direction.

From the Side of the Parents

(i) Indifference of the parents to school work.

(ii) Busy life of the parents and lack of time to contact teachers.

(iii) Ignorance on the part of the parents that they can render any assistance to the child in his work.

(iv) Their suspicious nature regarding the motives of school authorities.

Cooperation Sought

In view of the mass illiteracy in our country, the initiative for the home-school cooperation rests upon the teachers. To quote S.

Balakrishna Joshi, "Parental cooperation cannot be had by learned discourses on the subject or by periodical pamphlets posted to the parties. It cannot be created overnight. We cannot wake up one fine morning and find the parents pitch forked into cooperation. It is based on a series of silent acts of sincere service to children. It is the natural consumption of devoted deeds of dedication at the shrine of Duty." All possible avenues should be explored to establish contacts with the parents. Following are some of the main methods of securing cooperation of the parents and to make them interested in school work.

Good Treatment. Whenever the parents visit the school they should be shown proper courtesy. Patient hearing should be given to their complaints.

Personal Contacts. The parents of those children who do not show good results in monthly tests or terminal examinations, may be requested to visit the school. Positive suggestions regarding the future progress of the children should be given to them. Frank and free talks would result in active cooperation.

School Reports. These include:

Casual Letters. These should be used only when it is not possible to have personal contact with the parents. The parents of those students who reside in the hostel may have to be contacted through letters.

Progress Reports. These are sent to the parents from time to time. It is a useful device to keep in touch with the parents. Progress report should be very comprehensive, touching all the different aspects of the life of the child—mental, moral, physical, academic and aesthetic, etc.

Participation by the Parents in School Programmes. (a) Some parents can lend a helping hand in raising funds for the school. Their help should be secured. This will develop in them a sense of belongingness to the school. There are many other ways through which the parents can help the school authorities, e.g., donating or lending books, giving stipends to the poor students, arranging mid-day meals for the poor, etc.

(b) The school authorities should not hesitate to utilise the knowledge, skill and experience of the parents in supplementing class teaching. A doctor may be requested to give lectures on Hygiene and Physiology. Similarly, the services of the parents in other fields may be utilised.

Home Visits by the Teachers. These should always be friendly. The false notions of prestige should not stand in the way.

Association of the Parents in the Management of the School. Representation should be given to the parents on the board's management. But in some cases this may prove very harmful to the efficient working of the school.

Making the School as a Centre of Community Service. National, social and cultural functions should be organised in the school. Labour weeks may be organised wherein students render some social service to the community.

Formation of Parent-Teacher Association. The meetings of the association provide an opportunity to the parents to make suggestions for the improvement of the school. The head and the members of the staff acquaint the parents with the current thought and practices of education. The sphere of the working of such associations should be clearly defined so as to avoid unnecessary interference on the part of the parents in the internal organisation of the school. It would be better if the parents of the students of one class are invited to meet the teachers of that class, at one time. The smaller the group, the better would be the results.

In the end we may again stress the importance of making the parents interested in school work. "The ordinary machinery for good school life," writes Thring, "is a thing of calculation and measurement but all discussion is in vain unless parents are interested."

Importance of the Parents 'Day from the Teachers' View-point

(i) They get an opportunity to acquaint the parents with the various activities of the school.

(ii) They get an opportunity to explain to the parents what future plans the school has for the welfare of the students.

(iii) They get an opportunity to request the parents to render assistance to the school.

(iv) They get an opportunity to exchange views.

Parents' View-point

(i) It provides them an excellent opportunity to see the working of the school.

(ii) It provides them an opportunity to know what their children are doing at school.

(iii) It enables them to discuss certain specific problems of their children with the teachers.

From Pupils' View-point

(i) They feel immense joy when they see their parents visiting the school.

(ii) They try to put in their best for making the programme a success. Esprit de Corps is developed in them and they feel love for the school.

It should be a full working day. The parents should be taken round the school so that they may see how the classes are held and where their children sit. They should get an occasion to see the actual teaching done in the school.

Different co-curricular activities such as debates, dramatics, etc. may be organised.

Children's work like calligraphy, models, maps, charts, etc. may be exhibited in one of the rooms of the schools.

The parents may be taken to special rooms, e.g. Geography, History, Science, Craft etc.

School sports may be organised on this day or it may take the form of prize distribution or School Annual Day.

Adequate preparations should be made so as to give a good show of school activities. A light refreshment to the parents may be served if the funds allow.